Pivot Tables In Depth

For
Microsoft Excel 2016

Suljan Qeska

ISBN: 9781973401469

Contents

Appendix: Custom Sorting

How to use this book?

This book is written in the form of a tutorial. To make best use of it download the files used in the book by going to http://www.intelligent-courses.com/ebooks/pivot-tables-in-depth-for-microsoft-excel-2016-downloads.

This book has many illustrations and even though it has been designed in the form of a tutorial you can still learn how to use Pivot Tables simply by reading it.

At the end of this book you should be able to:

- Build Pivot Tables using multiple fields

- Understand how all summary functions used in calculating value fields are calculated

- Build Pivot Tables using custom calculations

- Understand how custom calculations work and how they are calculated

- Filter Pivot Tables with all types of filters available including Slicers and Timelines

- Group items within a field, build Calculated fields and Calculated items and use Solve Order correctly with Calculated Items

- Format a Pivot Table to your requirements including the ability to choose which rows or columns are displayed

- Use Pivot Table Options effectively

- Build Pivot Charts

- Build Pivot Tables from different data sources

- Have a basic understanding of what OLAP is

- Build OLAP Pivot Tables and drill through them

- Use Named Sets

CHAPTER 1

What are Pivot tables?

Pivot Tables are a feature of Microsoft Excel through which you can easily summarize data that comes in the form of a database and present it in tables.

With Pivot Tables you can build cross-tabulations and frequency distributions of your data. You can also build custom fields on which you can compute the same calculations as the ones you can compute on fields that are already in your data.

Figure 1.1 illustrates a typical data range which can be analysed using Pivot Tables. Each column header in Fig 1.1 (for e.g. Year, Month etc) in Pivot Table terminology is a field.

	A	B	C	D	E	F	G	H	I	J
1	Year	Month	Date	Production Line	Manager	Shift	Product	Units produced	Price per unit	Revenue
2	2015	January	01/01/2015	Line A	Steven Robertson	Day	Chocolate Bars	54,300	$1.25	$67,875
3	2015	January	01/01/2015	Line A	Steven Robertson	Day	Biscuits	25,600	$1.75	$44,800
4	2015	January	01/01/2015	Line A	Douglass Robinson	Night	Crackers	12,356	$2.00	$24,712
5	2015	January	01/01/2015	Line A	Douglass Robinson	Night	Candies	38,000	$2.50	$95,000
6	2015	January	01/01/2015	Line B	Asim Khan	Day	Cream Cakes	11,500	$1.00	$11,500
7	2015	January	01/01/2015	Line B	Asim Khan	Day	Small Cakes	45,000	$2.50	$112,500
8	2015	January	01/01/2015	Line B	Steve Black	Night	Chocolate Croissants	22,478	$1.80	$40,460
9	2015	January	01/01/2015	Line B	Steve Black	Night	Muffins	28,700	$2.10	$60,270
10	2015	January	01/01/2015	Line C	Robert Frog	Day	Ice Cream	52,000	$4.00	$208,000
11	2015	January	01/01/2015	Line C	Robert Frog	Day	Frozen Yoghurt	44,000	$4.50	$198,000
12	2015	January	01/01/2015	Line C	Julian Teacher	Night	Ice Cream	53,200	$4.00	$212,800
13	2015	January	01/01/2015	Line C	Julian Teacher	Night	Frozen Yoghurt	41,000	$4.50	$184,500
14	2015	February	01/02/2015	Line A	Douglass Robinson	Day	Chocolate Bars	49,990	$1.25	$62,488
15	2015	February	01/02/2015	Line A	Douglass Robinson	Day	Biscuits	23,200	$1.75	$40,600
16	2015	February	01/02/2015	Line A	Steven Robertson	Night	Crackers	11,200	$2.00	$22,400
17	2015	February	01/02/2015	Line A	Steven Robertson	Night	Candies	35,000	$2.50	$87,500
18	2015	February	01/02/2015	Line B	Steve Black	Day	Cream Cakes	10,000	$1.00	$10,000
19	2015	February	01/02/2015	Line B	Steve Black	Day	Small Cakes	42,000	$2.50	$105,000
20	2015	February	01/02/2015	Line B	Asim Khan	Night	Chocolate Croissants	21,765	$1.80	$39,177
21	2015	February	01/02/2015	Line B	Asim Khan	Night	Muffins	26,123	$2.10	$54,858
22	2015	February	01/02/2015	Line C	Julian Teacher	Day	Ice Cream	50,000	$4.00	$200,000
23	2015	February	01/02/2015	Line C	Julian Teacher	Day	Frozen Yoghurt	41,000	$4.50	$184,500

Warehouse (+)

Fig 1.1: Typical data range used to build Pivot Table

Pivot Tables are very useful. For e.g. if you had a range of data in Excel and tried to summarize it using Excel functions, it would prove to be very cumbersome. With Pivot Tables data can be summarized in a few clicks.

Similarly if the data you wanted to analyse was in a database such as, a Microsoft Access Database, rather than write SQL code to summarize this data, by connecting your database tables to Excel you can build summaries at any level you like and only in a few clicks using the Pivot Tables feature. Hence Pivot Tables are a life saver in this respect. They will save you time and resources and enable you to extract meaningful information out of your data easily. With their Online Analytical Processing (OLAP) feature they will empower you to summarize data from different data sources at many levels and drill down to any level you like in a few clicks.

Pivot Tables can summarize data from a worksheet, a database, a text file, and many other data sources.

Once a Pivot Table is built, information within it can be re-arranged in a few clicks. For example, one field previously in a Pivot Table column can be moved to a Pivot Table row and vice versa. The value field (the field or fields on which calculations are done) or the calculation on it can be changed in a matter of seconds. Data can be grouped, for example the *Product* field in the data source used in this book, see the *Product* column in the data range shown in Fig 1.1, can be grouped into *Frozen desserts, Biscuits and Crackers, Cakes, Candies and Chocolate Flavoured* (or any other combination you like) and summary data can be calculated for each of these groups just like for an individual item within the *Product* field.

This is only the tip of the Iceberg. This book will aim to uncover the whole iceberg and empower you with the use of a great tool.

1.1 Pivot Table Terminology

Understanding Pivot Table terminology is an important requirement on the road to mastering the use of Pivot Tables.

Manager	(Multiple Items) 🔽			
Revenue		**Year** 🔽		
Production Line 🔽 **Shift** 🔽		**2015**	**2016**	**Grand Total**
⊟ **Line A**		$1,406,344	$1,521,451	$2,927,795
	Day	$677,340	$735,639	$1,412,979
	Night	$729,005	$785,811	$1,514,816
⊟ **Line B**		$1,355,361	$1,457,890	$2,813,251
	Day	$745,846	$784,465	$1,530,311
	Night	$609,515	$673,425	$1,282,940
⊟ **Line C**		$4,869,651	$5,097,258	$9,966,909
	Day	$2,478,361	$2,621,397	$5,099,758
	Night	$2,391,290	$2,475,860	$4,867,150
Grand Total		$7,631,356	$8,076,598	$15,707,954

Fig 1.2: Pivot Table with a filter field

Below are some of the most frequently used terms. Refer to the figure above for better understanding:

Row field: A field whose items are listed in rows in a Pivot Table. There may be multiple row fields in a Pivot Table. In the figure above *Production Line* and *Shift* are row fields.

Column field: A field whose items are listed in columns in a Pivot Table. There may be multiple column fields in a Pivot Table. In the figure above *Year* is a column field.

Value area: The area of cells in a Pivot Table where the summary data is contained. In the figure above the value area is the area where all the *Revenue* data is.

Value field: A field that is placed in the **Σ Values** area of the **PivotTable Fields List**. On value fields calculations such as Sum, Count, Min etc. are computed which are then displayed on the value area. In Fig 1.2 *Revenue* is a value field.

Filter field: This is a field that acts like a filter and shows a sliced version of the Pivot Table based on the selected item or items within. In Fig 1.2 *Manager* is a filter field.

Grand Totals: The totals for all cells in a row, column or both (in the Value area) displayed in their own row or column. Putting it differently a Grand Total is the sum of all cells in the value area under a row, column or both and is displayed in its own row or column. In Fig 1.2 the Grand Totals are found in the last row and column of the Pivot Table.

Subtotals: A row or column that displays the totals for a group of items in the value area. In Fig 1.2 the rows in bold are subtotals.

Item: This is an element within a field that is placed in rows or columns. Each item is the header of a row or column in a Pivot Table depending on whether the field it is part of is a row or column field. In Fig 1.2 *Day* and *Night* are items within *Shift. Line A, Line B* and *Line C* are items within *Production Line. 2015* and *2016* are items within *Year.*

Source data: This is the data the Pivot Table is built upon. It can reside in the same worksheet or a different one, in a different workbook, in a text file or in an external database.

Group: This is a group of different items combined into a single item and it is treated as such. Groups can be built manually, i.e. you manually select which items to group, or automatically.

1.2 Let's start building our first Pivot Table

The best way to learn Pivot Tables is by doing them. We will build our first Pivot Table by using the data from Fig 1.1. This data is from a fictional packing warehouse which has three production lines that work with two shifts. Each shift has a line manager. The data we have is monthly units produced and monthly revenue by *Product, Shift* and *Production line.*

If you haven't downloaded the required files please do so now. A link to the data is found in the '*How to use this book*' section.

Let's suppose that you are the warehouse manager and you want to know the total unit production for each *Production line* by year.

To do this select all the data and then go to the **Insert** tab and in the **Tables** group click on the **PivotTable** button as shown in Fig 1.3.

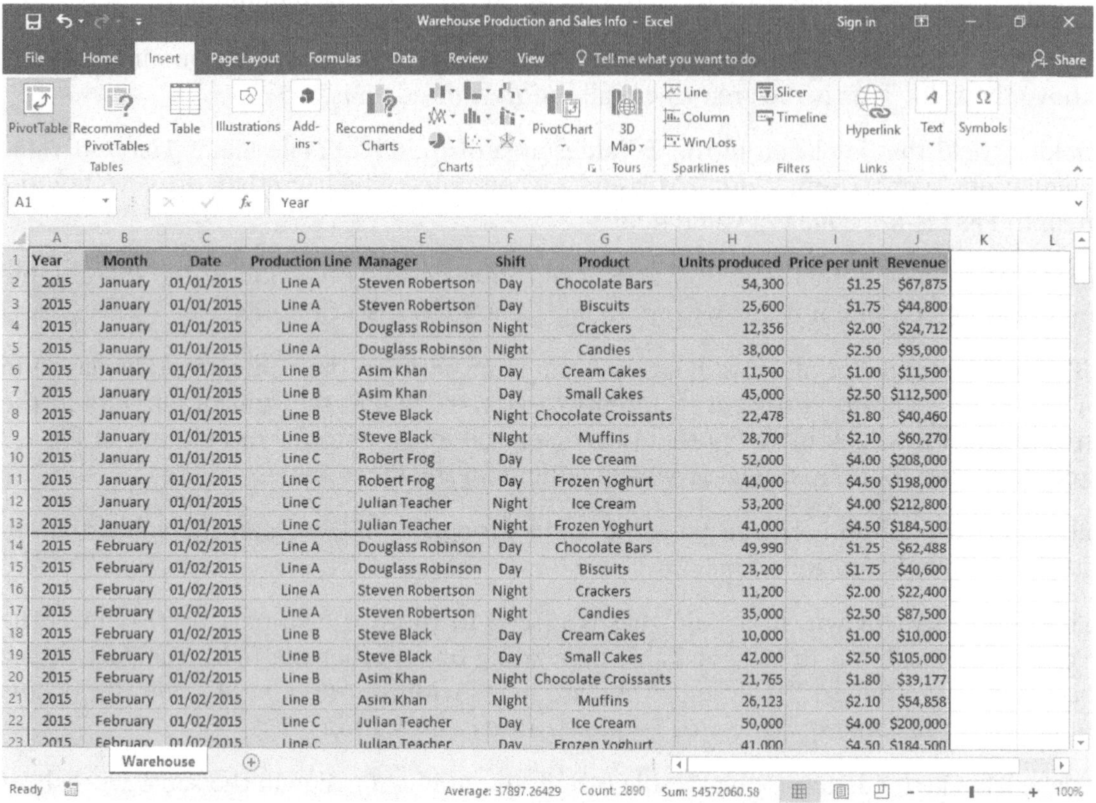

Year	Month	Date	Production Line	Manager	Shift	Product	Units produced	Price per unit	Revenue
2015	January	01/01/2015	Line A	Steven Robertson	Day	Chocolate Bars	54,300	$1.25	$67,875
2015	January	01/01/2015	Line A	Steven Robertson	Day	Biscuits	25,600	$1.75	$44,800
2015	January	01/01/2015	Line A	Douglass Robinson	Night	Crackers	12,356	$2.00	$24,712
2015	January	01/01/2015	Line A	Douglass Robinson	Night	Candies	38,000	$2.50	$95,000
2015	January	01/01/2015	Line B	Asim Khan	Day	Cream Cakes	11,500	$1.00	$11,500
2015	January	01/01/2015	Line B	Asim Khan	Day	Small Cakes	45,000	$2.50	$112,500
2015	January	01/01/2015	Line B	Steve Black	Night	Chocolate Croissants	22,478	$1.80	$40,460
2015	January	01/01/2015	Line B	Steve Black	Night	Muffins	28,700	$2.10	$60,270
2015	January	01/01/2015	Line C	Robert Frog	Day	Ice Cream	52,000	$4.00	$208,000
2015	January	01/01/2015	Line C	Robert Frog	Day	Frozen Yoghurt	44,000	$4.50	$198,000
2015	January	01/01/2015	Line C	Julian Teacher	Night	Ice Cream	53,200	$4.00	$212,800
2015	January	01/01/2015	Line C	Julian Teacher	Night	Frozen Yoghurt	41,000	$4.50	$184,500
2015	February	01/02/2015	Line A	Douglass Robinson	Day	Chocolate Bars	49,990	$1.25	$62,488
2015	February	01/02/2015	Line A	Douglass Robinson	Day	Biscuits	23,200	$1.75	$40,600
2015	February	01/02/2015	Line A	Steven Robertson	Night	Crackers	11,200	$2.00	$22,400
2015	February	01/02/2015	Line A	Steven Robertson	Night	Candies	35,000	$2.50	$87,500
2015	February	01/02/2015	Line B	Steve Black	Day	Cream Cakes	10,000	$1.00	$10,000
2015	February	01/02/2015	Line B	Steve Black	Day	Small Cakes	42,000	$2.50	$105,000
2015	February	01/02/2015	Line B	Asim Khan	Night	Chocolate Croissants	21,765	$1.80	$39,177
2015	February	01/02/2015	Line B	Asim Khan	Night	Muffins	26,123	$2.10	$54,858
2015	February	01/02/2015	Line C	Julian Teacher	Day	Ice Cream	50,000	$4.00	$200,000
2015	February	01/02/2015	Line C	Julian Teacher	Day	Frozen Yoghurt	41,000	$4.50	$184,500

Fig 1.3: Selecting all data and clicking on the **PivotTable** button

Once we do this Excel outputs a **Create PivotTable** dialog box that looks as in Fig 1.4. This dialog box is composed of three parts.

In the first part we choose the data we want to analyse. This can be in the current workbook as in this case, in another Excel workbook, or in an external data source. How to build Pivot Tables using external data sources will be covered in chapter 10. The rest of the book will be based on building Pivot Tables using Excel data ranges.

In the second part of the dialog box we can select where we want our Pivot Table to be placed. This can be in a new worksheet or in the current one. In this case we will choose a new

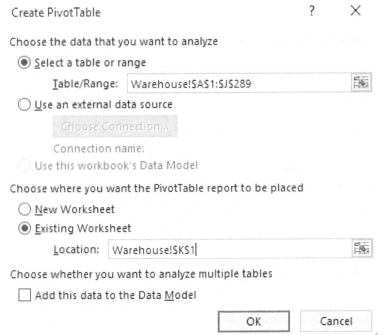

Fig 1.4: Create PivotTable dialog box

worksheet. If you want to build a Pivot Table in the existing worksheet instead, select the second option and in the **Location** box input the cell you want the Pivot Table to start. In this case the **Create PivotTable** dialog box will look as in Fig 1.5.

Create PivotTable   ?   ×

Choose the data that you want to analyze

◉ Select a table or range

    Table/Range: Warehouse!$A$1:$J$289

○ Use an external data source

    Choose Connection...

    Connection name:

    Use this workbook's Data Model

Choose where you want the PivotTable report to be placed

○ New Worksheet

◉ Existing Worksheet

    Location: Warehouse!$K$1

Choose whether you want to analyze multiple tables

☐ Add this data to the Data Model

      OK   Cancel

Fig 1.5: Create PivotTable dialog box with **Existing Worksheet** selected as Pivot Table location

The third part of the **Create PivotTable** dialog box requests from you to let Excel know if you would like the data added to the **Workbook Data Model**. By doing this you will be able to connect this data range to other data already in the **Workbook Data Model** or to data that will be added later which can be Excel based or from other data sources. The **Workbook Data Model** is then used to build **OLAP** Pivot Tables. More on this in chapter 10.

In this case we will leave the box in front of **Add this data to the Data Model** unchecked.

Now let's click on the **OK** button. A new worksheet will be created with an empty Pivot Table within just like in Fig 1.6.

Once a Pivot Table is built two more tabs are added to the Ribbon area under **PivotTable Tools**. These tabs are used to edit Pivot Tables. In this book we will be covering most of the features within both of these.

At the moment the Pivot Table we built does not have any data and that is because we haven't added any to it yet. For a start we want to build a simple Pivot Table where we can show *Total Units Produced* by *Production Line* and *Year*. To do this we click on each field in the **PivotTables Fields List**, which can be seen on the right, and drag it to the appropriate area. In this case we will be dragging *Production Line* to **Rows**, *Year* to **Columns** and *Units produced* to ∑ **Values**.

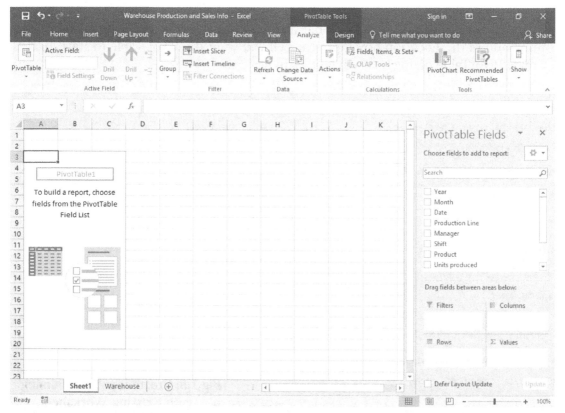

Fig 1.6: New Pivot Table ready to be built

If you just clicked a field, rather than clicked and then dragged it, Excel will choose automatically where to place it. Click on it again and simply drag it to the correct area.

As in Fig 1.7 we should now have:

Columns: Year

Rows: Production Line

Σ Values: Units produced

In Fig 1.7 we have our first Pivot Table which shows *Sum of Units Produced* by *Production Line* and *Year*. Some of the things that we may notice is that the data is not formatted well and perhaps we wouldn't call the value field as *Sum of Units produced* but something more meaningful such as *Total Units Produced*.

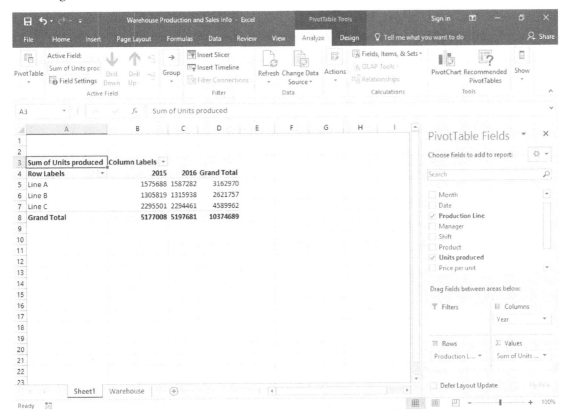

Fig 1.7: First Pivot Table built

To do these and more we click on the name of the value field (Sum of Units produced) in the Σ **Values** area. Once we do this we get the menu in Fig 1.8.

Most of the options in the menu in Fig 1.8 are self-explanatory. We can basically move *Units produced* to any other area or up and down the Σ **Values** area when there is more than one field in it.

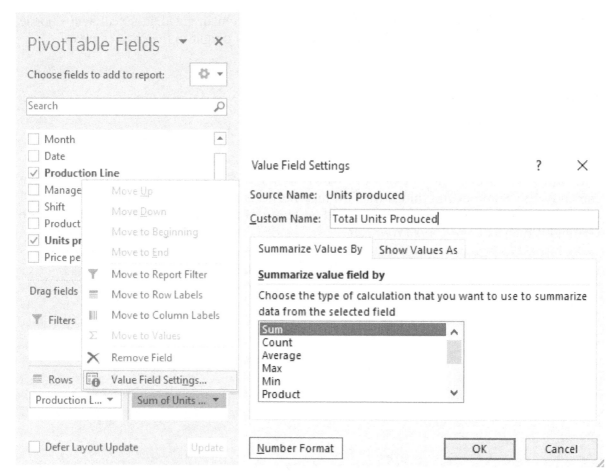

Fig 1.8: Accessing **Value Field Settings** from the Σ **Values** area

Fig 1.9: Value Field Settings dialog box

Let's click on the **Value Fields Settings** button in order to do some formatting on the *Sum of Units produced* field. After clicking this button the **Value Field Settings** dialog box will pop up as in Fig 1.9.

We will go through all the options in this dialog box in detail in chapter 2. For now click on the **Number Format** button so that we can edit the number format of the Pivot Table and tick the checkbox before **Use the 1000 separator(,)** and set the **Decimal places:** to 0 to make the production numbers more legible.

Once you have done this let's also change the name of the field from *Sum of Units produced* to *Total Units Produced*. This can be done by inputting the new name in the custom name box at the top and then click **OK**.

After finishing with the **Value Field Settings** dialog box click on the **Design** tab and in the **PivotTable Styles** group select a style of your liking. Simply click on the one you like and the Pivot Table formatting will be updated automatically.

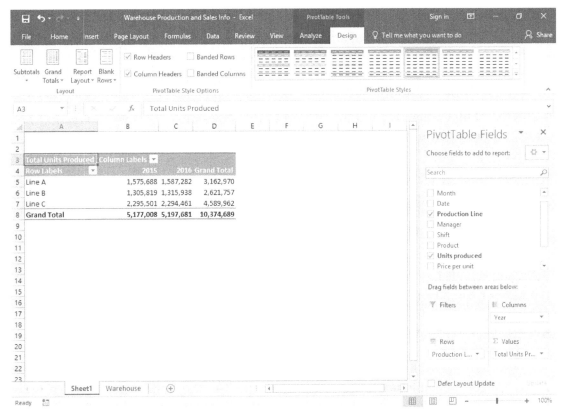

Fig 1.10: First Pivot Table formatted successfully

Now that we have done some basic editing we can see that our Pivot Table looks much more readable. Notice that the name of the value field has changed both in the Pivot Table and in the **PivotTable Fields List** and the Pivot Table looks nicer with the new style.

1.3 Using multiple fields in a Pivot Table

One of the most useful features of a Pivot Table is that you can use multiple fields in all areas i.e. in **Rows, Columns, ∑ Values** and **Filters**.

Let's say that the warehouse manager wants to see the *Revenue* generated by the warehouse by:

- Production Line

- Product

- Shift

- Year

and rather than just seeing *Total Revenue* he also wants to see *Revenue* by *Production Line* and *Product* as a *% of Shift Revenue* in a *Year* and as a *% of a Year's Revenue*. This information can help him determine which *Product or Production Line* generates most *Revenue* as a percentage of the *Total Revenue*.

To do this let's build a new Pivot Table where in the **Rows** area we have *Production Line* and *Product*, in the **Columns** area we have *Year* and *Shift* and in the **∑ Values** area we have *Revenue* <u>twice</u>.

To display *Revenue* as a % of *Shift* and *Year Revenue* we need to do a few more things.

- First rename the first *Revenue* field as *Total Revenue* and change the number format to $ with no decimal places.

- Second, right click on the second *Revenue* field in the **∑ Values** area and in the **Value Field Settings** dialog box let's leave the calculation type in the **Summarize Values By** tab as **Sum** and let's go to the **Show Values As** tab and instead of **No Calculation** let's choose **% of Column Total** as in columns we have *Year* and *Shift* which will be our division base as per warehouse manager's request.

And finally let's do some design work.

- Let's change the name of the second *Revenue* field in the **Value Field Settings** dialog box to *% of Total Revenue* and let's click on the **Number Format** button and change the format to **Percentage** and remove decimal places.

- In the **Design** tab let's keep the **Report Layout** as **Show in Compact Form** and in the **Blank Rows** section let's click on **Insert Blank Line after Each Item** to make the table easier to read.

The Pivot Table will now look as in Fig 1.11 and congratulations you have just built a complex Pivot Table which only took a minute to build but which conveys a lot of useful information which otherwise would have been more difficult and more time consuming to obtain.

From this Pivot Table a warehouse manager can see that *Frozen Yoghurt* and *Ice Cream* produced by *Line C* are the warehouse's most profitable products which need more attention. Perhaps the best line manager needs employing for this line and the best workers. The manager should also make sure that engineers and spare parts are readily available for this production line even more so than for the other lines.

A warehouse manager knows that demand for products can be seasonal hence he would also want to know if there are any differences by month. As a Pivot Table expert, you know that this can be done quickly by moving the *Month* field to the **Filters** area. Now we have a Pivot Table like the one in Fig 1.12 where we can easily filter data by month.

Row Labels	Column Labels				2015 Total Revenue	2015 % of Total Revenue
	⊟2015					
	Day		Night			
	Total Revenue	% of Total Revenue	Total Revenue	% of Total Revenue		
⊟Line A	$1,356,136	17%	$1,458,450	20%	$2,814,586	18%
Biscuits	$538,395	7%		0%	$538,395	4%
Candies		0%	$1,153,840	15%	$1,153,840	8%
Chocolate Bars	$817,741	11%		0%	$817,741	5%
Crackers		0%	$304,610	4%	$304,610	2%
⊟Line B	$1,492,041	19%	$1,227,685	16%	$2,719,726	18%
Chocolate Croissants		0%	$494,613	7%	$494,613	3%
Cream Cakes	$141,893	2%		0%	$141,893	1%
Muffins		0%	$733,072	10%	$733,072	5%
Small Cakes	$1,350,148	17%		0%	$1,350,148	9%
⊟Line C	$4,906,800	63%	$4,788,600	64%	$9,695,400	64%
Frozen Yoghurt	$2,394,360	31%	$2,226,200	30%	$4,620,560	30%
Ice Cream	$2,512,440	32%	$2,562,400	34%	$5,074,840	33%
Grand Total	$7,754,976	100%	$7,474,735	100%	$15,229,711	100%

Fig 1.11: Pivot Table with two fields in **Rows** and **Columns**

 This is only half of the table since the original one is two large to place here.

Month   March   .T

Row Labels	Column Labels				2015 Total Revenue	2015 % of Total Revenue
	⊟2015					
	Day		Night			
	Total Revenue	% of Total Revenue	Total Revenue	% of Total Revenue		
⊟Line A	$110,775	17%	$120,175	20%	$230,950	19%
Biscuits	$43,400	7%		0%	$43,400	3%
Candies		0%	$95,375	16%	$95,375	8%
Chocolate Bars	$67,375	11%		0%	$67,375	5%
Crackers		0%	$24,800	4%	$24,800	2%
⊟Line B	$121,375	19%	$100,530	16%	$221,905	18%
Chocolate Croissants		0%	$40,680	7%	$40,680	3%
Cream Cakes	$11,375	2%		0%	$11,375	1%
Muffins		0%	$59,850	10%	$59,850	5%
Small Cakes	$110,000	17%		0%	$110,000	9%
⊟Line C	$401,340	63%	$394,000	64%	$795,340	64%
Frozen Yoghurt	$193,500	31%	$180,000	29%	$373,500	30%
Ice Cream	$207,840	33%	$214,000	35%	$421,840	34%
Grand Total	$633,490	100%	$614,705	100%	$1,248,195	100%

Fig 1.12: Pivot Table with *Month* in the **Filters** area and filtered by March

CHAPTER 2

Managing Calculations and more with Value Field Settings and Field Settings

Value Field Settings and **Field Settings** are settings for value fields and row or column fields respectively. They are very important as through them Pivot Tables gain a high degree of flexibility, from managing custom calculations to managing formats. In this chapter we will be looking at both in detail.

2.1 Value Field Settings

The **Value Field Settings** dialog box can be accessed either by clicking on the value field name in the Σ **Values** area as already shown in the previous chapter or by right clicking anywhere on the value area of the Pivot Table and then clicking on the **Value Field Settings...** button as shown in Fig 2.1.

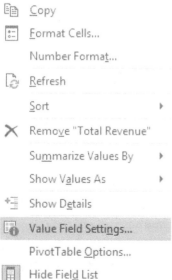

Fig 2.1: Accessing the **Value Field Settings** dialog box by right clicking on a Pivot Table cell

Value Field Settings can also be accessed by clicking on the value area of a Pivot Table and then going to the **Analyze** tab, **Active Field** group and then clicking on the **Field Settings** button as in Fig 2.2.

Fig 2.2: Accessing the **Value Field Settings** dialog box through the **Analyze** tab

In the **Value Field Settings** dialog box in Fig 2.3 we can edit the value field name and give it a custom name by editing the **Custom Name** box.

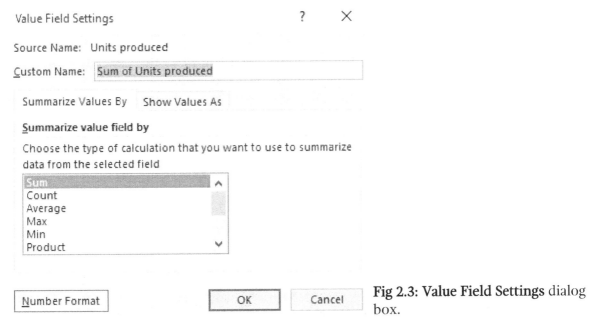

Fig 2.3: Value Field Settings dialog box.

We can also edit the number format by clicking the **Number Format** button and selecting the appropriate format.

The two most powerful features of this dialog box lie in the **Summarize Values By** and **Show Values As** tabs. Let's look at both of them.

2.1.1 Summarize Values By Tab

In the **Summarize Values By** tab we can choose how to summarize a value field. The default calculation is the **Sum**.

The **Sum** is calculated as follows. For any combination of fields in the **Rows**, **Columns** and **Filters** areas the **Sum** of the value field's cells in the source data that relate to that combination is shown in a Pivot Table cell. If a different calculation is selected then that calculation is performed for the same combination of cells.

For e.g. in Fig 2.4 the value of the cell where *Line A* and *2015* cross is the **Sum** of all cells under the *Units produced* column in the source data where in the same row there are *Line A* and *2015* cells under *Production Line* and *Year* columns respectively.

Total Units Produced	Column Labels		
Row Labels	2015	2016	Grand Total
Line A	1,575,688	1,587,282	3,162,970
Line B	1,305,819	1,315,938	2,621,757
Line C	2,295,501	2,294,461	4,589,962
Grand Total	5,177,008	5,197,681	10,374,689

Fig 2.4: The units produced for *Production Line A* and *Year 2015* are 1,575,688

In Fig 2.5 we have filtered the cells from the *Units Produced* column where *Year* is *2015* and *Production Line* is *Line A*. As you can see the total **Sum** of these filtered cells equals the value of the Pivot Table cell where *Line A* and *2015* cross (see Fig 2.4).

	A	B	C	D	E	F	G	H	I	J
1	Ye	Month	Date	Production Li	Manager	Shi	Product	Units produce	Price per ur	Reven
2	2015	January	01/01/2015	Line A	Steven Robertson	Day	Chocolate Bars	54,300	$1.25	$67,875
3	2015	January	01/01/2015	Line A	Steven Robertson	Day	Biscuits	25,600	$1.75	$44,800
4	2015	January	01/01/2015	Line A	Douglass Robinson	Night	Crackers	12,356	$2.00	$24,712
5	2015	January	01/01/2015	Line A	Douglass Robinson	Night	Candies	38,000	$2.50	$95,000
14	2015	February	01/02/2015	Line A	Douglass Robinson	Day	Chocolate Bars	49,990	$1.25	$62,488
15	2015	February	01/02/2015	Line A	Douglass Robinson	Day	Biscuits	23,200	$1.75	$40,600
16	2015	February	01/02/2015	Line A	Steven Robertson	Night	Crackers	11,200	$2.00	$22,400
17	2015	February	01/02/2015	Line A	Steven Robertson	Night	Candies	35,000	$2.50	$87,500
26	2015	March	01/03/2015	Line A	Steven Robertson	Day	Chocolate Bars	53,900	$1.25	$67,375
27	2015	March	01/03/2015	Line A	Steven Robertson	Day	Biscuits	24,800	$1.75	$43,400
28	2015	March	01/03/2015	Line A	Douglass Robinson	Night	Crackers	12,400	$2.00	$24,800
29	2015	March	01/03/2015	Line A	Douglass Robinson	Night	Candies	38,150	$2.50	$95,375
38	2015	April	01/04/2015	Line A	Douglass Robinson	Day	Chocolate Bars	53,700	$1.25	$67,125
39	2015	April	01/04/2015	Line A	Douglass Robinson	Day	Biscuits	24,500	$1.75	$42,875
40	2015	April	01/04/2015	Line A	Steven Robertson	Night	Crackers	12,250	$2.00	$24,500
41	2015	April	01/04/2015	Line A	Steven Robertson	Night	Candies	37,700	$2.50	$94,250
50	2015	May	01/05/2015	Line A	Steven Robertson	Day	Chocolate Bars	54,794	$1.25	$68,493
51	2015	May	01/05/2015	Line A	Steven Robertson	Day	Biscuits	26,100	$1.75	$45,675
52	2015	May	01/05/2015	Line A	Douglass Robinson	Night	Crackers	12,666	$2.00	$25,332
53	2015	May	01/05/2015	Line A	Douglass Robinson	Night	Candies	39,000	$2.50	$97,500
62	2015	June	01/06/2015	Line A	Douglass Robinson	Day	Chocolate Bars	53,234	$1.25	$66,543
63	2015	June	01/06/2015	Line A	Douglass Robinson	Day	Biscuits	25,555	$1.75	$44,721

Sheet1 | Warehouse

Ready   48 of 288 records found   Average: 32,827   Count: 48   Sum: 1,575,688   100%

Fig 2.5: The **Sum** of the *Units produced* column cells filtered by *Year 2015* and *Production Line A* equates to 1,575,688 units which is the same as the Pivot Table cell value in Fig 2.4 where *Line A* and *2015* cross

In the **Summarize Values By** tab we have a selection of 11 calculations, the **Sum** included, to choose from. In the table below the description of each calculation is shown.

Function	Description
Sum	The sum of values in a set of data. The set is based on the combination of row and column field items that relate to a Pivot Table cell. This is the default function for numeric data.
Count	The number of data values in a set of data. The set is based on the combination of row and column field items that relate to a Pivot Table cell. The Count summary function works the same as the COUNTA function i.e. counts the number of non-blank cells. Count is the default function in a Pivot Table for data other than numbers.
Average	The average of values in a set of data. The set is based on the combination of row and column field items that relate to a Pivot Table cell.
Max	The largest value in a set of data. The set is based on the combination of row and column field items that relate to a Pivot Table cell.
Min	The smallest value in a set of data. The set is based on the combination of row and column field items that relate to a Pivot Table cell.
Product	The product of values in a set of data. The set is based on the combination of row and column field items that relate to a Pivot Table cell.
Count Numbers	The number of data values that are numbers in a set of data. The set is based on the combination of row and column field items that relate to a Pivot Table cell. The Count Numbers summary function works the same as the worksheet COUNT function.
StDev	An estimate of the standard deviation of a population, where the sample is a subset of the entire population. The sample is a set of data based on the combination of row and column field items that relate to a Pivot Table cell. The StDev formula used is: $$\sqrt{\left(\frac{\sum (x-\bar{x})^2}{(n-1)}\right)}$$
StDevp	The standard deviation of a population, where the population is all the data to be summarized. The data to be summarized is a set of data based on the combination of row and column field items that relate to a Pivot Table cell. The StDevp formula used is: $$\sqrt{\left(\frac{\sum (x-\bar{x})^2}{n}\right)}$$

Var	An estimate of the variance of a population, where the sample is a subset of the entire population. The sample is a set of data based on the combination of row and column field items that relate to a Pivot Table cell. The Var formula used is: $$\sum \frac{(x- \bar{x})^2}{(n- 1)}$$
Varp	The variance of a population, where the population is all of the data to be summarized. The data to be summarized is a set of data based on the combination of row and column field items that relate to a Pivot Table cell. The Varp formula used is: $$\sum \frac{(x- \bar{x})^2}{n}$$

Table 2.1: Summarize Values By calculations description

2.1.2 Show Values As Tab

In the **Show Values As** tab we can display values on a Pivot Table as custom calculations. All we need to do is select a calculation from the list of calculations available from the tab. This list of calculations can be accessed by clicking the drop-down button in the drop-down box under the **Show values as** section.

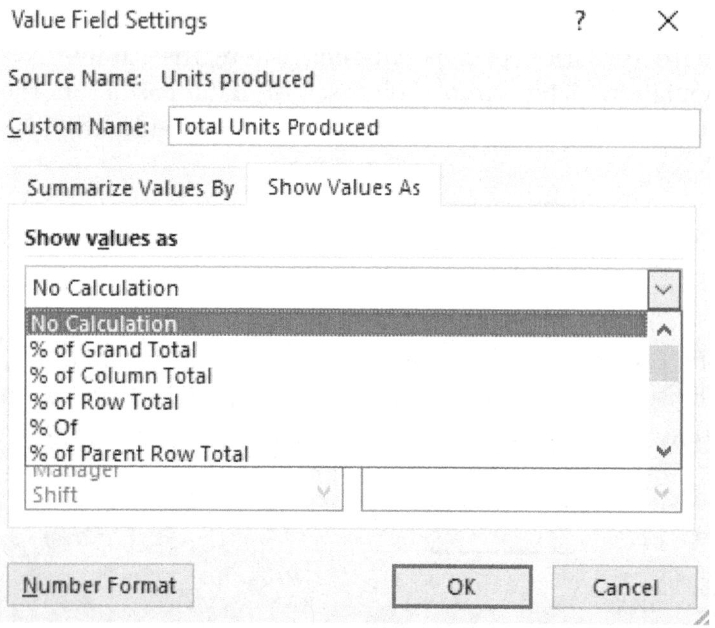

Value Field Settings ? ✕

Source Name: Units produced

Custom Name: Total Units Produced

Summarize Values By   Show Values As

Show values as

No Calculation
- No Calculation
- % of Grand Total
- % of Column Total
- % of Row Total
- % Of
- % of Parent Row Total

Manager
Shift

Number Format   OK   Cancel

Fig 2.6: Show values as calculation list

Apart from the **Show Values As** tab, custom calculations can also be accessed by right clicking on a value cell and then in the menu that pops up by going to **Show Values As.** When pointing the mouse to the latter a list of calculations to select from will appear as in Fig 2.7.

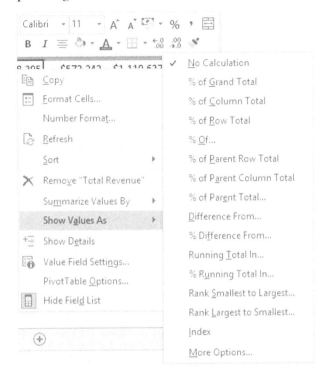

Fig 2.7: **Show Values As** calculations list

In total there are 15 calculations to choose from.

1. No Calculation

2. % of Grand Total

3. % of Column Total

4. % of Row Total

5. % Of

6. % of Parent Row Total

7. % of Parent Column Total

8. % of Parent Total

9. Difference from

10. % Difference From

11. Running Total In

12. % Running Total In

13. Rank Smallest to Largest

14. Rank Largest to Smallest

15. Index

Let's look at each calculation in detail.

No Calculation

This option will leave the value fields as they are depending on the summary function that you have chosen in the **Summarize Values By** tab. For e.g. if you have chosen the Sum of Revenue then the Pivot Table will only show the **Sum**.

% of Grand Total

This calculation will show the value of a cell as a % of the **Grand Total** value for all columns and rows. The **Grand Total** value itself will be 100%. This is the cell where the intersection of the last column and the last row takes place. In Fig 2.8 the **Grand Total** is circle 2. The **% of Grand Total** in circle 3 is calculated as the value in circle 1 divided by the value in circle 2.

Total Units Produced	Column Labels		
Row Labels	2015	2016	Grand Total
Line A	1 1,575,688	1,587,282	3,162,970
Line B	1,305,819	1,315,938	2,621,757
Line C	2,295,501	2,294,461	2 4,589,962
Grand Total	5,177,008	5,197,681	10,374,689

Total Units Produced	Column Labels		
Row Labels	2015	2016	Grand Total
Line A	3 15.19%	15.30%	30.49%
Line B	12.59%	12.68%	25.27%
Line C	22.13%	22.12%	44.24%
Grand Total	49.90%	50.10%	100.00%

Fig 2.8: % of Grand Total in 3 is calculated as $(1/2)*100 = (1,575,688/10,374,689)*100=15.19\%$

% of Column Total

This calculation will show the value of a cell as **% of** the **Column Total**. This means that the value of each cell will be divided by the value of the total for the column this cell is in. In this case column totals will be 100%. In Fig 2.9 the **Column Total** for the first column is circle 2.

The **% of Column Total** in circle 3 is calculated as the value in circle 1 divided by the value in circle 2.

Total Units Produced	Column Labels		
Row Labels	**2015**	**2016**	**Grand Total**
Line A	1 1,575,688	1,587,282	3,162,970
Line B	1,305,819	1,315,938	2,621,757
Line C	2,295,501	2,294,461	4,589,962
Grand Total	2 5,177,008	5,197,681	10,374,689

Total Units Produced	Column Labels		
Row Labels	**2015**	**2016**	**Grand Total**
Line A	3 30.44%	30.54%	30.49%
Line B	25.22%	25.32%	25.27%
Line C	44.34%	44.14%	44.24%
Grand Total	100.00%	100.00%	100.00%

Fig 2.9: % of Column Total in 3 is calculated as $(1/2)*100 = (1,575,688/5,177,008)*100=30.44\%$

% of Row Total

This calculation will show the value of a cell as **% of** the **Row Total**. This means that the value of each cell will be divided by the value of the total for the row this cell is in. In this case row totals will be 100%. In Fig 2.10 the **Row Total** for the first row is circle 2. The **% of Row Total** in circle 3 is calculated as the value in circle 1 divided by the value in circle 2.

Total Units Produced	Column Labels		
Row Labels	**2015**	**2016**	**Grand Total**
Line A	1 1,575,688	1,587,282	3,162,970
Line B	1,305,819	1,315,938 2	2,621,757
Line C	2,295,501	2,294,461	4,589,962
Grand Total	5,177,008	5,197,681	10,374,689

Total Units Produced	Column Labels		
Row Labels	**2015**	**2016**	**Grand Total**
Line A	3 49.82%	50.18%	100.00%
Line B	49.81%	50.19%	100.00%
Line C	50.01%	49.99%	100.00%
Grand Total	49.90%	50.10%	100.00%

Fig 2.10: % of Row Total in 3 is calculated as $(1/2)*100 = (1,575,688/3,162,970)*100=49.82\%$

% Of ...

In this option you can choose what the value cells should be divided by. You can only choose from items of fields you already have in the **Rows** or **Columns** areas.

In Fig 2.11 we have a Pivot Table which shows the *Sum of Revenue* by *Month* and *Year*.

Sum of Revenue	Year		
Month	2015	2016	Grand Total
January	$1,260,417	$1,326,231	$2,586,649
February	$1,182,823	$1,249,315	$2,432,138
March	$1,248,195	$1,347,664	$2,595,859
April	$1,237,010	$1,304,882	$2,541,892
May	$1,268,263	$1,345,825	$2,614,088
June	$1,248,297	$1,340,332	$2,588,629
July	$1,301,202	$1,369,796	$2,670,998
August	$1,277,925	$1,346,617	$2,624,541
September	$1,256,384	$1,352,311	$2,608,695
October	$1,293,890	$1,381,815	$2,675,704
November	$1,313,026	$1,401,244	$2,714,270
December	$1,342,279	$1,422,301	$2,764,581
Grand Total	$15,229,711	$16,188,334	$31,418,045

Fig 2.11: *Revenue* by *Month* and *Year*

Now let's suppose that we want this table presented differently. We would like to see January as a base month whereas all the other months will be shown as a % of January's Revenue. To do this right click on any value cell and then choose **Show Values As...** and then **% Of...** . When you do this a dialog box as in Fig 2.12 will pop up.

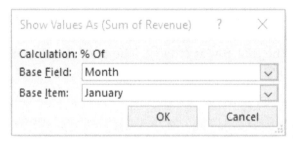

Fig 2.12: Show Values As dialog box

In this dialog box select **Base Field** as *Month* and **Base Item** as *January* and then click **OK**. The Pivot Table will now look as in Fig 2.13.

Sum of Revenue	Year		
Month	2015	2016	Grand Total
January	100.00%	100.00%	100.00%
February	93.84%	94.20%	94.03%
March	99.03%	101.62%	100.36%
April	98.14%	98.39%	98.27%
May	100.62%	101.48%	101.06%
June	99.04%	101.06%	100.08%
July	103.24%	103.28%	103.26%
August	101.39%	101.54%	101.46%
September	99.68%	101.97%	100.85%
October	102.66%	104.19%	103.44%
November	104.17%	105.66%	104.93%
December	106.49%	107.24%	106.88%
Grand Total			

Fig 2.13: Pivot Table with **% Of** January's Revenue

In the **% Of...** calculation we also have the option to choose from the **(previous)** or **(next)** base item in the base field. In the Pivot Table in Fig 2.12 if we chose **(previous)** as the **base item** and *Month* as the **base field** then the values would have been shown as a % of the previous month.

 The **Base Field** for the **% Of** calculation should always be chosen from one of the fields already in the table. If we went to the **% Of** calculation through a right click on the Pivot Table and then by clicking on **Show Values As** and then **% Of...** this wouldn't be a problem as in the **Show Values As** dialog box we would only have the fields on the Pivot Table to choose from. However if we went through the **Show Values As tab** as shown in Fig 2.14 we would have access to all fields. In this case use only the fields already in the table as **Base Fields** otherwise you will be getting Errors or Blank cells as a result depending on your Pivot Table options.

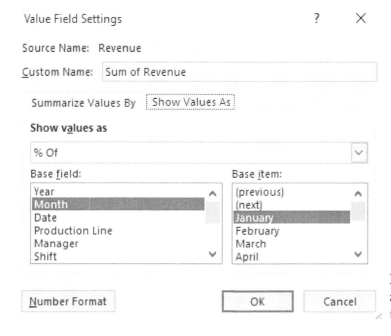

Fig 2.14: Options available when accessing **% Of** calculation from the **Show Values As** tab

% of Parent Row Total

If you have more than one field in **Rows**, then when the **% of Parent Row Total** calculation is selected, the figures in the Pivot Table will be shown as a % of the parent row field's item totals which are also referred to as subtotals.

To understand this better let's look at an example. Fig 2.15 shows a Pivot Table with two fields in **Rows**.

Sum of Revenue		Year		
Production Line ▾	Shift ▾	2015	2016	Grand Total
⊟ Line A		$2,814,586	$3,059,037	$5,873,623
	Day	$1,356,136	$1,467,168	$2,823,304
	Night	$1,458,450	$1,591,869	$3,050,319
⊟ Line B		$2,719,726	$2,954,936	$5,674,662
	Day	$1,492,041	$1,594,026	$3,086,067
	Night	$1,227,685	$1,360,910	$2,588,595
⊟ Line C		$9,695,400	$10,174,361	$19,869,760
	Day	$4,906,800	$5,166,116	$10,072,916
	Night	$4,788,600	$5,008,245	$9,796,845
Grand Total		$15,229,711	$16,188,334	$31,418,045

Fig 2.15: Pivot Table with *Production Line* and *Shift* in the **Rows** area

In Fig 2.15 the parent row field is *Production Line*. If we apply the **% of Parent Row Total** calculation then *Day* and *Night* cells under *Line A* will be divided by *Line A* subtotals, *Day* and *Night* cells under *Line B* will be divided by *Line B* subtotals and the same for *Day* and *Night* items under *Line C*. The subtotals themselves will be shown as a % of the **Column Totals.**

The new Pivot Table will look like in Fig 2.16.

Sum of Revenue		Year		
Production Line ▾	Shift ▾	2015	2016	Grand Total
⊟ Line A		18.48%	18.90%	18.70%
	Day	48.18%	47.96%	48.07%
	Night	51.82%	52.04%	51.93%
⊟ Line B		17.86%	18.25%	18.06%
	Day	54.86%	53.94%	54.38%
	Night	45.14%	46.06%	45.62%
⊟ Line C		63.66%	62.85%	63.24%
	Day	50.61%	50.78%	50.69%
	Night	49.39%	49.22%	49.31%
Grand Total		100.00%	100.00%	100.00%

Fig 2.16: Pivot Table with **% of Parent Row Total** calculation

% of Parent Column Total

If you have more than one field in the **Columns** area then the figures in the Pivot Table will be shown as a % of the parent column field's subtotals.

Fig 2.17 shows a Pivot Table with two fields in **Columns**.

Sum of Revenue	Year	Shift						Grand Total
	2015		2015 Total	2016		2016 Total	Grand Total	
Production Line	Day	Night		Day	Night			
Line A	$1,356,136	$1,458,450	$2,814,586	$1,467,168	$1,591,869	$3,059,037	$5,873,623	
Line B	$1,492,041	$1,227,685	$2,719,726	$1,594,026	$1,360,910	$2,954,936	$5,674,662	
Line C	$4,906,800	$4,788,600	$9,695,400	$5,166,116	$5,008,245	$10,174,361	$19,869,760	
Grand Total	$7,754,976	$7,474,735	$15,229,711	$8,227,310	$7,961,024	$16,188,334	$31,418,045	

Fig 2.17: Pivot Table with two fields in the **Columns** area

In Fig 2.17 the parent column field is *Year*. If we apply the **% of Parent Column Total** calculation then *Day* and *Night* cells under *2015* will be divided by the *2015* subtotals, *Day* and *Night* cells under *2016* will be divided by the *2016* subtotals. The subtotals themselves will be shown as a % of the **Row Totals**.

The new Pivot Table will look like in Fig 2.18.

Sum of Revenue	Year	Shift					Grand Total
	2015		2015 Total	2016		2016 Total	Grand Total
Production Line	Day	Night		Day	Night		
Line A	48.18%	51.82%	47.92%	47.96%	52.04%	52.08%	100.00%
Line B	54.86%	45.14%	47.93%	53.94%	46.06%	52.07%	100.00%
Line C	50.61%	49.39%	48.79%	50.78%	49.22%	51.21%	100.00%
Grand Total	50.92%	49.08%	48.47%	50.82%	49.18%	51.53%	100.00%

Fig 2.18: Pivot Table with **% of Parent Column Total** calculation

% of Parent Total

With **% of Parent Row Total** and **% of Parent Column Total** you don't get to choose which subtotals to divide by unless you change the parent field. With **% of Parent Total** you do. This is better understood when you have more than one subtotal available. Fig 2.19 shows a table with three fields in **Rows**.

Sum of Revenue			Year		
Production Line ▼ Shift ▼	Product	▼	2015	2016	Grand Total
⊟ Line A			$2,814,586	$3,059,037	$5,873,623
	⊟ Day		$1,356,136	$1,467,168	$2,823,304
		Chocolate Bars	$817,741	$894,926	$1,712,667
		Biscuits	$538,395	$572,242	$1,110,637
	⊟ Night		$1,458,450	$1,591,869	$3,050,319
		Candies	$1,153,840	$1,270,313	$2,424,153
		Crackers	$304,610	$321,556	$626,166
⊟ Line B			$2,719,726	$2,954,936	$5,674,662
	⊟ Day		$1,492,041	$1,594,026	$3,086,067
		Small Cakes	$1,350,148	$1,416,090	$2,766,238
		Cream Cakes	$141,893	$177,936	$319,829
	⊟ Night		$1,227,685	$1,360,910	$2,588,595
		Muffins	$733,072	$811,093	$1,544,165
		Chocolate Croissants	$494,613	$549,817	$1,044,430
⊟ Line C			$9,695,400	$10,174,361	$19,869,760
	⊟ Day		$4,906,800	$5,166,116	$10,072,916
		Ice Cream	$2,512,440	$2,708,699	$5,221,139
		Frozen Yoghurt	$2,394,360	$2,457,417	$4,851,777
	⊟ Night		$4,788,600	$5,008,245	$9,796,845
		Ice Cream	$2,562,400	$2,740,257	$5,302,657
		Frozen Yoghurt	$2,226,200	$2,267,989	$4,494,188
Grand Total			$15,229,711	$16,188,334	$31,418,045

Fig 2.19: Pivot Table with three fields in the **Rows** area

Now let's right click on any value cell and then select **Show Values As** and click on **% of Parent Total**. (Note that if we had more than one value field in the Pivot Table then we would right click on the value cells of the value field we want to apply the calculation on.) The **Show Value As** dialog box will appear (Fig 2.20). In this dialog box we can choose the field whose subtotals we want to use as a base to divide by. In this case only *Production Line* and *Shift* are valid selections. If we choose *Product* the Pivot Table will be filled with 100% values. Let's choose *Production Line* and click **OK**.

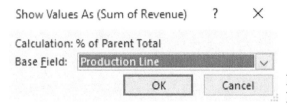

Fig 2.20: Show Values As dialog box for the **% of Parent Total** calculation

The updated Pivot Table will now look like in Fig 2.21.

Sum of Revenue			Year		
Production Line	Shift	Product	2015	2016	Grand Total
Line A			100.00%	100.00%	100.00%
	Day		48.18%	47.96%	48.07%
		Chocolate Bars	29.05%	29.26%	29.16%
		Biscuits	19.13%	18.71%	18.91%
	Night		51.82%	52.04%	51.93%
		Candies	41.00%	41.53%	41.27%
		Crackers	10.82%	10.51%	10.66%
Line B			100.00%	100.00%	100.00%
	Day		54.86%	53.94%	54.38%
		Small Cakes	49.64%	47.92%	48.75%
		Cream Cakes	5.22%	6.02%	5.64%
	Night		45.14%	46.06%	45.62%
		Muffins	26.95%	27.45%	27.21%
		Chocolate Croissants	18.19%	18.61%	18.41%
Line C			100.00%	100.00%	100.00%
	Day		50.61%	50.78%	50.69%
		Ice Cream	25.91%	26.62%	26.28%
		Frozen Yoghurt	24.70%	24.15%	24.42%
	Night		49.39%	49.22%	49.31%
		Ice Cream	26.43%	26.93%	26.69%
		Frozen Yoghurt	22.96%	22.29%	22.62%
Grand Total					

Fig 2.21: Pivot Table with **% of Parent Total** calculation

All the values from *Product* and *Shift* have been divided by their respective *Production Line* subtotals. If we chose *Shift* as a base field then all the values except for *Production Line* values will be divided by their respective *Shift* subtotals as in Fig 2.22.

In contrast, if we were to choose **% Parent Row Total** instead then the *Product* cells would be divided by their respective *Shift* subtotals and the *Shift* cells would be divided by their respective *Production Line* subtotals and lastly *Production Line* cells would be divided by their respective *Column Totals*.

It is important to notice that if we had multiple fields in both the **Rows** and **Columns** areas then the **% of Parent Total** calculation will allow us to use, as a division base, fields from both **Rows** or **Columns**. Whereas, **% of Parent Row Total** and **% of Parent Column Total** calculations allow only the use of fields from **Rows** and **Columns** respectively.

Difference From ...

The **Difference From** calculation allows you to subtract one value cell from another value cell within the same value field. What this means is that you can subtract for e.g. *Revenue* from *Revenue* but not *Revenue* from *Units produced*.

To understand this calculation better let's look at an example. Let's build a Pivot Table

Sum of Revenue			Year		
Production Line	Shift	Product	2015	2016	Grand Total
Line A					
	Day		100.00%	100.00%	100.00%
		Chocolate Bars	60.30%	61.00%	60.66%
		Biscuits	39.70%	39.00%	39.34%
	Night		100.00%	100.00%	100.00%
		Candies	79.11%	79.80%	79.47%
		Crackers	20.89%	20.20%	20.53%
Line B					
	Day		100.00%	100.00%	100.00%
		Small Cakes	90.49%	88.84%	89.64%
		Cream Cakes	9.51%	11.16%	10.36%
	Night		100.00%	100.00%	100.00%
		Muffins	59.71%	59.60%	59.65%
		Chocolate Croissants	40.29%	40.40%	40.35%
Line C					
	Day		100.00%	100.00%	100.00%
		Ice Cream	51.20%	52.43%	51.83%
		Frozen Yoghurt	48.80%	47.57%	48.17%
	Night		100.00%	100.00%	100.00%
		Ice Cream	53.51%	54.71%	54.13%
		Frozen Yoghurt	46.49%	45.29%	45.87%
Grand Total					

Fig 2.22: Pivot Table with **% of Parent Total** calculation when *Shift* is used as a base field

where we have *Revenue* twice in Σ **Values**, *Month* in **Rows** and *Year* in **Columns**. In this case we want to have both *Revenue* and the difference in *Revenue Month on Month* in the same Pivot Table. The Pivot Table will look like in Fig 2.23.

	Year		Values				
		2015		2016		Total Sum of Revenue	Total Sum of Revenue2
Month	Sum of Revenue	Sum of Revenue2	Sum of Revenue	Sum of Revenue2			
January	$1,260,417	$1,260,417	$1,326,231	$1,326,231	$2,586,649	$2,586,649
February	$1,182,823	$1,182,823	$1,249,315	$1,249,315	$2,432,138	$2,432,138
March	$1,248,195	$1,248,195	$1,347,664	$1,347,664	$2,595,859	$2,595,859
April	$1,237,010	$1,237,010	$1,304,882	$1,304,882	$2,541,892	$2,541,892
May	$1,268,263	$1,268,263	$1,345,825	$1,345,825	$2,614,088	$2,614,088
June	$1,248,297	$1,248,297	$1,340,332	$1,340,332	$2,588,629	$2,588,629
July	$1,301,202	$1,301,202	$1,369,796	$1,369,796	$2,670,998	$2,670,998
August	$1,277,925	$1,277,925	$1,346,617	$1,346,617	$2,624,541	$2,624,541
September	$1,256,384	$1,256,384	$1,352,311	$1,352,311	$2,608,695	$2,608,695
October	$1,293,890	$1,293,890	$1,381,815	$1,381,815	$2,675,704	$2,675,704
November	$1,313,026	$1,313,026	$1,401,244	$1,401,244	$2,714,270	$2,714,270
December	$1,342,279	$1,342,279	$1,422,301	$1,422,301	$2,764,581	$2,764,581
Grand Total	**$15,229,711**	**$15,229,711**	**$16,188,334**	**$16,188,334**	**$31,418,045**	**$31,418,045**

Fig 2.23: Pivot Table with *Revenue* twice in the Σ **Values** area

Let's do a right click on a value cell under *Sum of Revenue2*, select **Value Field Settings** and go to the **Show Values As** tab and select the **Difference From...** calculation from the drop down list. In the list box under **Base Field** select *Month* whereas in the list box under **Base Item** select *(previous)* as in Fig 2.24. In the **Custom Name** box let's change the name from *Sum of Revenue2* to *Monthly Diff* and then click **OK**.

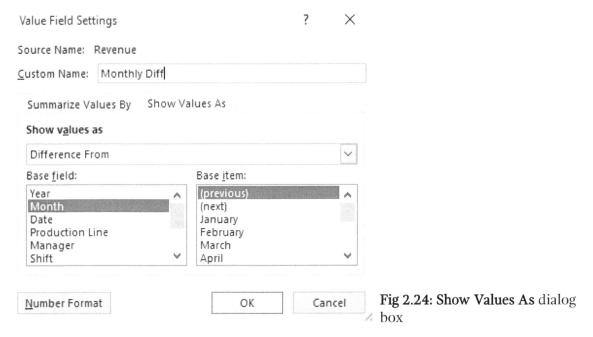

Fig 2.24: Show Values As dialog box

Now let's remove **Grand Totals** from rows to make the Pivot Table more readable. To do this go to the **Design** tab and in the **Layout** group click on **Grand Totals** and then select **On for Columns Only**. The new Pivot Table will look like in Fig 2.25.

Month	Sum of Revenue (2015)	Monthly Diff (2015)	Sum of Revenue (2016)	Monthly Diff (2016)
January	$1,260,417		$1,326,231	
February	$1,182,823	-$77,595	$1,249,315	-$76,916
March	$1,248,195	$65,372	$1,347,664	$98,349
April	$1,237,010	-$11,185	$1,304,882	-$42,782
May	$1,268,263	$31,253	$1,345,825	$40,942
June	$1,248,297	-$19,966	$1,340,332	-$5,493
July	$1,301,202	$52,905	$1,369,796	$29,464
August	$1,277,925	-$23,278	$1,346,617	-$23,179
September	$1,256,384	-$21,541	$1,352,311	$5,695
October	$1,293,890	$37,506	$1,381,815	$29,503
November	$1,313,026	$19,137	$1,401,244	$19,429
December	$1,342,279	$29,253	$1,422,301	$21,057
Grand Total	$15,229,711		$16,188,334	

Fig 2.25: Pivot Table with **Difference From** calculation

% Difference From

The **% Difference From** calculation is the same as the **Difference From** one except that we are showing the difference as a % of the **Base Item** rather than in real terms.

Using the Pivot Table above let's right click on a value cell under *Monthly Diff.* Then let's select **Show Values As** and click on **% Difference From...** . Fill the **Show Values As** dialog box as in Fig 2.26 and click **OK**.

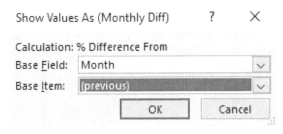

Fig 2.26: Show Values As dialog box filled for the **% Difference From** calculation

In the new Pivot Table rename *Monthly Diff* as *% Monthly Diff.* The Pivot Table will look like in Fig 2.27.

Month	2015 Sum of Revenue	2015 % Monthly Diff	2016 Sum of Revenue	2016 % Monthly Diff
January	$1,260,417		$1,326,231	
February	$1,182,823	-6.16%	$1,249,315	-5.80%
March	$1,248,195	5.53%	$1,347,664	7.87%
April	$1,237,010	-0.90%	$1,304,882	-3.17%
May	$1,268,263	2.53%	$1,345,825	3.14%
June	$1,248,297	-1.57%	$1,340,332	-0.41%
July	$1,301,202	4.24%	$1,369,796	2.20%
August	$1,277,925	-1.79%	$1,346,617	-1.69%
September	$1,256,384	-1.69%	$1,352,311	0.42%
October	$1,293,890	2.99%	$1,381,815	2.18%
November	$1,313,026	1.48%	$1,401,244	1.41%
December	$1,342,279	2.23%	$1,422,301	1.50%
Grand Total	**$15,229,711**		**$16,188,334**	

Fig 2.27: Pivot Table with **% Difference From** calculation

A quick verification calculation indeed shows that **% Difference** and **% Difference From** are the same calculation but expressed differently. If we divide -$77,595 (difference of February 2015 from January 2015) by $1,260,417 (total January 2015) we get -6.16% which is the number we have in Fig 2.27.

Running Total In

If you want to build cumulative data for e.g. over a period of time or over a number of items you can use the **Running Total In** custom calculation.

Let's build a Pivot Table where we have *Year* in **Columns**, *Product* in **Rows** and *Revenue* twice in Σ **Values**. The Pivot Table will look like in Fig 2.28.

Year		Values		
	2015		2016	
Product	Sum of Revenue	Sum of Revenue2	Sum of Revenue	Sum of Revenue2
Ice Cream	$5,074,840	$5,074,840	$5,448,956	$5,448,956
Frozen Yoghurt	$4,620,560	$4,620,560	$4,725,405	$4,725,405
Small Cakes	$1,350,148	$1,350,148	$1,416,090	$1,416,090
Candies	$1,153,840	$1,153,840	$1,270,313	$1,270,313
Chocolate Bars	$817,741	$817,741	$894,926	$894,926
Muffins	$733,072	$733,072	$811,093	$811,093
Biscuits	$538,395	$538,395	$572,242	$572,242
Chocolate Croissants	$494,613	$494,613	$549,817	$549,817
Crackers	$304,610	$304,610	$321,556	$321,556
Cream Cakes	$141,893	$141,893	$177,936	$177,936
Grand Total	$15,229,711	$15,229,711	$16,188,334	$16,188,334

Fig 2.28: Pivot Table set up for **Running Total In** calculation

Let's right click on any value cell under *Sum of Revenue2*. Next let's select **Show Values As...** and then click on **Running Total In...** . In the **Show Values As** dialog box put *Product* as **Base Field** and click **OK** (Fig 2.29).

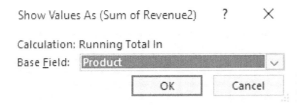

Fig 2.29: **Show Values As** dialog box for **Running Total In** custom calculation

In this case the only possible selections are *Product* and *Year* since these are the only fields we have in **Rows** or **Columns** areas. If we wanted to use *Year* we would need to move Σ *Values* to the **Rows** area so that value fields will get listed in rows and not in columns.

In the new Pivot Table rename *Sum of Revenue2* to *Cumulative Revenue*. The new Pivot Table should now look like in Fig 2.30 with the *Running Total* column next to the *Revenue* column.

% Running Total In

% Running Total In is essentially cumulative data over a period of time or series of items divided by the **Row** or **Column Total** for the **Base Field** and expressed as a percentage. Whether the **Row** or **Column Total** will be used in the calculation will depend on whether the **Base Field** is in the **Rows** area or the **Columns** area. In Fig 2.30 the **% Running Total In** for each *Product* item would be the **Running Total In** *(Cumulative Revenue)* for each *Product* item in a given year divided by the **Column Total** for *Product* in the same year.

Product	2015 Sum of Revenue	2015 Cumulative Revenue	2016 Sum of Revenue	2016 Cumulative Revenue
Biscuits	$538,395	$538,395	$572,242	$572,242
Candies	$1,153,840	$1,692,235	$1,270,313	$1,842,555
Chocolate Bars	$817,741	$2,509,976	$894,926	$2,737,481
Chocolate Croissants	$494,613	$3,004,589	$549,817	$3,287,298
Crackers	$304,610	$3,309,199	$321,556	$3,608,854
Cream Cakes	$141,893	$3,451,092	$177,936	$3,786,790
Frozen Yoghurt	$4,620,560	$8,071,651	$4,725,405	$8,512,196
Ice Cream	$5,074,840	$13,146,491	$5,448,956	$13,961,151
Muffins	$733,072	$13,879,563	$811,093	$14,772,244
Small Cakes	$1,350,148	$15,229,711	$1,416,090	$16,188,334
Grand Total	$15,229,711		$16,188,334	

Fig 2.30: Pivot Table with **Running Total In** calculation named as *Cumulative Revenue*

In the Pivot Table from Fig 2.30 let's right click on any cell under *Cumulative Revenue* and then click on **Show Values As** and finally on **% Running Total In**. In the **Show Values As** dialog box leave *Product* as **Base Field** and click **OK** (Fig 2.31).

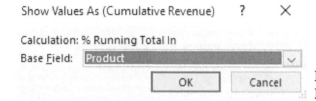

Fig 2.31: Show Values As dialog box with **% Running Total In** calculation

Rename *Cumulative Revenue* as *Cumulative Revenue in %*. Now the Pivot Table should look like in Fig 2.32.

Product	2015 Sum of Revenue	2015 Cumulative Revenue in %	2016 Sum of Revenue	2016 Cumulative Revenue in %
Biscuits	$538,395	3.54%	$572,242	3.53%
Candies	$1,153,840	11.11%	$1,270,313	11.38%
Chocolate Bars	$817,741	16.48%	$894,926	16.91%
Chocolate Croissants	$494,613	19.73%	$549,817	20.31%
Crackers	$304,610	21.73%	$321,556	22.29%
Cream Cakes	$141,893	22.66%	$177,936	23.39%
Frozen Yoghurt	$4,620,560	53.00%	$4,725,405	52.58%
Ice Cream	$5,074,840	86.32%	$5,448,956	86.24%
Muffins	$733,072	91.13%	$811,093	91.25%
Small Cakes	$1,350,148	100.00%	$1,416,090	100.00%
Grand Total	$15,229,711		$16,188,334	

Fig 2.32: Pivot table with **% Running Total In** calculation named as *Cumulative Revenue in %*

Rank Smallest to Largest

This calculation assigns a rank to a value cell in relation to other value cells for the same base field. A value of *1* is assigned to the smallest value and a value of *N* to the largest.

 If a field that is ranked has a parent field then the ranking for this field will be done for each parent field item separately.

Let's build a new Pivot Table with *Product* in **Rows**, *Year* in **Columns** and *Revenue* and *Price per unit* in **Σ Values** and without **Row Totals**. Revenue will be calculated as **Sum** whereas *Price per unit* as **Max**. This Pivot Table will look like the one in Fig 2.33.

| Product | Year ▼ Values | | | |
| | 2015 | | 2016 | |
▼	Sum of Revenue	Max of Price per unit	Sum of Revenue	Max of Price per unit
Biscuits	$538,395	1.75	$572,242	1.85
Candies	$1,153,840	2.5	$1,270,313	2.75
Chocolate Bars	$817,741	1.25	$894,926	1.35
Chocolate Croissants	$494,613	1.8	$549,817	1.99
Crackers	$304,610	2	$321,556	2.1
Cream Cakes	$141,893	1	$177,936	1.25
Frozen Yoghurt	$4,620,560	4.5	$4,725,405	4.6
Ice Cream	$5,074,840	4	$5,448,956	4.3
Muffins	$733,072	2.1	$811,093	2.3
Small Cakes	$1,350,148	2.5	$1,416,090	2.6
Grand Total	**$15,229,711**	**4.5**	**$16,188,334**	**4.6**

Fig 2.33: Pivot Table built for **Rank Smallest to Largest** calculation

Let's click on any value cell under *Max of Price per unit* and then right click, select **Show Values As** and then click on **Rank Smallest to Largest...** . In the **Show Values As** dialog box set *Product* as the **Base Field** and click **OK** (Fig 2.34).

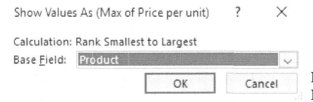

Fig 2.34: Show Values As dialog box for the **Rank Smallest to Largest** calculation

In the new Pivot Table rename *Max of Price per unit* to *Rank Price S to L*. The new Pivot Table will now look like in Fig 2.35.

Product	Year		Values	
	2015		2016	
	Sum of Revenue	Rank Price S to L	Sum of Revenue	Rank Price S to L
Biscuits	$538,395	3	$572,242	3
Candies	$1,153,840	7	$1,270,313	8
Chocolate Bars	$817,741	2	$894,926	2
Chocolate Croissants	$494,613	4	$549,817	4
Crackers	$304,610	5	$321,556	5
Cream Cakes	$141,893	1	$177,936	1
Frozen Yoghurt	$4,620,560	9	$4,725,405	10
Ice Cream	$5,074,840	8	$5,448,956	9
Muffins	$733,072	6	$811,093	6
Small Cakes	$1,350,148	7	$1,416,090	7
Grand Total	$15,229,711		$16,188,334	

Fig 2.35: Pivot Table with *Price per unit* ranked from smallest to largest

Rank Largest to Smallest

This calculation is the same as the **Rank Smallest to Largest** except that now the largest value is assigned a rank of *1* and the smallest a rank of *N*.

Right click on any value cell under *Rank Price S to L* in the Pivot Table from Fig 2.35 and then click on **Show Values As** and then on **Rank Largest to Smallest**. In the **Show Values As** dialog box keep *Product* as **Base Field** and click **OK**.

Show Values As (Rank Price S to L)   ?   X

Calculation: Rank Largest to Smallest
Base Field: Product

OK   Cancel

Fig 2.36: Show Values As dialog box for **Rank Largest to Smallest**

In the new Pivot Table rename *Rank Price S to L* to *Rank Price L to S*. The new Pivot Table will now look like in Fig 2.37.

Index

The **Index** custom calculation is used to compare an item's value in proportion to a **Row** or **Column Total** for this item *versus* this item's **Row** or **Column Total** in proportion to the **Grand Total**.

For example the **Index** will show how a production line does relative to all production lines in one year, compared to how this production line does relative to all production lines in all years combined.

To understand this better let's build a Pivot Table with *Production Line* in **Rows**, *Year* in

Columns and *Revenue* in Σ **Values** twice. The new Pivot Table will look like in Fig 2.38.

Product	2015 Sum of Revenue	2015 Rank Price L to S	2016 Sum of Revenue	2016 Rank Price L to S
Biscuits	$538,395	7	$572,242	8
Candies	$1,153,840	3	$1,270,313	3
Chocolate Bars	$817,741	8	$894,926	9
Chocolate Croissants	$494,613	6	$549,817	7
Crackers	$304,610	5	$321,556	6
Cream Cakes	$141,893	9	$177,936	10
Frozen Yoghurt	$4,620,560	1	$4,725,405	1
Ice Cream	$5,074,840	2	$5,448,956	2
Muffins	$733,072	4	$811,093	5
Small Cakes	$1,350,148	3	$1,416,090	4
Grand Total	$15,229,711		$16,188,334	

Fig 2.37: Pivot Table with *Price per unit* ranked from largest to smallest

Production Line	2015 Sum of Revenue	2015 Sum of Revenue2	2016 Sum of Revenue	2016 Sum of Revenue2	Total Sum of Revenue	Total Sum of Revenue2
Line A	$2,814,586	$2,814,586	$3,059,037	$3,059,037	$5,873,623	$5,873,623
Line B	$2,719,726	$2,719,726	$2,954,936	$2,954,936	$5,674,662	$5,674,662
Line C	$9,695,400	$9,695,400	$10,174,361	$10,174,361	$19,869,760	$19,869,760
Grand Total	$15,229,711	$15,229,711	$16,188,334	$16,188,334	$31,418,045	$31,418,045

Fig 2.38: Pivot Table prior to applying the **Index** calculation

Right click on any value cell under *Sum of Revenue2*, click on **Value Field Settings** and go to the **Show Values As** tab. In the drop-down list select the **Index** calculation. In the **Custom Name** box rename *Sum of Revenue2* as *Revenue Index* and then click **OK** (Fig 2.39).

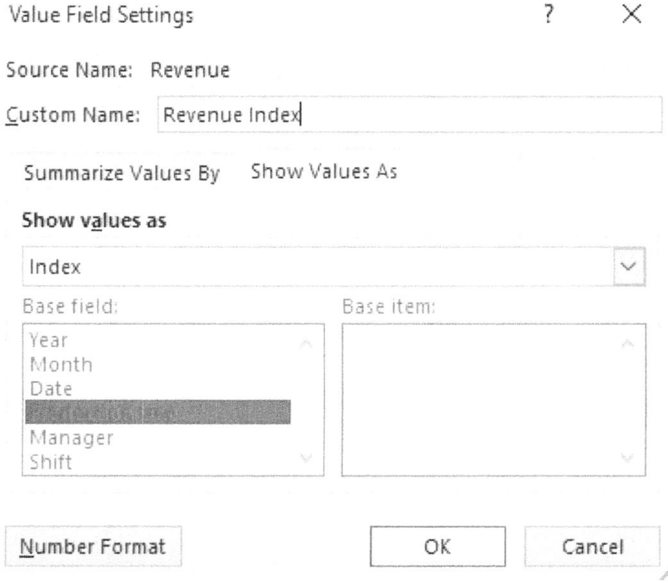

Fig 2.39: The **Show Values As** tab with the **Index** calculation selected

The new Pivot Table will now look like in Fig 2.40.

Year	Values					
	2015		2016		Total Sum of Revenue	Total Revenue Index
Production Line	Sum of Revenue	Revenue Index	Sum of Revenue	Revenue Index		
Line A	$2,814,586	0.989	$3,059,037	1.011	$5,873,623	1
Line B	$2,719,726	0.989	$2,954,936	1.011	$5,674,662	1
Line C	$9,695,400	1.007	$10,174,361	0.994	$19,869,760	1
Grand Total	$15,229,711	1	$16,188,334	1	$31,418,045	1

Fig 2.40: Pivot Table with *Revenue* in a year indexed against *Revenue* in all years

The above Pivot Table shows that in *2015 Revenue* from *Line A* and *Line B* has been relatively lower than *Revenue* from these production lines in both years taken together.

The formula for the **Index** calculation is:

$$Index = \frac{(Cell\ Value) \div (Column\ Total)}{(Row\ Total) \div (Grand\ Total)}$$

$$ALSO$$

$$Index = \frac{(Cell\ Value) \div (Row\ Total)}{(Column\ Total) \div (Grand\ Total)}$$

$$BOTH\ EQUAL$$

$$Index = \frac{(Cell\ Value) \times (Grand\ Total)}{(Row\ Total) \times (Column\ Total)}$$

Let's put the formula to work.

According to the above formula the *Revenue Index* for *Line A* and *2015* should be:

Index = ($2,814,586*$31,418,045)/($5,873,623*$15,229,711)

= ($88,428,789,604,370/$89,453,580,812,953)

= **0.989**

Using the **Index** formula we calculated the same **Index** as the one calculated by Excel which confirms that this is the formula used for computing the **Index** calculation.

2.2 Field Settings

Field settings are options available for fields in **Filters**, **Columns** or **Rows** areas. We can access **Field Settings** by clicking on the name of the field in the **PivotTable Fields List's Filters, Columns** or **Rows** areas and then selecting **Field Settings...** . In the example below I have selected **Field Settings** for the *Year* field (Fig 2.41).

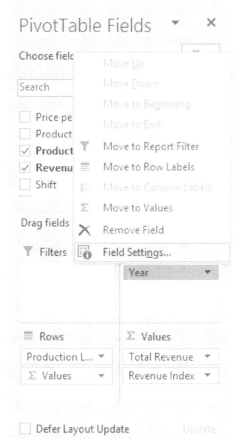

Fig 2.41: Accessing **Field Settings** through the **PivotTable Fields List**

If we click on the **Field Settings...** button we get the **Field Settings** dialog box as in Fig 2.42. In this dialog box as in the **Value Field Settings** dialog box we can change the number format, when the field is numeric, and give the field a custom name.

The **Field Settings** dialog box has two tabs. The **Subtotals & Filters** tab and the **Layout & Print** tab.

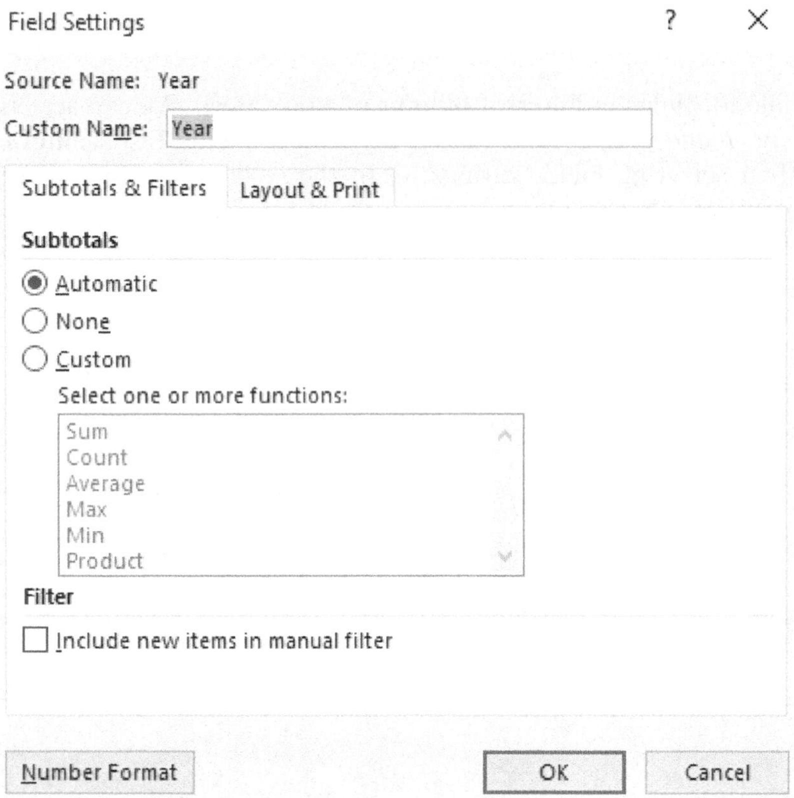

Fig 2.42: Field Settings dialog box for the *Year* field

2.2.1 Subtotals & Filters Tab

The **Subtotals & Filters** tab has two sections, the **Subtotals** and the **Filter** sections.

Subtotals Section

In the **Subtotals** section of the **Subtotals & Filters** tab we can select how to calculate the **Subtotals**. The choices for calculation types are **Automatic**, **None** or **Custom**. There is a total of 11 calculations under **Custom**. The definitions for these calculations are the same as the ones explained in Table 2.1.

Let's build a Pivot Table where we have *Production Line* and *Product* in **Rows**, *Year* in **Columns** and *Revenue* in ∑ **Values**. Then go to the **Design** tab and in the **Layout** group click on **Subtotals** and then click on **Show all Subtotals at Bottom of Group**. The Pivot Table will look like in Fig 2.43.

If we click on any cell under *Production Line* and then right click and select **Field Settings...**, a dialog box as in Fig 2.44 will appear.

Sum of Revenue		Year		
Production Line ▾	Product ▾	2015	2016	Grand Total
⊟ Line A				
	Biscuits	$538,395	$572,242	$1,110,637
	Candies	$1,153,840	$1,270,313	$2,424,153
	Chocolate Bars	$817,741	$894,926	$1,712,667
	Crackers	$304,610	$321,556	$626,166
Line A Total		$2,814,586	$3,059,037	$5,873,623
⊟ Line B				
	Chocolate Croissants	$494,613	$549,817	$1,044,430
	Cream Cakes	$141,893	$177,936	$319,829
	Muffins	$733,072	$811,093	$1,544,165
	Small Cakes	$1,350,148	$1,416,090	$2,766,238
Line B Total		$2,719,726	$2,954,936	$5,674,662
⊟ Line C				
	Frozen Yoghurt	$4,620,560	$4,725,405	$9,345,965
	Ice Cream	$5,074,840	$5,448,956	$10,523,796
Line C Total		$9,695,400	$10,174,361	$19,869,760
Grand Total		$15,229,711	$16,188,334	$31,418,045

Fig 2.43: Pivot Table ready for subtotals editing

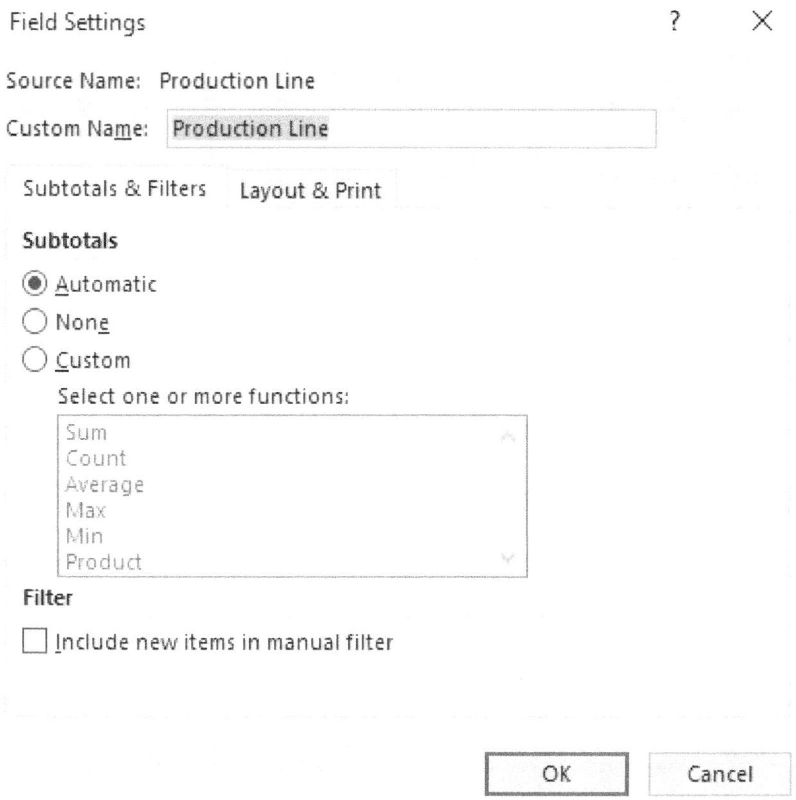

Field Settings   ?   ✕

Source Name: Production Line

Custom Name: Production Line

Subtotals & Filters   Layout & Print

Subtotals

◉ Automatic

◯ None

◯ Custom

Select one or more functions:

```
Sum
Count
Average
Max
Min
Product
```

Filter

☐ Include new items in manual filter

OK   Cancel

Fig 2.44: Field Settings dialog box for *Production Line*

As you can see under the **Subtotals** section the **Automatic** option has been selected by default. This is basically the **Sum** as you can notice from the Pivot Table.

If we select the **None** option then the **Subtotals** will be removed from the Pivot Table.

If we select the **Custom** option then we have a choice of 11 calculations to calculate the Subtotals such as the Sum, Average, Max, etc.

What is also important to note is that under **Custom** we can select more than one calculation at the same time, if we wanted to, as it can be clearly seen in Fig 2.45.

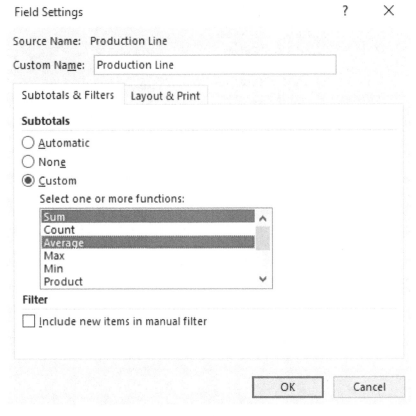

Fig 2.45: Selecting more than one function for the subtotals

For this exercise let's select the **Sum** and the **Average**. The Pivot Table will now look as in Fig 2.46.

Filter Section

In the **Filter** section we have a checkbox and the statement **Include new items in manual filter**.

Sum of Revenue		Year		
Production Line	Product	2015	2016	Grand Total
Line A				
	Biscuits	$538,395	$572,242	$1,110,637
	Candies	$1,153,840	$1,270,313	$2,424,153
	Chocolate Bars	$817,741	$894,926	$1,712,667
	Crackers	$304,610	$321,556	$626,166
Line A Sum		**$2,814,586**	**$3,059,037**	**$5,873,623**
Line A Average		**$58,637**	**$63,730**	**$61,184**
Line B				
	Chocolate Croissants	$494,613	$549,817	$1,044,430
	Cream Cakes	$141,893	$177,936	$319,829
	Muffins	$733,072	$811,093	$1,544,165
	Small Cakes	$1,350,148	$1,416,090	$2,766,238
Line B Sum		**$2,719,726**	**$2,954,936**	**$5,674,662**
Line B Average		**$56,661**	**$61,561**	**$59,111**
Line C				
	Frozen Yoghurt	$4,620,560	$4,725,405	$9,345,965
	Ice Cream	$5,074,840	$5,448,956	$10,523,796
Line C Sum		**$9,695,400**	**$10,174,361**	**$19,869,760**
Line C Average		**$201,987**	**$211,966**	**$206,977**
Grand Total		**$15,229,711**	**$16,188,334**	**$31,418,045**

Fig 2.46: Pivot Table with two subtotals calculations

Perhaps the average revenue figure for **Subtotals** is not what you expected. Perhaps you expected that the average should have been the average of the **Sums** by *Product* (already in the table) which, for *Line A* and *2015* would have been $703,646.5 or at least you would have found this a more useful number. Well this is not the case as the **Average** for **Subtotals** is the *Average Monthly Revenue* generated by each *Shift* in the *Year 2015* or *2016*. This is important because you need to know how these metrics are calculated in order to display the correct figures in your Pivot Table. *If you want the average of the sums then you will need to build a Pivot Table using the above Pivot Table as a data source OR simply use worksheet functions and present it in a table close-by.*

☐ **Include new items in manual filter**

This option is not selected by default.

If you had a Pivot Table with *Production Line* in **Rows**, *Year* in **Columns** and *Revenue* in Σ **Values** and you wanted your Pivot Table to display only the *Year 2015* you would manually filter this in the Pivot Table as in Fig 2.47. If you update the source data with *Year 2017* data and refresh the Pivot Table then:

- If **Include new items in manual filter** option **IS NOT SELECTED** when the Pivot Table is refreshed only *Year 2015* will continue to appear in the Pivot Table.

- If **Include new items in manual filter** option **IS SELECTED** when the Pivot Table is refreshed both *Year 2015* and *Year 2017* will appear in the Pivot Table.

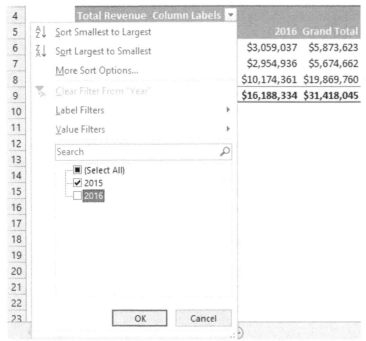

Fig 2.47: Manually filtering the *Year 2015* in the Pivot Table

2.2.2 Layout & Print tab

Using the latest Pivot Table we built let's do a right click under *Production Line* and select **Field Settings...** . In the **Field Settings** dialog box that pops up there is a second tab named as the **Layout & Print** tab (see Fig 2.48). The tab is divided in two sections where we have a few options that are mainly to do with formatting and printing a Pivot Table.

Layout Section

The **Layout** options in the **Layout & Print** tab are similar to the ones in the **Design** tab, **Layout** group. These options can be understood better when we have two or more fields in either **Rows** or **Columns** areas.

There is one important difference between the **Layout** options in the **Design** tab and the **Layout** options in the **Layout & Print** tab under **Field Settings**. **Layout** options in the **Design** tab apply to the whole Pivot Table, that is, to all the fields, however **Layout** options in the **Layout & Print** tab apply to the selected field only.

For e.g. if we have three fields in the **Rows** area we can have the **Outline form** for the first field and the **Compact form** for the next two fields.

Field Settings   ?   ✕

Source Name: Production Line

Custom Name: | Production Line |

Subtotals & Filters | Layout & Print |

Layout

◉ Show item labels in outline form

   ☐ Display labels from the next field in the same column (compact form)

   ☐ Display subtotals at the top of each group

◯ Show item labels in tabular form

☐ Repeat item labels

☐ Insert blank line after each item label

☐ Show items with no data

Print

☐ Insert page break after each item

    | OK | | Cancel | **Fig 2.48**: The **Layout & Print** tab

We can have **Repeat item labels** for one field but not for the others and we can **Insert blank line after each item label** for one field but not for the others.

This basically gives you a higher degree of flexibility. You can't get this flexibility from the **Design** tab as your choices apply to all fields at the same time.

We won't unnecessarily go through all the combinations here however let's look at an example with mixed options so you can see this flexibility in practice.

Lets' build a Pivot Table with *Production Line, Shift* & *Product* in **Rows**, *Year* in **Columns** and *Revenue* in Σ **Values**. Once the Pivot Table has been built go to the **Design** tab, click on **Report Layout** and then click **Show in Outline Form**. This will put the entire Pivot Table in **Outline form**.

Now let's right click any cell under *Shift* and select **Field Settings...** and then click on the **Layout & Print** tab. Fill in the options as in Fig 2.49 and click **OK**.

Now right click any cell under *Production Line* and select **Field Settings...** . In the dialog box that opens click on the **Layout & Print** tab. Fill the options as in Fig 2.50 and click **OK**.

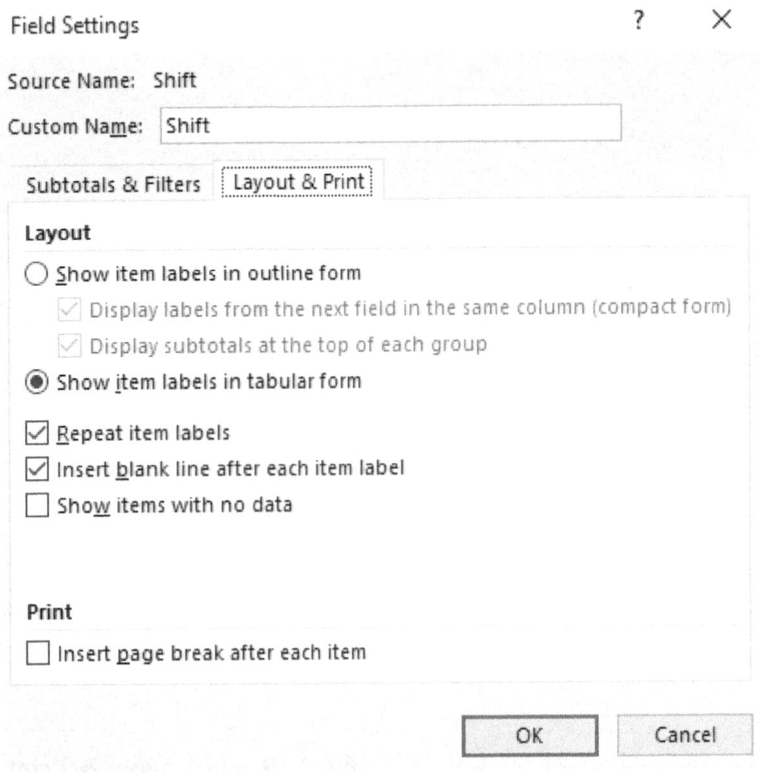

Field Settings   ?   ✕

Source Name: Shift

Custom Name: Shift

Subtotals & Filters | Layout & Print

Layout

○ Show item labels in outline form

  ☑ Display labels from the next field in the same column (compact form)

  ☑ Display subtotals at the top of each group

◉ Show item labels in tabular form

☑ Repeat item labels

☑ Insert blank line after each item label

☐ Show items with no data

Print

☐ Insert page break after each item

[OK] [Cancel]

Fig 2.49: Layout & Print tab with all the options that need selecting for the *Shift* field

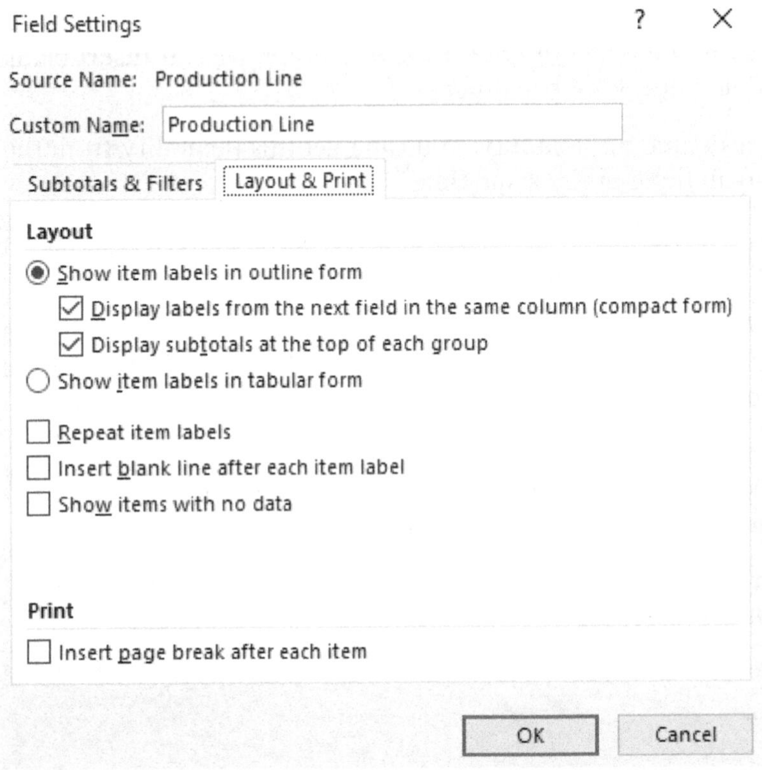

Field Settings   ?   ✕

Source Name: Production Line

Custom Name: Production Line

Subtotals & Filters | Layout & Print

Layout

◉ Show item labels in outline form

  ☑ Display labels from the next field in the same column (compact form)

  ☑ Display subtotals at the top of each group

○ Show item labels in tabular form

☐ Repeat item labels

☐ Insert blank line after each item label

☐ Show items with no data

Print

☐ Insert page break after each item

[OK] [Cancel]

Fig 2.50: Layout & Print tab with all the options that need selecting for the *Production Line* field

Now we should see an updated Pivot Table as in Fig 2.51.

Sum of Revenue		Column Labels ▼		
Row Labels ▼	Product	2015	2016	Grand Total
⊟ Line A		$2,814,586	$3,059,037	$5,873,623
⊟ Day	Biscuits	$538,395	$572,242	$1,110,637
Day	Chocolate Bars	$817,741	$894,926	$1,712,667
Day Total		$1,356,136	$1,467,168	$2,823,304
⊟ Night	Candies	$1,153,840	$1,270,313	$2,424,153
Night	Crackers	$304,610	$321,556	$626,166
Night Total		$1,458,450	$1,591,869	$3,050,319
⊟ Line B		$2,719,726	$2,954,936	$5,674,662
⊟ Day	Cream Cakes	$141,893	$177,936	$319,829
Day	Small Cakes	$1,350,148	$1,416,090	$2,766,238
Day Total		$1,492,041	$1,594,026	$3,086,067
⊟ Night	Chocolate Croissants	$494,613	$549,817	$1,044,430
Night	Muffins	$733,072	$811,093	$1,544,165
Night Total		$1,227,685	$1,360,910	$2,588,595
⊟ Line C		$9,695,400	$10,174,361	$19,869,760
⊟ Day	Frozen Yoghurt	$2,394,360	$2,457,417	$4,851,777
Day	Ice Cream	$2,512,440	$2,708,699	$5,221,139
Day Total		$4,906,800	$5,166,116	$10,072,916
⊟ Night	Frozen Yoghurt	$2,226,200	$2,267,989	$4,494,188
Night	Ice Cream	$2,562,400	$2,740,257	$5,302,657
Night Total		$4,788,600	$5,008,245	$9,796,845
Grand Total		$15,229,711	$16,188,334	$31,418,045

Fig 2.51: Pivot Table with different layout options for different fields

As you can see from the new Pivot Table we have a few mixed features.

- *Shift* has repeating item labels but *Production Line* does not.

- *Shift* and *Product* are in **Tabular Form** whereas *Production Line* and *Shift* are in **Outline Form**.

- There is a blank line only after each *Shift* item.

Again note that you wouldn't be able to get this layout using the **Design** tab.

☐ **Show items with no data**

This option is not selected by default.

In the **Layout section** we have the option to show items with no data by ticking the **Show items with no data** checkbox.

If we have two or more fields in **Rows** or **Columns** and some items from a field relate to one parent field item but not to another parent field item then if this option is selected all items from a field will be shown for each parent field item rather than only for those that relate to it.

Value cells for items that don't have any data will be shown in the Pivot Table either empty or as zeros depending on Pivot Table options.

Let's try and understand this better through an example. Let's build a Pivot Table with *Shift* and *Product* in **Rows**, *Year* in **Columns** and *Revenue* in **Σ Values**.

The Pivot Table when this option is not selected will look like in Fig 2.52.

Sum of Revenue		Column Labels		
Row Labels	Product	2015	2016	Grand Total
⊟ **Day**		**$7,754,976**	**$8,227,310**	**$15,982,286**
	Biscuits	$538,395	$572,242	$1,110,637
	Chocolate Bars	$817,741	$894,926	$1,712,667
	Cream Cakes	$141,893	$177,936	$319,829
	Frozen Yoghurt	$2,394,360	$2,457,417	$4,851,777
	Ice Cream	$2,512,440	$2,708,699	$5,221,139
	Small Cakes	$1,350,148	$1,416,090	$2,766,238
⊟ **Night**		**$7,474,735**	**$7,961,024**	**$15,435,759**
	Candies	$1,153,840	$1,270,313	$2,424,153
	Chocolate Croissants	$494,613	$549,817	$1,044,430
	Crackers	$304,610	$321,556	$626,166
	Frozen Yoghurt	$2,226,200	$2,267,989	$4,494,188
	Ice Cream	$2,562,400	$2,740,257	$5,302,657
	Muffins	$733,072	$811,093	$1,544,165
Grand Total		$15,229,711	$16,188,334	$31,418,045

Fig 2.52: Pivot Table with **Show items with no data** NOT selected

Right click on any *Product* item under *Product* and go to the **Layout section** under **Layout & Print** tab in the **Field Settings** dialog box and tick the checkbox before **Show items with no data** and then click **OK**. The updated Pivot Table will show *Product* items with no data for each *Shift* as in Fig 2.53.

In the Pivot Table in Fig 2.53 we can see that *Candies* for e.g. are only produced in the *Night Shift* and *Biscuits* only in the *Day Shift* yet they show under both *Shifts* due to the option we selected.

Print Section
☐ **Insert page break after each item**

This option is not selected by default.

Essentially it can get each row field item in a Pivot Table printed on a new page.

Sum of Revenue	Column Labels ▼		
Row Labels ▼ Product	2015	2016	Grand Total
⊟ Day	$7,754,976	$8,227,310	$15,982,286
Biscuits	$538,395	$572,242	$1,110,637
Candies			
Chocolate Bars	$817,741	$894,926	$1,712,667
Chocolate Croissants			
Crackers			
Cream Cakes	$141,893	$177,936	$319,829
Frozen Yoghurt	$2,394,360	$2,457,417	$4,851,777
Ice Cream	$2,512,440	$2,708,699	$5,221,139
Muffins			
Small Cakes	$1,350,148	$1,416,090	$2,766,238
⊟ Night	$7,474,735	$7,961,024	$15,435,759
Biscuits			
Candies	$1,153,840	$1,270,313	$2,424,153
Chocolate Bars			
Chocolate Croissants	$494,613	$549,817	$1,044,430
Crackers	$304,610	$321,556	$626,166
Cream Cakes			
Frozen Yoghurt	$2,226,200	$2,267,989	$4,494,188
Ice Cream	$2,562,400	$2,740,257	$5,302,657
Muffins	$733,072	$811,093	$1,544,165
Small Cakes			
Grand Total	$15,229,711	$16,188,334	$31,418,045

Fig 2.53: Pivot Table showing items with no data

Let's rebuild the Pivot Table from Fig 2.51 and right click on one of the *Shift* items and then select **Field Settings....** In the **Layout & Print** tab tick the checkbox before **Insert page break after each item** and then press **OK**.

Sum of Reve	Column La ▼		
Row Labe ▼ Product	2015	2016	Grand Total
⊟ Line A	$2,814,586	$3,059,037	$5,873,623
⊟ Day			
Biscuits	$538,395	$572,242	$1,110,637
Chocolate Bars	$817,741	$894,926	$1,712,667
Day Total	$1,356,136	$1,467,168	$2,823,304
⊟ Night			
Candies	$1,153,840	$1,270,313	$2,424,153
Crackers	$304,610	$321,556	$626,166
Night Total	$1,458,450	$1,591,869	$3,050,319
⊟ Line B	$2,719,726	$2,954,936	$5,674,662
⊟ Day			
Cream Cakes	$141,893	$177,936	$319,829
Small Cakes	$1,350,148	$1,416,090	$2,766,238
Day Total	$1,492,041	$1,594,026	$3,086,067
⊟ Night			
Chocolate Croissants	$494,613	$549,817	$1,044,430
Muffins	$733,072	$811,093	$1,544,165
Night Total	$1,227,685	$1,360,910	$2,588,595
⊟ Line C	$9,695,400	$10,174,361	$19,869,760
⊟ Day			
Frozen Yoghurt	$2,394,360	$2,457,417	$4,851,777
Ice Cream	$2,512,440	$2,708,699	$5,221,139
Day Total	$4,906,800	$5,166,116	$10,072,916
⊟ Night			
Frozen Yoghurt	$2,226,200	$2,267,989	$4,494,188
Ice Cream	$2,562,400	$2,740,257	$5,302,657
Night Total	$4,788,600	$5,008,245	$9,796,845
Grand Total	$15,229,711	$16,188,334	$31,418,045

Fig 2.54: Page Breaks after each *Shift* item

Let's go to the **View** tab and click on **Page Break View**. In Fig 2.54 we can clearly see how each *Shift* item including any items from a child field (i.e. *Product*) will now get printed on a new page.

Now let's remove the page break after each *Shift* item and let's put it after each *Production Line* item. To do this untick the **Insert page break after each item** checkbox in *Shift's* **Field Settings** dialog box and then go and tick it in the *Production Line's* **Field Settings** dialog box.

Now each *Production Line* data will get printed on a new page as in Fig 2.55.

Sum of Reve	Product	Column La		
Row Labe	Product	2015	2016	Grand Total
Line A		$2,814,586	$3,059,037	$5,873,623
Day				
	Biscuits	$538,395	$572,242	$1,110,637
	Chocolate Bars	$817,741	$894,926	$1,712,667
Day Total		$1,356,136	$1,467,168	$2,823,304
Night				
	Candies	$1,153,840	$1,270,313	$2,424,153
	Crackers	$304,610	$321,556	$626,166
Night Total		$1,458,450	$1,591,869	$3,050,319
Line B		$2,719,726	$2,954,936	$5,674,662
Day				
	Cream Cakes	$141,893	$177,936	$319,829
	Small Cakes	$1,350,148	$1,416,090	$2,766,238
Day Total		$1,492,041	$1,594,026	$3,086,067
Night				
	Chocolate Croissants	$494,613	$549,817	$1,044,430
	Muffins	$733,072	$811,093	$1,544,165
Night Total		$1,227,685	$1,360,910	$2,588,595
Line C		$9,695,400	$10,174,361	$19,869,760
Day				
	Frozen Yoghurt	$2,394,360	$2,457,417	$4,851,777
	Ice Cream	$2,512,440	$2,708,699	$5,221,139
Day Total		$4,906,800	$5,166,116	$10,072,916
Night				
	Frozen Yoghurt	$2,226,200	$2,267,989	$4,494,188
	Ice Cream	$2,562,400	$2,740,257	$5,302,657
Night Total		$4,788,600	$5,008,245	$9,796,845
Grand Total		$15,229,711	$16,188,334	$31,418,045

Fig 2.55: New page breaks after each *Production Line* item

CHAPTER 3

Filters, Slicers and Timelines

Filtering is very important in making sure that you display the data you want on a Pivot Table. There are many ways you can filter data and we will explore each one in detail.

3.1 Filters Area

The **Filters** area is used to contain fields whose items we intend to use as filters for our Pivot Table.

This simply means: Build a Pivot Table using as a data source only the rows where the items of the field or fields in the **Filters** area equate to any value or values that you want. An important feature of the **Filters** area is that it can contain multiple fields.

To understand this feature better let's look at an example. Using the same data source we have used so far in this book let's build a Pivot Table with *Product* in **Rows**, *Year* in **Columns** and *Revenue* in **Σ Values**.

It does make sense to compare *Product Revenue* by *Year* however sometimes it makes sense to compare a *Month* in a *Year* to the same *Month* in another *Year*. Therefore, in this case we want to filter by a third group which will be *Month*. So let's put *Month* in the **Filters** area.

The **PivotTable Fields List** should look like in Fig 3.1.

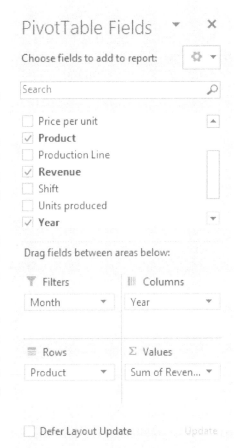

Fig 3.1: **PivotTable Fields List** with all the fields in the right place

Right click in the value area of the Pivot Table and select **Value Field Settings...** . In the **Value Field Settings** dialog box change the **number format** to $ with no decimal places and rename *Sum of Revenue* to *Total Revenue*. The new Pivot table will now look as in Fig 3.2.

Month	(All)		

Total Revenue	Column Labels		
Row Labels	2015	2016	Grand Total
Biscuits	$538,395	$572,242	$1,110,637
Candies	$1,153,840	$1,270,313	$2,424,153
Chocolate Bars	$817,741	$894,926	$1,712,667
Chocolate Croissants	$494,613	$549,817	$1,044,430
Crackers	$304,610	$321,556	$626,166
Cream Cakes	$141,893	$177,936	$319,829
Frozen Yoghurt	$4,620,560	$4,725,405	$9,345,965
Ice Cream	$5,074,840	$5,448,956	$10,523,796
Muffins	$733,072	$811,093	$1,544,165
Small Cakes	$1,350,148	$1,416,090	$2,766,238
Grand Total	$15,229,711	$16,188,334	$31,418,045

Fig 3.2: Pivot Table with *Month* in the **Filters** area

Note though that this Pivot Table as it is won't look any different to the one built without any filters. This is because we have selected **(All)** months in the *Month* filter. To compare *January 2015* with *January 2016* for e.g. we will need to select only *January* from the **Filters** drop-down menu. See Fig 3.3.

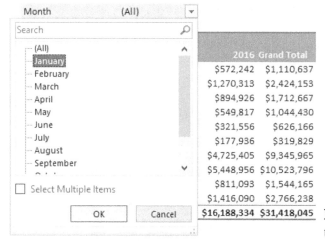

Fig 3.3: List of months to select from for the *Month* filter

Click on the drop-down button in the cell next to *Month,* select *January* and then click **OK**. Now the Pivot Table data will be filtered by the month of *January* in both years.

Notice that at the end of the list in Fig 3.3 there is the **Select Multiple Items** checkbox. If you tick this checkbox then you will be able to select more than one month to filter by. For e.g. you can select the first quarter of a year to compare results year on year.

In Fig 3.4 we can see how the Pivot Table looks like after it has been filtered by *January*. Notice the **Funnel icon** that appears in the Pivot Table next to the *Month* field in the **PivotTable-Fields List**. If we click this icon in either we will get the filter list as in Fig 3.3.

Month	January	▼

Total Revenue	Column Labels ▼		
Row Labels ▼	2015	2016	Grand Total
Biscuits	$44,800	$45,512	$90,312
Candies	$95,000	$101,167	$196,167
Chocolate Bars	$67,875	$75,462	$143,337
Chocolate Croissants	$40,460	$43,842	$84,302
Crackers	$24,712	$25,131	$49,843
Cream Cakes	$11,500	$13,691	$25,191
Frozen Yoghurt	$382,500	$386,170	$768,670
Ice Cream	$420,800	$450,769	$871,569
Muffins	$60,270	$66,183	$126,453
Small Cakes	$112,500	$118,305	$230,805
Grand Total	$1,260,417	$1,326,231	$2,586,649

Fig 3.4: Pivot Table filtered by *January*

As already mentioned we can have multiple filters at the same time through which we can drill down the data further. All we need to do is select a new field in the **PivotTable Fields List** and drag it to the **Filters** area.

So let's drag *Manager* to the **Filters** area. Then click on the drop down button in the cell next to the field name and select *Douglass Robinson*. Now the Pivot Table has been filtered to *January* and to *Douglass Robinson* as *Manager*.

Manager	Douglass Robinson	▼
Month	January	▼

Total Revenue	Column Labels	▼	
Row Labels ▼	2015	2016	Grand Total
Candies	$95,000	$101,167	$196,167
Crackers	$24,712	$25,131	$49,843
Grand Total	$119,712	$126,298	$246,010

Fig 3.5: Pivot Table filtered by *Month* and *Manager*

3.2 Label and Value Filters

Of the various ways to filter data in Pivot Tables two of these are the **Label** and **Value Filters**. The **Label** and **Value Filters** are filters used on fields that reside in **Columns** or **Rows** areas. These labels are accessible from:

- The drop-down button next to **Column labels** or **Row labels** when a Pivot Table is in **Compact form**

- The drop-down button next to a field's name in a Pivot Table when it is in **Outline** or **Tabular form**

- The **PivotTable Fields List's** areas section by clicking on the name of the field.

In the Pivot Table from Fig 3.5 let's remove *Month* and *Manager* from the **Filters** area and let's click on the drop-down button next to **Row Labels**. Once the drop down button is clicked we have a menu drop down as in Fig 3.6 from which we can access **Label** or **Value Filters**. In this case let's select **Label Filters** since we want to filter based on the name of items in the *Product* field.

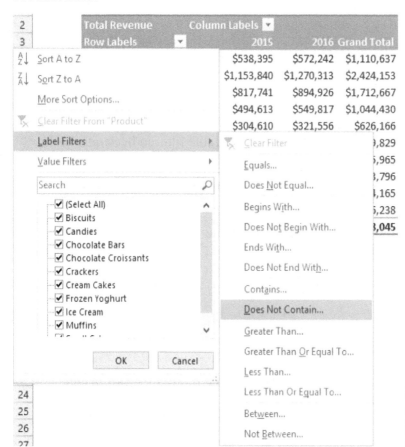

Fig 3.6: Menu from where we can access **Label** or **Value Filters** once the button next to **Row Labels** has been clicked

In **Label Filters** we have a total of 14 conditions through which to filter data. They can be seen in Fig 3.6. In this case let's choose the condition '**Does Not Contain...**' and use the word *'Chocolate'*. Once we do this then any *Product* item that contains the word *Chocolate* will be removed from the Pivot Table. You might have already noticed from Fig 3.7 that I have not written the entire word *Chocolate* but opted to go for a shortcut and use the * instead of writing the whole word. The * will include any words that start with 'Choc' but do not necessarily end in 'olate'. They can end in any combination of letters. This type of shortcuts are just meant to make your life easier as well as to increase your options when filtering.

The filtered Pivot Table looks like in Fig 3.8.

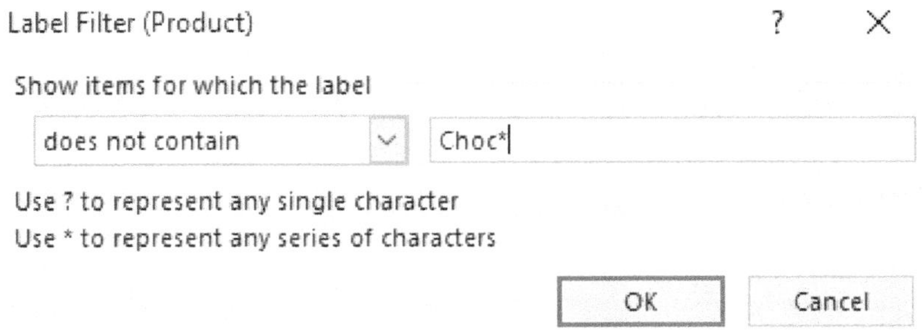

Label Filter (Product)   ? ✕

Show items for which the label

| does not contain | ∨ | Choc* |

Use ? to represent any single character
Use * to represent any series of characters

OK   Cancel

Fig 3.7: Label Filter dialog box

Total Revenue	Column Labels ▼		
Row Labels ⊐	2015	2016	Grand Total
Biscuits	$538,395	$572,242	$1,110,637
Candies	$1,153,840	$1,270,313	$2,424,153
Crackers	$304,610	$321,556	$626,166
Cream Cakes	$141,893	$177,936	$319,829
Frozen Yoghurt	$4,620,560	$4,725,405	$9,345,965
Ice Cream	$5,074,840	$5,448,956	$10,523,796
Muffins	$733,072	$811,093	$1,544,165
Small Cakes	$1,350,148	$1,416,090	$2,766,238
Grand Total	$13,917,357	$14,743,591	$28,660,948

Fig 3.8: Pivot Table with *Products* that don't contain the word *Chocolate*

Now we will look at **Value Filters** and for this we will build a new Pivot Table. Instead of using *Product* in **Rows** we will use *Price per unit*. The updated Pivot Table looks as in Fig 3.9.

Total Revenue	Column Labels ▼		
Row Labels ▼	2015	2016	Grand Total
$1.00	$141,893		$141,893
$1.25	$817,741	$177,936	$995,678
$1.35		$894,926	$894,926
$1.75	$538,395		$538,395
$1.80	$494,613		$494,613
$1.85		$572,242	$572,242
$1.99		$549,817	$549,817
$2.00	$304,610		$304,610
$2.10	$733,072	$321,556	$1,054,628
$2.30		$811,093	$811,093
$2.50	$2,503,988		$2,503,988
$2.60		$1,416,090	$1,416,090
$2.75		$1,270,313	$1,270,313
$4.00	$5,074,840		$5,074,840
$4.30		$5,448,956	$5,448,956
$4.50	$4,620,560		$4,620,560
$4.60		$4,725,405	$4,725,405
Grand Total	$15,229,711	$16,188,334	$31,418,045

Fig 3.9: Updated Pivot Table with *Price per unit* in place of *Product*

Let's click on the drop-down button next to **Row Labels.** A menu as in Fig 3.10 will appear.

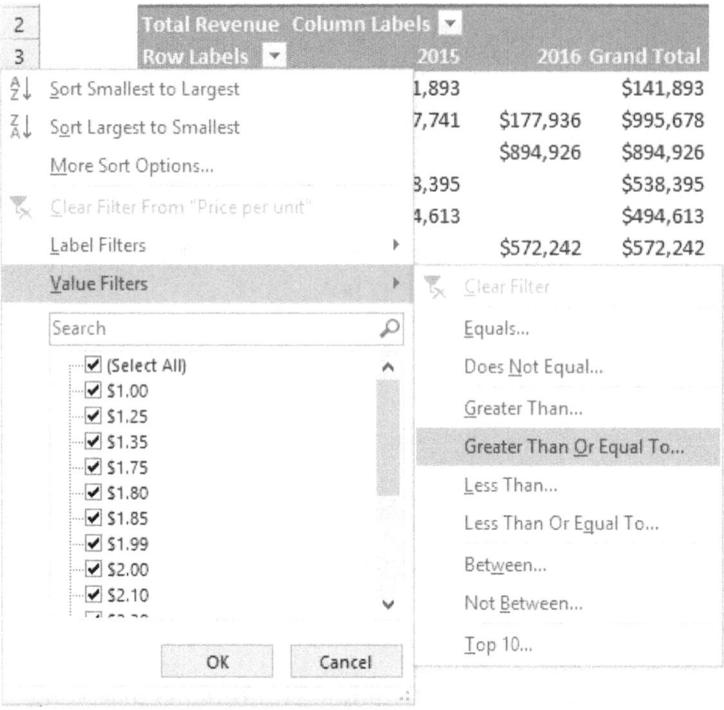

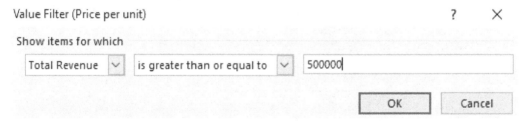

Fig 3.10: The Value Filters

As you can see from Fig 3.10 we have a total of 9 conditions available in **Value Filters**.

Let's say that I wanted to filter the data by all *Prices per unit* that generated a revenue greater than or equal to $500,000 in any year. Then I would go to **Value Filters** by clicking the drop down button next to **Row Labels** and then selecting **Greater Than Or Equal To...** . Now put 500,000 in the dialog box and click **OK** (Fig 3.11).

Value Filter (Price per unit)		? X
Show items for which		
Total Revenue ∨	is greater than or equal to ∨	500000
		OK Cancel

Fig 3.11: Value Filter dialog box

The new Pivot Table now looks like in Fig 3.12.

As you might have already noticed the **Value Filters** conditions filter column or row fields in combination with value fields which in this case is *Total Revenue*.

To apply a filter on the *Price per Unit* or *Year* values we would need to use the **Manual** or the **Label Filters.**

Total Revenue	Column Labels ▼		
Row Labels ↓⊤	2015	2016	Grand Total
$1.25	$817,741	$177,936	$995,678
$1.35		$894,926	$894,926
$1.75	$538,395		$538,395
$1.85		$572,242	$572,242
$1.99		$549,817	$549,817
$2.10	$733,072	$321,556	$1,054,628
$2.30		$811,093	$811,093
$2.50	$2,503,988		$2,503,988
$2.60		$1,416,090	$1,416,090
$2.75		$1,270,313	$1,270,313
$4.00	$5,074,840		$5,074,840
$4.30		$5,448,956	$5,448,956
$4.50	$4,620,560		$4,620,560
$4.60		$4,725,405	$4,725,405
Grand Total	$14,288,595	$16,188,334	$30,476,929

Fig 3.12: Pivot Table after **Value Filter** on *Price per unit* has been applied

3.3 Manual Filter

Through a **Manual Filter** we can manually select the items of the field we want to filter.

Let's clear the filters from the Pivot Table in Fig 3.12. To clear a filter whether from **Manual, Label** or **Value Filters** we click on the **Clear Filter From** "*Name of Field*" button as in Fig 3.13.

Once the filter has been cleared the Pivot Table will return to its original form. In the cleared Pivot Table click on the drop-down button next to **Row Labels** as in Fig 3.14. In this menu, we can see the list of *Price per unit* items with a checkbox in front. If we don't want to show an item in a Pivot Table then we simply untick the checkbox in front of its name in this list.

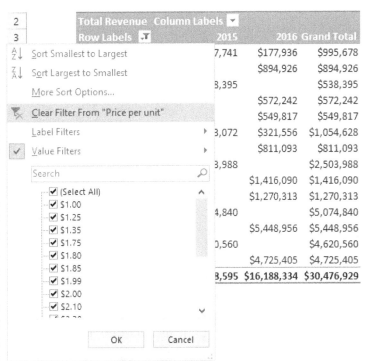

Fig 3.13: Using the **Clear Filter From** "*Name of Field*" button to clear **Manual, Value** or **Label filters**

In Fig 3.14 the tick has been removed from a few *Price per unit* items. Do the same and click the **OK** button.

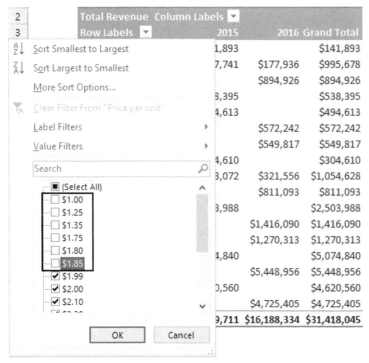

Fig 3.14: Pivot Table ready to be manually filtered

Now we have a manually filtered Pivot Table as in Fig 3.15.

Total Revenue Column Labels ▼			
Row Labels ▼	2015	2016	Grand Total
$1.99		$549,817	$549,817
$2.00	$304,610		$304,610
$2.10	$733,072	$321,556	$1,054,628
$2.30		$811,093	$811,093
$2.50	$2,503,988		$2,503,988
$2.60		$1,416,090	$1,416,090
$2.75		$1,270,313	$1,270,313
$4.00	$5,074,840		$5,074,840
$4.30		$5,448,956	$5,448,956
$4.50	$4,620,560		$4,620,560
$4.60		$4,725,405	$4,725,405
Grand Total	$13,237,069	$14,543,230	$27,780,299

Fig 3.15: Manually filtered Pivot Table

Manual filtering can also be accessed from the **PivotTable Fields List's Fields Section**. If you want to filter from the **Fields Section** click on the name of the field you want to filter and a menu as the one in Fig 3.14 will appear where you can make your selection. If used from the **Fields Section** manual filtering will only work if a field is already in the Pivot Table.

3.4 Slicers

Slicers are another way of filtering data. They graphically show which items are filtered and which aren't.

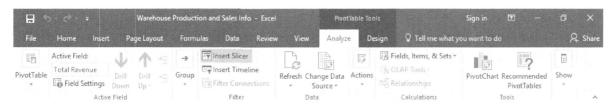

Fig 3.16: Accessing the **Slicer** feature through the **Analyze** tab

Let's say that I want to build a Pivot Table that displays *Revenue* by *Product* and *Year* but only when a product has made more than $50,000 a month. None of the filter options we

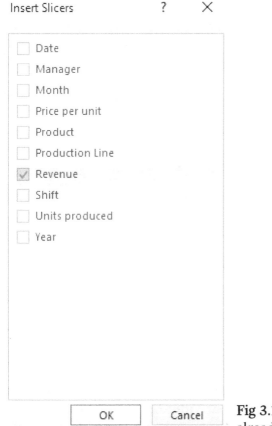

Fig 3.17: The **Insert Slicers** dialog box with *Revenue* already selected

have talked about so far allows me to do this. For e.g. the **Value Filter** will only work on the total *Sum of Revenue* by *Product* and does not work on monthly data.

This is when a **Slicer** comes to play. A **Slicer** works independently of the Pivot Table and can filter using fields that are not used in the Pivot Table. It filters the data at granular level i.e. the data before calculations such as the **Sum** or **Average** are done.

Let's continue using the Pivot Table where we have *Product* in **Rows**, *Year* in **Columns** and *Revenue* in **Σ Values**.

Click anywhere on the Pivot Table to activate the **Analyze** and **Design** tabs. Go to the **Analyze** tab and then click on **Insert Slicer** in the **Filter** group (Fig 3.16).

The **Insert Slicers** dialog box as in Fig 3.17 will appear. In the list of available fields tick on the checkbox before *Revenue* and press **OK**.

A box with a list of all *Revenue* values and all of them pre-selected will appear in the spreadsheet as in Fig 3.18.

Fig 3.18: Revenue Slicer

Now let's select the revenues $50,000 and over. An easy way to do this is to click on the first value (in this case $50,011) and then press and hold the <u>Shift</u> button on the keyboard and after scrolling to the end click on the last value you want to select. All the values in between will be selected for you. The Pivot Table updates automatically.

After selecting a set of values if we want to clear the filter we click the **Clear Filter** button on the top right corner of the **Slicer's** box.

To select a set of values in a **Slicer** you can also use the **Multi-Select** feature. This feature is accessible through the **Multi-Select** button next to the **Clear Filter** button and also by right clicking a **Slicer** and selecting **Multi-Select "Name of Slicer"**. This can be seen in Figures 3.20 and 3.21.

Fig 3.19: Clearing the filter in a **Slicer** by clicking on the **Clear Filter** button (encircled)

Fig 3.20: Multi-Select button

If you click the **Multi-Select** button, then by clicking a value within a **Slicer**, <u>when all values in the **Slicer** are selected</u>, instead of selecting it, you deselect it. This works with a range of values too. It can be handy if you want <u>to filter out</u> only a few values.

If you have <u>no selected values</u> or you have <u>selected only a few</u>, when enabled, **Multi-Select** works the opposite way, i.e. you can select multiple values or multiple ranges of values.

To disable this feature you either click on the **Multi-Select** button in the **Slicer** or right click on the **Slicer** itself and select **Multi-Select "Name of Slicer"**. Fig 3.22 shows an example where values have been deselected using the **Multi-Select** feature.

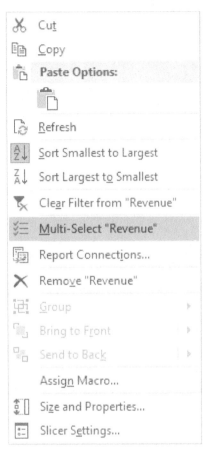

Fig 3.21: Accessing **Multi-Select** by right clicking the **Slicer**

Fig 3.22: Using the **Multi-Select** feature to deselect some values

You can sort values in **Slicers A-Z** or **Z-A** and **Smallest to Largest** or **Largest to Smallest**. To do this right click on the **Slicer** and select **Sort Smallest to Largest** or **Sort Largest to Smallest** if your data is numeric or **Sort A to Z** or **Sort Z to A** if it isn't. See Fig 3.23.

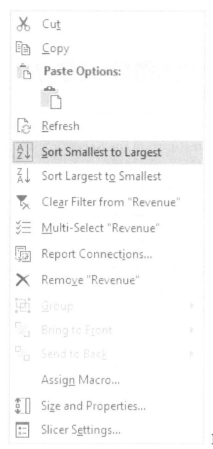

Fig 3.23: Sorting data within a **Slicer**

An interesting fact about **Slicers** is that we can have multiple **Slicers** per Pivot Table and this makes them even more useful.

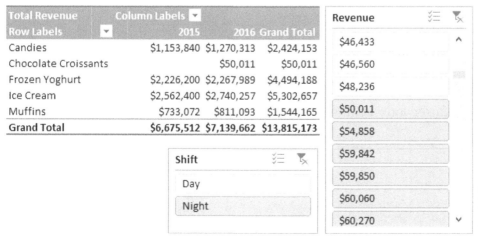

Total Revenue	Column Labels ▾		
Row Labels ▾	2015	2016	Grand Total
Candies	$1,153,840	$1,270,313	$2,424,153
Chocolate Croissants		$50,011	$50,011
Frozen Yoghurt	$2,226,200	$2,267,989	$4,494,188
Ice Cream	$2,562,400	$2,740,257	$5,302,657
Muffins	$733,072	$811,093	$1,544,165
Grand Total	$6,675,512	$7,139,662	$13,815,173

Revenue
- $46,433
- $46,560
- $48,236
- $50,011
- $54,858
- $59,842
- $59,850
- $60,060
- $60,270

Shift
- Day
- Night

Fig 3.24: Pivot Table filtered by two **Slicers**

To build a new **Slicer** click anywhere on the Pivot Table and then go to the **Analyze** tab and click on **Insert Slicer** in the **Filter** group. The **Insert Slicers** dialog box as in Fig 3.17 will appear again. Click the checkbox before the *Shift* field. In the new **Slicer** filter by the *Night* shift.

The Pivot Table with two filters applied through **Slicers** will look as in Fig 3.24. Congratulations, now you have a Pivot Table which shows data only for the *Night Shift* and only from months with *Revenue* higher than $50,000.

After building a new **Slicer** or when selecting an already built one the **Slicer Tools Options** tab appears as in Fig 3.25. In this tab we have a few options and features on the **Slicer**.

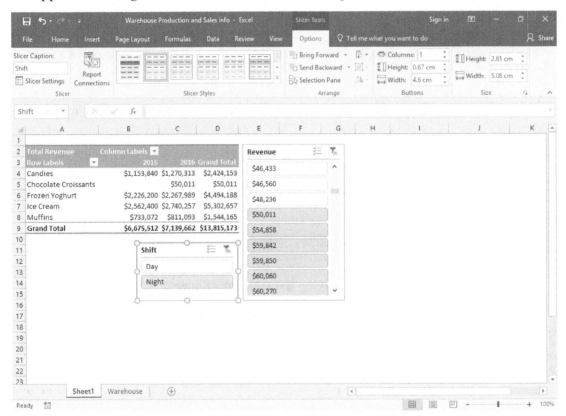

Fig 3.25: Slicer Tools Options tab showing when selecting a **Slicer**

Fig 3.26 gives us a closer look at the **Slicer Tools Options** tab which is divided into 5 groups.

1. Slicer

2. Slicer Styles

3. Arrange

4. Buttons

5. Size

Fig 3.26: A close look at the **Slicer Tools Options** tab

3.4.1 Slicer group

In here we have:

Slicer caption

This is the name of the selected **Slicer**. The name can be changed by editing it in the box.

Slicer Settings

These are the settings for the **Slicer**. If you click on this button the **Slicer Settings** dialog box will pop up as in Fig 3.27. This dialog box is also accessible by right clicking on a **Slicer** and selecting **Slicer Settings...** .

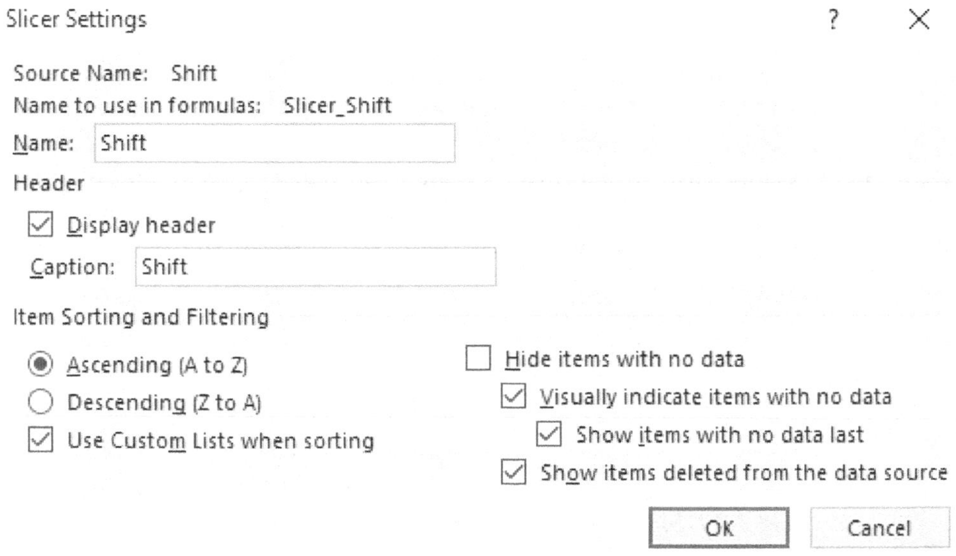

Slicer Settings   ?   ✕

Source Name: Shift
Name to use in formulas: Slicer_Shift
Name: Shift

Header

☑ Display header

Caption: Shift

Item Sorting and Filtering

◉ Ascending (A to Z)   ☐ Hide items with no data

◯ Descending (Z to A)   ☑ Visually indicate items with no data

☑ Use Custom Lists when sorting   ☑ Show items with no data last

                                         ☑ Show items deleted from the data source

                              OK   Cancel

Fig 3.27: Slicer Settings dialog box

In **Slicer Settings' Header** section you can change the name (or keep the automatically generated one) of the **Slicer Header** which is the same as the one in the **Slicer Caption** we mentioned above or choose not to display it at all.

In the **Item Sorting and Filtering** section you can also choose how to sort and filter the data. Sorting can be done using the usual ascending or descending methods or by using **Custom Lists. Custom Sorting Lists** are explained in the **Appendix.** These lists can be very useful when you want to sort by a list that is neither alphabetically nor numerically sorted.

Fig 3.28 shows the **Revenue Slicer** sorted in descending order.

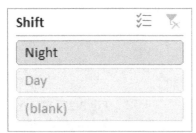

Fig 3.28: The **Revenue Slicer** with data sorted in descending order

In the filtering part you can choose how to deal with items which have no data or have been deleted from the data source.

Let's understand how these options work by running a few tests. First let's clear the filter from the *Shift* **Slicer**. Then in the data source let's delete all *Day Shift* cells and **Refresh** the Pivot Table. With the options **Show items deleted from the data source, Visually indicate items with no data** and **Show items with no data last** selected the *Day* button in the **Slicer** is dimmed (indicating no data) and we have a new button named *(blank)* showing last as in Fig 3.29 indicating that now we have blank data in place.

Fig 3.29: Slicer after *Day Shift* rows have been deleted

If we untick **Show items deleted from data source** in **Slicer Settings** the dimmed *Day* button will disappear and the **Slicer** will look as in Fig 3.30.

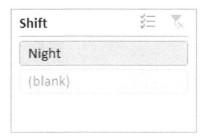

Fig 3.30: Slicer after **Show items deleted from data source** has been deselected

Next, if we tick the checkbox before **Hide items with no data**, only the *Night* button will be shown in the **Slicer** as in Fig 3.31:

Fig 3.31: Slicer with **Hide items with no data** option selected

If we have the **Hide items with no data** checkbox unticked and **Show items deleted from the data source** ticked in **Slicer Settings** we will revert back to the **Slicer** in Fig 3.29.

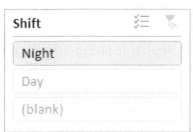

Fig 3.32: Slicer with all filtering options selected

Let's untick the **Show items with no data last** checkbox. The *Day* button now moves above the *Night* one as in Fig 3.33.

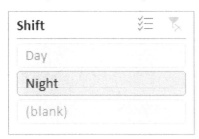

Fig 3.33: Slicer after **Show items with no data last** option has been deselected

And finally let's untick the **Visually indicate items with no data** checkbox. The *Day* and *(blank)* buttons are no longer dimmer as in Fig 3.34.

Fig 3.34: Slicer after **Visually indicate items with no data** option has been deselected

Report Connections

Let's say that we have multiple Pivot Tables in a workbook, which could be on the same worksheet or on different ones, and we want filtered the same way. Would we need to filter each Pivot Table separately?

No, we can use the same **Slicer** to filter multiple Pivot Tables and this can be done through the **Report Connections** feature.

To see how the **Report Connections** feature works let's proceed with an example.

First let's rename our Pivot Table from Fig 3.25. To do this click anywhere on the table and then click on the **Analyze** tab, then on **PivotTable** group and in the **PivotTable Name Box** write the name *ProductRevenueByYear*.

Then let's name the first Pivot Table we built in the first chapter. If it is not already on your workbook then build a new separate Pivot Table which has *Production Line* in **Rows**, *Year* in **Columns** and *Revenue* in **Σ Values**. Once built follow the naming instructions above and name this table as *LineProductionByYear*.

Select the **Revenue Slicer** and in the **Slicer Tools Options** tab click on **Report Connections**. The **Report Connections** dialog box will appear as in Fig 3.35.

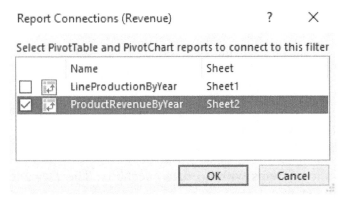

Fig 3.35: **Report Connections** dialog box

In the **Report Connections** dialog box you can see that the *ProductRevenueByYear* table is already filtered by the **Revenue Slicer**. To get the *LineProductionByYear* table filtered by the same **Slicer** we simply click on the checkbox before its name and then click **OK**.

Now we have both tables filtered by the same **Slicer**. Check your *LineProductionByYear* table. The figures should be lower now that this table is connected to the **Revenue Slicer**.

If we want to remove the connection to a Pivot Table we simply untick the checkbox before its name in the **Report Connections** dialog box and then click **OK** and the **Slicer** will no longer be connected to this Pivot Table.

3.4.2 Slicer Styles group

In the **Slicer Tools Options** tab we can change the look and feel of a **Slicer** by using the **Slicer Styles** group.

Select the **Revenue Slicer** and then go to **Slicer Tools Options** and pick up a new slicer style. To do this scroll through slicer styles by using the **Up/down** buttons, circle 1 in Fig 3.36, and then click on any of the styles that you like. You can also see all available styles or choose to build a new slicer style by clicking the **More** button, circle 2 in Fig 3.36.

Slicer Styles

Fig 3.36: **Slicer Styles** with **Up/down** buttons and **More** button encircled

If you click the **More** button, **Slicer Styles** will expand enabling you to see all available styles plus offering you the possibility to build your own slicer style.

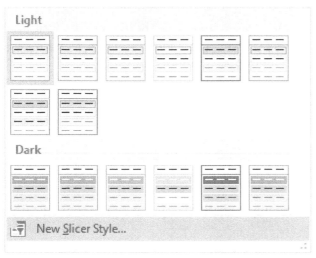

Fig 3.37: **Slicer Styles** expanding by pressing the **More** button

If we click on the **New Slicer Style...** button the **New Slicer Style** dialog box will pop up.

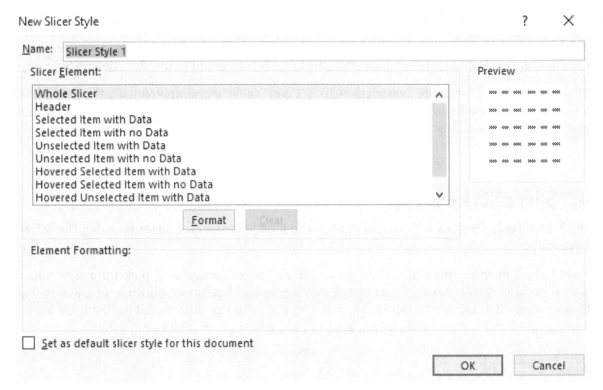

Fig 3.38: The **New Slicer Style** dialog box

In the dialog box you can name your **New Slicer Style** by writing its name in the **Name** box.

You can edit each **Slicer Element** by selecting it and then clicking on the **Format** button. After changing each element you can see the changes in the **Preview** window located at the right of the box.

If you want to clear the formatting of an element you can select the **Slicer Element** and then click the **Clear** button. The formatting that is applied to an element is described under the **Element Formatting** section of the dialog box when this element is selected.

We can also choose to set a **Slicer Style** as default for the current document by clicking on the checkbox before the **Set as default slicer style for this document** statement.

Now go ahead and build your own custom style according to your preferences.

Once a custom style has been built it will appear at the top of the **Slicer Styles** box as in Fig 3.39.

You can modify, duplicate, delete, or set as default a custom style by right clicking on it and selecting the desired action.

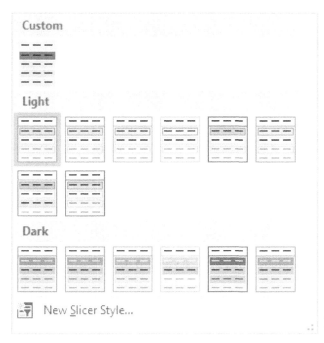

Fig 3.39: Custom style showing on top of the **Slicer Styles** box

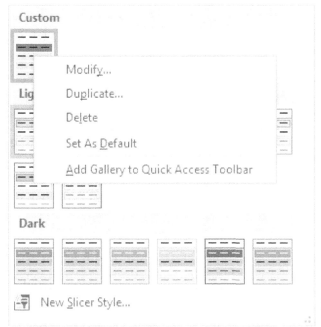

Fig 3.40: Modifying, duplicating, deleting, or setting as default a custom style

Once you pick a style it will be used instantly by the **Slicer**. The **Revenue Slicer** will now have a new look.

Fig 3.41: Revenue Slicer with new style applied

3.4.3 Arrange group

In the **Arrange** group of the **Slicer Tools Options** tab you can arrange your data in a few ways:

1. If you have more than one **Slicer** and you have them on top of each other, you can bring forward the **selected (i.e. clicked on) Slicer,** or bring to front, by clicking the **Bring Forward** button and then in the drop down, choose **Bring Forward** or **Bring to Front**.

2. The **Send Backward** button works in the opposite way. You can send backward a selected **Slicer** by clicking **Send Backward** and then again **Send Backward** or you can send to back by clicking on **Send Backward** and then **Send to Back**.

3. By using the **Align Objects** button you can change the placement of your **Slicers** on the page. You can **Snap to Grid** or **Snap to Shape**. If these options are selected, whenever you resize or move a **Slicer**, it will align or "snap to" the nearest line or intersection of lines in the grid, even if the grid is not visible, or to the nearest shape. You can also choose whether to **View Gridlines** in the worksheet or not.

4. Using the **Group** option you can group **Slicers** together and move them as if they were one object. This option is normally greyed out. However, once you select more than one **Slicer** at the same time this option becomes available. Formatting however can only be done through **Slicer Styles** and with one **Slicer** at a time.

5. In the **Arrange** group you can also access the **Selection Pane** which looks like in Fig 3.42:

In the **Selection Pane** you can do a few things with **Slicers**:

- You can show or hide them all by clicking the **Show All** and **Hide All** buttons.

- You can show or hide a **Slicer** by clicking on the eye icon next to its name.

- If you have **Slicers** on top of each other you can move a **Slicer** up or down by selecting a **Slicer**'s name and then by using the up or down buttons in the top right corner.

- You can rename a **Slicer** by double clicking on its name and then typing the new name. *Note that this is the* **Name** *in the* **Slicer Settings** *and not the* **Caption (or Slicer Header)** *which is what appears as the name of a* **Slicer** *in the workbook.*

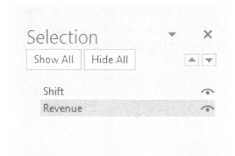

3.4.4 Buttons group

In the **Buttons** group of the **Slicer Tool Options** tab we can change the height and width of each button and choose how many columns of buttons to display in a **Slicer**.

Let's select the **Shift Slicer** and instead of 1 column let's display 2 and let's change the height of buttons to 1 cm. Now the **Slicer** will look like in Fig 3.43.

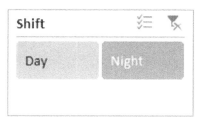

Fig **3.43**: The **Shift Slicer** with two columns of buttons

Fig **3.42: Selection Pane** for **Slicers**

3.4.5 Size group

In the **Size** group we can change the height and width of a **Slicer**. We also have a few more format options which are accessible by clicking the small **Size and Properties** button located at the bottom right corner of the group, encircled in Fig 3.44.

Fig **3.44: Size and Properties** button encircled

If we click this button a new pane called **Format Slicer** will be displayed as in Fig 3.45 where we have a few options on formatting the **Slicer**. **Format Slicer** can also be accessed by right clicking on a **Slicer** and selecting **Size and Properties...** .

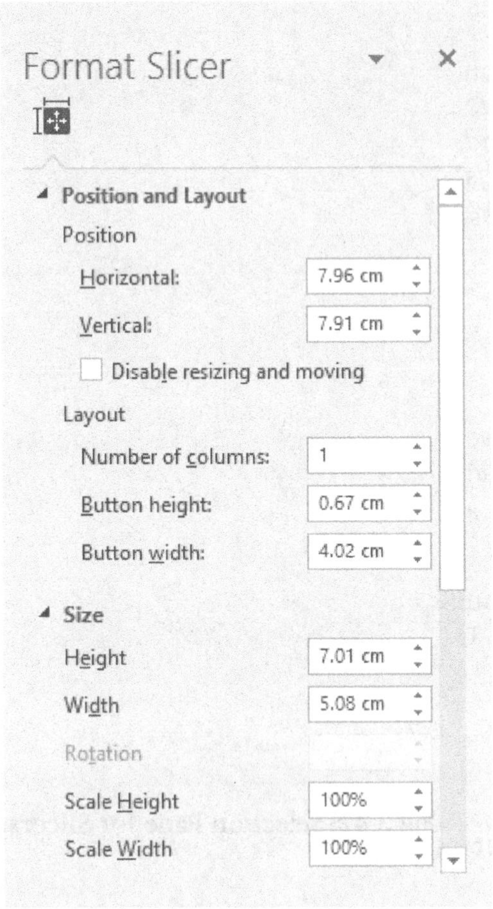

Fig 3.45: **Format Slicer** pane for **Slicers** 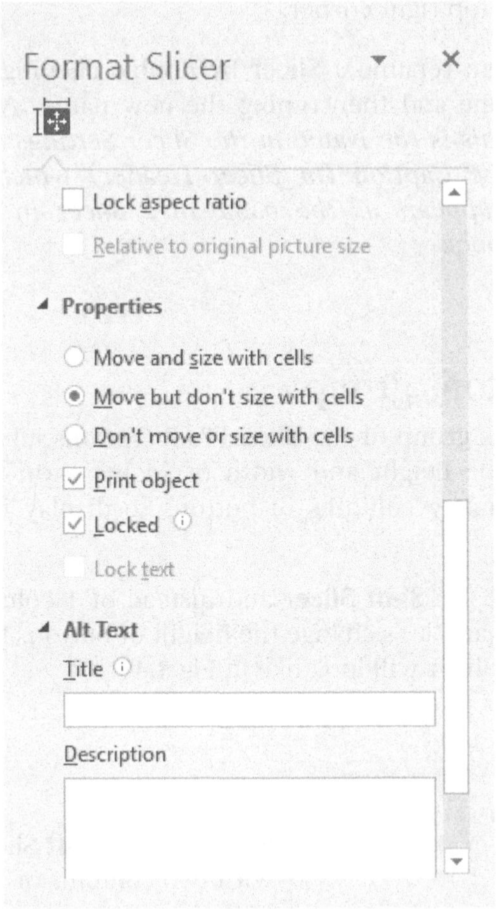   Fig 3.46: **Format Slicer** pane continued

In the **Format Slicer pane** apart from changing the height and width of a **Slicer** we have a few more sophisticated options such as:

- **Position: Horizontal & Vertical**. The Rows and Columns in a spreadsheet act like the X & Y axis of a graph. In the **Horizontal** and **Vertical** boxes under **Position** you can specify the coordinates of the selected **Slicer** in the worksheet.

- **Layout:** These are the options available in the **Buttons** group. You can change how many buttons you can have per column as well as what the height and width of each button should be.

- **Scale Height & Width:** Change the height and width proportionally to current size.

- **Lock aspect ratio:** Tick this box to maintain the original proportion while resizing. Untick it to resize to a different proportion.

You also have **Properties** such as:

- **Move and size with cells**: To have the selected **Slicer** move and resize when you move or resize the underlying cells or chart, click this option. This is useful if you want to sort shapes or objects with their underlying cells. If this is the case the shapes can be no taller than the row or wider than the column that you want to sort. *(A cell is resized by resizing either of its corresponding row or column or both. These options can be useful when building dashboards so play around with them to understand them better.)*

- **Move but don't size with cells**: To have the selected **Slicer** move but not resize when you move or resize the underlying cells or chart, click this option.

- **Don't move or size with cells:** To prevent the selected **Slicer** from moving and resizing with cells, click this option.

- **Print object**: To print the selected **Slicer** when you print a worksheet, tick this checkbox.

- **Locked:** To prevent the selected **Slicer** from being changed, moved, resized or deleted, select this checkbox. You must also select **Lock text** if you want to prevent text within the selected object from being changed. This option has no effect unless the sheet is protected.

- **Lock text:** To keep text in the selected **Slicer** from being selected or edited, tick this check box.

Alt Text

Alt Text or alternative text is descriptive text added to an image. In this case they provide alternative text-based representation of the information contained in a **Slicer**. This information is useful for people with vision or cognitive impairments who may not be able to see or understand the information contained in a **Slicer**.

3.5 Timelines

A **Timeline** is yet another way to filter your Pivot Table. However, it is only used with <u>date fields</u>. It is similar to a **Slicer** but with extra functionality that makes filtering by date a breeze.

Let's use the same Pivot Table that we used to learn about the **Slicer**, where we had *Product* in **Rows**, *Year* in **Columns** and *Revenue* in Σ **Values**.

Click anywhere on the Pivot Table and go to the **Analyze** tab and then in the **Filter** group click on **Insert Timeline**. The **Insert Timelines** dialog box will appear is in Fig 3.47.

Fig 3.47: The **Insert Timelines** dialog box

Click on the checkbox before *Date* and then click on the **OK** button.

After doing this a **Timeline** that looks as in Fig 3.48 will be displayed.

Fig 3.48: Timeline based on the *Date* field

If we click on the **Timeline** we will notice that a new tab named **Timeline Tools Options** will now appear (Fig 3.49).

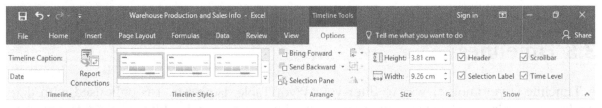

Fig 3.49: Timeline Tools Options tab

This is very similar to the **Slicer Tools Options** tab but with fewer options to choose from.

Let's look at what we can do with a **Timeline**.

3.5.1 Timeline group

In the **Timeline** group we can change the name of a **Timeline** by changing the **Timeline Caption**. Let's go ahead and change this from **Date** to **Filter By Date**.

The **Timeline** now has a new title and will look as in Fig 3.50.

Fig 3.50: Changing the **Timeline Caption** to a more meaningful name

Report Connections

If we have more than one Pivot Table that we want to filter by the same **Timeline** we go to **Timeline Tools Options** tab and click on **Report Connections** and then in the **Report Connections** dialog box tick the checkbox before the name of the Pivot Table/s we want to filter and click **OK**. See Fig 3.51.

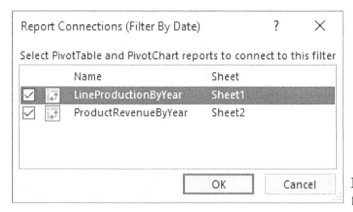

Fig 3.51: Selecting a second table to filter by the **Filter By Date Timeline**

If we no longer want to filter a Pivot Table with a particular **Timeline** we can go to the **Report Connections** dialog box for that **Timeline** and untick the checkbox before the name of the Pivot Table we want to stop filtering.

3.5.2 Timeline Styles group

In the **Timeline Styles** group we can select one of the predefined styles Excel comes with to format a **Timeline** or we can build our own style.

To select a predefined style you can click the **Up/Down** buttons to see the styles available or click the **More** button (Fig 3.52) to access all available styles and the **New Timeline Style...** button as in Fig 3.53.

Timeline Styles

Fig 3.52: 1: The **Up/Down** buttons; 2: The **More** button

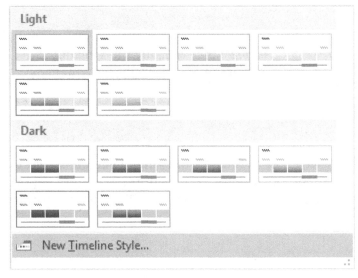

Fig 3.53: **Timeline Styles** available as standard

If you click on the **New Timeline Style...** button the **New Timeline Style** dialog box will pop up as shown in Fig 3.54.

At the top of the dialog box you can write the name of your **Timeline Style** in the **Name** box.

In the **Timeline Element** box you can edit each **Timeline Element** by selecting it and then clicking on the **Format** button. Upon changing each element you can see the changes in the **Preview** window located at the right of the box.

If you want to clear the formatting of an element you can select the element in the **Timeline Element** box and then click the **Clear** button.

New Timeline Style   ?   ✕

Name: | Timeline Style 1 |

Timeline Element: Preview

| **Whole Timeline** |
| **Header** |
| **Selection Label** |
| **Time Level** |
| **Period Labels 1** |
| **Period Labels 2** |
| **Selected Time Block** |
| **Unselected Time Block** |
| Selected Time Block Space |

Format   Clear

Element Formatting:

Left, Right, Top, Bottom Borders; Shaded

☐ Set as default timeline style for this document

OK   Cancel

Fig 3.54: New Timeline Style dialog box

The formatting that is already applied to an element is described under the **Element Formatting** section of the dialog box when an element has been selected.

Custom

Light

Dark

New Timeline Style...

Fig 3.55: Custom **Timeline Style** appearing at the top of the **Timeline Styles** box

We can choose to set a **Timeline Style** as default for the current workbook by clicking on the checkbox before the **Set as default timeline style for this document** statement.

Now go ahead and build your own custom style according to your preferences.

Once a custom style has been built it will appear at the top of **Timeline Styles** box as in Fig 3.55.

You can modify, duplicate, delete, or set as default a custom style by right clicking on it and selecting the desired action.

Fig 3.56: How to modify, duplicate, delete, or set as default a custom style

3.5.3 Arrange group

Fig 3.57: Options available under the **Arrange** group

In the **Arrange** group of the **Timeline Tools Options** tab you have a few ways to arrange your **Timelines**:

1. If you have more than one **Timeline** or **Timelines & Slicers** and you have them on top of each other you can bring the **selected Timeline** forward or to the front by clicking the **Bring Forward** button. If you click the drop down button next to the **Bring Forward** button you get two options. **Bring Forward** and **Bring to Front**. The **Bring to Front** button brings a **Timeline** to the very front.

2. The **Send Backward** button as labelled does the opposite. If you click the drop down button next to the **Send Backward** button you get two options. **Send Backward** and **Send to Back**. The **Send to Back** button sends a **Timeline** to the very back.

3. Using the **Align Objects** button you can change the placement of your **Timelines** on the page. You can **Snap to Grid** or **Snap to Shape**. If the **Snap to Grid** option is selected whenever you resize or move a **Timeline** it will align or "snap to" the nearest line or intersection of lines in the grid even if the grid is not visible. If the **Snap to Shape** option is selected it will align or "snap to" the nearest shape. You also have the option to **View Gridlines** in the worksheet if you wanted to.

4. When having more than one **Timeline** or **Slicer** selected, by using the **Group** button you can group **Timelines** together, including **Timelines** and **Slicers**, and move them as if they were one object. Formatting can only be done through **Timeline Styles** and only with one **Timeline** at a time.

5. If you want to **Ungroup** grouped **Timelines** or **Slicers** you can double click on any one of them and then click on **Ungroup** from the **Arrange** group. You can also click and then right click one of them and then go to **Group** and select **Ungroup**.

6. In the **Arrange** group you can access the **Selection Pane** which is common to **Timelines** and **Slicers** and looks like in Fig 3.58.

In the **Selection Pane** you can do a few things with **Timelines & Slicers**:

- You can show or hide them all by clicking the **Show All** or **Hide All** buttons.

- You can move a **Timeline** up or down visually if you have **Timelines** and **Slicers** on top of each other first by selecting a **Timeline**'s or **Slicer**'s name and then by using the up or down buttons in the top right corner.

- You can show or hide a **Timeline** by clicking on the eye button next to its name.

You can rename a **Timeline** by double clicking on its name and then typing the new name. *Note that this is the **Name** similar to the one found in the **Slicer Settings** and not the*

Fig 3.58: Selection pane

Timeline Caption which is what appears as the name of a **Timeline** in the workbook. Changes to this will not affect the name of the **Timeline** in this case '**Filter By Date**'.

3.5.4 Size group

In the **Size** group you can change the height and width of a **Timeline**. In the same group, if you click the **Size and Properties** button encircled in Fig 3.59, you can access the **Format Timeline pane** shown in Fig 3.60 & Fig 3.61. This pane can also be accessed by right clicking on a **Timeline** and selecting **Size and Properties...** .

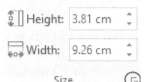

Size   Fig 3.59: The **Size** group with **Size and Properties** button encircled

In the **Format Timeline pane** apart from changing the height and width of a **Timeline** we have a few more sophisticated options such as:

- **Position: Horizontal & Vertical**. The Rows and Columns in a spreadsheet act like the X & Y axis of a graph. In the **Horizontal** and **Vertical** boxes under **Position** you can specify the coordinates of a **Timeline** in the worksheet.

- **Scale Height & Width**. Change the height and width in proportion to the current size.

- **Lock aspect ratio**. Tick box to maintain original proportion while resizing. Untick it to resize to a different proportion.

You also have **Properties** such as:

- **Move and size with cells**: To have a **Timeline** move and resize when you move or resize the underlying cells or chart, click this option. This is useful if you want to sort shapes or objects with their underlying cells. The shapes can be no taller than the row or wider than the column that you want to sort. *(A cell is resized by resizing either of its corresponding row or column or both.)*

- **Move but don't size with cells**: To have a **Timeline** move but not resize when you move or resize the underlying cells or chart, click this option.

- **Don't move or size with cells:** To prevent **Timelines** from moving and resizing with cells, click this option.

- **Print object**: To print the selected **Timeline** when you print a worksheet, tick this checkbox.

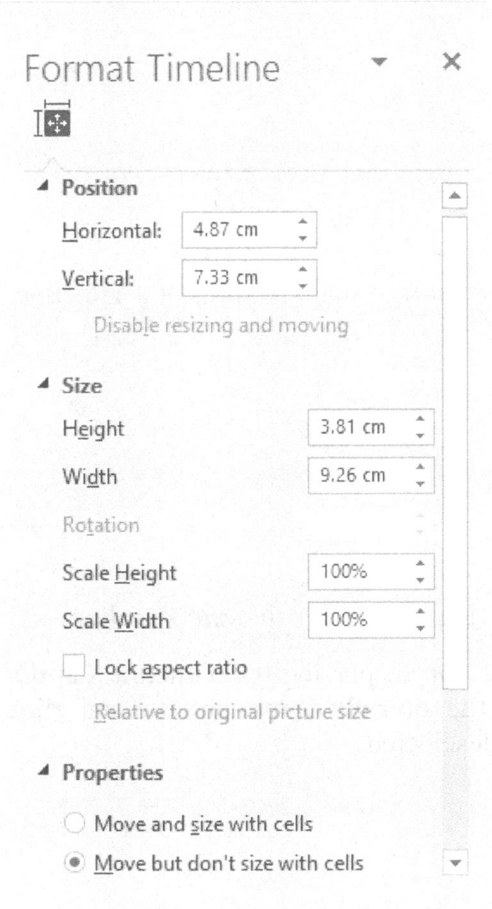

Format Timeline   ▾   ✕

⊿ **Position**
Horizontal: 4.87 cm
Vertical: 7.33 cm
    Disable resizing and moving

⊿ **Size**
Height   3.81 cm
Width   9.26 cm
Rotation
Scale Height   100%
Scale Width   100%
☐ Lock aspect ratio
    Relative to original picture size

⊿ **Properties**
◯ Move and size with cells
◉ Move but don't size with cells

◯ Don't move or size with cells
☑ Print object
☑ Locked ⓘ
    Lock text

⊿ **Alt Text**
Title ⓘ

Description

Fig 3.60: Format Timeline pane part 1 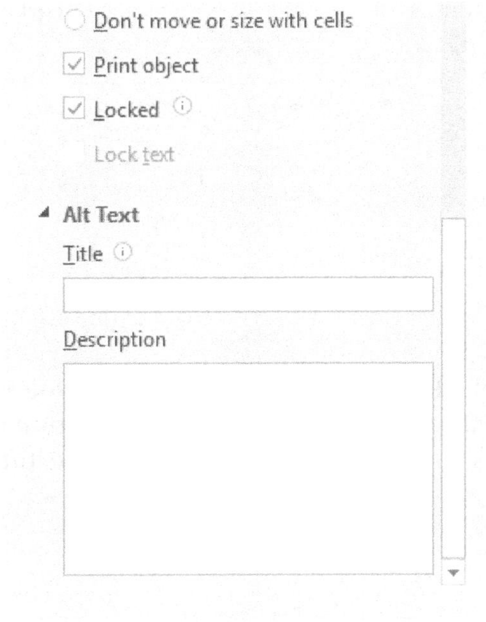   **Fig 3.61: Format Timeline pane** part 2

- **Locked:** To prevent a **Timeline** from being changed, moved, resized or deleted, tick this checkbox. You must also select **Lock text** if you want to prevent text within the selected object from being changed. This has no effect unless the sheet is protected.

- **Lock text:** To keep text in a **Timeline** from being selected or edited, select this checkbox.

Alt Text

Alt Text or alternative text is descriptive text added to an image. In this case they provide alternative text-based representation of the information contained in a **Timeline**. This information is useful for people with vision or cognitive impairments who may not be able to see or understand a **Timeline**.

3.5.5 Show group

Show   **Fig 3.62: Show** group

In the **Show** group you can decide whether to display or not four main features of a **Timeline**.

Fig 3.63: *Filter By Date* **Timeline**

Header: Unticking this feature means that you will stop displaying the **Timeline Caption** (in this case *Filter By Date*), the **Clear Filter** button on the top right corner and the **underline**. Fig 3.64 shows how a **Timeline** looks with this feature deselected.

Fig 3.64: Timeline without the **Header** feature

Scroll Bar: Unticking this feature will remove the scrollbar from a **Timeline**. The new **Timeline** will look like in Fig 3.65:

Fig 3.65: Removing the **scroll bar** from a **Timeline**

Selection Label: Unticking this feature removes the date selection range label from the **Timeline**. The new **Timeline** will look like in Fig 3.66.

Fig 3.66: Removing **Selection Label** from a **Timeline**

Time Level: Unticking the **Time Level** will remove the ability to select a **Time Level**. The new **Timeline** will look like in Fig 3.67.

Fig 3.67: Timeline after **Time Level** has been removed

3.5.6 Time Level

A **Timeline** has the option to filter data by Days, Months, Quarters or Years. To select how you want to see or filter the data in a **Timeline** click on the drop-down button in the top right corner and a list will be displayed as in Fig 3.68:

Fig 3.68: Time Levels available

Instead of MONTHS let's select QUARTERS and see how the **Timeline** will look like.

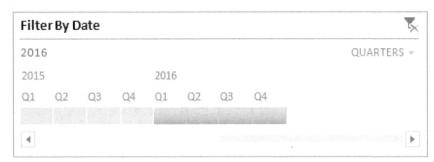

Fig 3.69: **Timeline** now showing data by QUARTERS

3.5.7 Filtering data with a Timeline

To **Filter** by date in a **Timeline** select the desired date range simply by clicking on the start of the period and then drag your mouse to the end of the required period. After doing this the Pivot Table or Pivot Tables associated with the **Timeline** will display data for the selected time period only. The **Timeline** will look like in Fig 3.70:

Fig 3.70: **Timeline** after selecting a range of Quarters

All the Pivot Tables associated with the **Timeline** will now summarize data for the year 2016 only.

If we want to remove the filter we just built then we simply press the **Clear All** button at the top right corner of the **Timeline**.

 With a **Timeline** you won't be able to select multiple periods by holding down the CTRL key for e.g. Q2 and Q3 in 2015 and then Q2 and Q3 in 2016. This can only be done with a **Slicer**.

CHAPTER 4

Formatting Pivot Tables with the Design Tab

We can change the look and feel of a Pivot Table by using the **Design** tab. If we click anywhere on a Pivot Table the **PivotTable Tools Analyze** and **Design** tabs will become visible as in Fig 4.1.

Fig 4.1: The **PivotTable Tools Analyze** and **Design** tabs

In the **Design** tab, we have a few options on formatting a Pivot Table organized under 3 groups.

1. Layout

2. PivotTable Style Options

3. Pivot Table Styles

4.1 Layout group

This part of the **Design** tab is concerned with the layout of a Pivot Table. To clearly see how these features work we need two or more fields in the **Rows** area. So let's build a Pivot Table where we have *Shift* and *Product* in **Rows**, *Year* in **Columns** and *Revenue* in **Σ Values** renamed as *Total Revenue*. This table will not be filtered in any way. The Pivot Table should look as in Fig 4.2.

Total Revenue	Column Labels ▼		
Row Labels ▼	2015	2016	Grand Total
⊟ **Day**	**$7,754,976**	**$8,227,310**	**$15,982,286**
Biscuits	$538,395	$572,242	$1,110,637
Chocolate Bars	$817,741	$894,926	$1,712,667
Cream Cakes	$141,893	$177,936	$319,829
Frozen Yoghurt	$2,394,360	$2,457,417	$4,851,777
Ice Cream	$2,512,440	$2,708,699	$5,221,139
Small Cakes	$1,350,148	$1,416,090	$2,766,238
⊟ **Night**	**$7,474,735**	**$7,961,024**	**$15,435,759**
Candies	$1,153,840	$1,270,313	$2,424,153
Chocolate Croissants	$494,613	$549,817	$1,044,430
Crackers	$304,610	$321,556	$626,166
Frozen Yoghurt	$2,226,200	$2,267,989	$4,494,188
Ice Cream	$2,562,400	$2,740,257	$5,302,657
Muffins	$733,072	$811,093	$1,544,165
Grand Total	**$15,229,711**	**$16,188,334**	**$31,418,045**

Fig 4.2: Pivot Table ready for layout manipulation

4.1.1 Subtotals

If we click the **Subtotals** button in the **Layout** group, we have four options available:

1. Do Not Show Subtotals. If we select this option, then the subtotals for the *Shift* field will be removed from the Pivot Table which will now look as in Fig 4.3:

Total Revenue	Column Labels ▼		
Row Labels ▼	2015	2016	Grand Total
⊟ **Day**			
Biscuits	$538,395	$572,242	$1,110,637
Chocolate Bars	$817,741	$894,926	$1,712,667
Cream Cakes	$141,893	$177,936	$319,829
Frozen Yoghurt	$2,394,360	$2,457,417	$4,851,777
Ice Cream	$2,512,440	$2,708,699	$5,221,139
Small Cakes	$1,350,148	$1,416,090	$2,766,238
⊟ **Night**			
Candies	$1,153,840	$1,270,313	$2,424,153
Chocolate Croissants	$494,613	$549,817	$1,044,430
Crackers	$304,610	$321,556	$626,166
Frozen Yoghurt	$2,226,200	$2,267,989	$4,494,188
Ice Cream	$2,562,400	$2,740,257	$5,302,657
Muffins	$733,072	$811,093	$1,544,165
Grand Total	**$15,229,711**	**$16,188,334**	**$31,418,045**

Fig 4.3: Pivot Table without subtotals

2. Show All Subtotals at Bottom of Group. If we select this option, the subtotals for the *Shift* field will be placed at the bottom of a group as in Fig 4.4:

Total Revenue	Column Labels		
Row Labels	2015	2016	Grand Total
⊟ Day			
Biscuits	$538,395	$572,242	$1,110,637
Chocolate Bars	$817,741	$894,926	$1,712,667
Cream Cakes	$141,893	$177,936	$319,829
Frozen Yoghurt	$2,394,360	$2,457,417	$4,851,777
Ice Cream	$2,512,440	$2,708,699	$5,221,139
Small Cakes	$1,350,148	$1,416,090	$2,766,238
Day Total	$7,754,976	$8,227,310	$15,982,286
⊟ Night			
Candies	$1,153,840	$1,270,313	$2,424,153
Chocolate Croissants	$494,613	$549,817	$1,044,430
Crackers	$304,610	$321,556	$626,166
Frozen Yoghurt	$2,226,200	$2,267,989	$4,494,188
Ice Cream	$2,562,400	$2,740,257	$5,302,657
Muffins	$733,072	$811,093	$1,544,165
Night Total	$7,474,735	$7,961,024	$15,435,759
Grand Total	$15,229,711	$16,188,334	$31,418,045

Fig 4.4: Subtotals showing at the bottom of a group

3. Show all Subtotals at Top of Group. If we select this option, the table will look as in Fig 4.2. Subtotals will appear at the same level as the *Shift* items.

4. Include Filtered Items in Totals. This option is explained in chapter 10 and is available only when we use multiple tables to build a Pivot Table.

4.1.2 Grand Totals

The **Grand Totals** button contains four options on displaying **Grand Totals** on a Pivot Table. They are:

1. Off for Rows and Columns. This option will completely remove the **Grand Totals** from both rows and columns as in Fig 4.5:

2. On for Rows and Columns. This option will bring **Grand Totals** back.

3. On for Rows Only. This option will keep **Grand Totals** for rows only as in Fig 4.6.

Total Revenue	Column Labels	
Row Labels	2015	2016
⊟ Day	$7,754,976	$8,227,310
Biscuits	$538,395	$572,242
Chocolate Bars	$817,741	$894,926
Cream Cakes	$141,893	$177,936
Frozen Yoghurt	$2,394,360	$2,457,417
Ice Cream	$2,512,440	$2,708,699
Small Cakes	$1,350,148	$1,416,090
⊟ Night	$7,474,735	$7,961,024
Candies	$1,153,840	$1,270,313
Chocolate Croissants	$494,613	$549,817
Crackers	$304,610	$321,556
Frozen Yoghurt	$2,226,200	$2,267,989
Ice Cream	$2,562,400	$2,740,257
Muffins	$733,072	$811,093

Fig 4.5: No **Grand Totals**

Total Revenue	Column Labels		
Row Labels	2015	2016	Grand Total
⊟ Day	$7,754,976	$8,227,310	$15,982,286
Biscuits	$538,395	$572,242	$1,110,637
Chocolate Bars	$817,741	$894,926	$1,712,667
Cream Cakes	$141,893	$177,936	$319,829
Frozen Yoghurt	$2,394,360	$2,457,417	$4,851,777
Ice Cream	$2,512,440	$2,708,699	$5,221,139
Small Cakes	$1,350,148	$1,416,090	$2,766,238
⊟ Night	$7,474,735	$7,961,024	$15,435,759
Candies	$1,153,840	$1,270,313	$2,424,153
Chocolate Croissants	$494,613	$549,817	$1,044,430
Crackers	$304,610	$321,556	$626,166
Frozen Yoghurt	$2,226,200	$2,267,989	$4,494,188
Ice Cream	$2,562,400	$2,740,257	$5,302,657
Muffins	$733,072	$811,093	$1,544,165

Fig 4.6: Grand Totals for rows only

4. On for Columns Only. This option will keep **Grand Totals** for columns only as in Fig 4.7.

Total Revenue	Column Labels	
Row Labels	2015	2016
⊟ Day	$7,754,976	$8,227,310
Biscuits	$538,395	$572,242
Chocolate Bars	$817,741	$894,926
Cream Cakes	$141,893	$177,936
Frozen Yoghurt	$2,394,360	$2,457,417
Ice Cream	$2,512,440	$2,708,699
Small Cakes	$1,350,148	$1,416,090
⊟ Night	$7,474,735	$7,961,024
Candies	$1,153,840	$1,270,313
Chocolate Croissants	$494,613	$549,817
Crackers	$304,610	$321,556
Frozen Yoghurt	$2,226,200	$2,267,989
Ice Cream	$2,562,400	$2,740,257
Muffins	$733,072	$811,093
Grand Total	$15,229,711	$16,188,334

Fig 4.7: Grand Totals for columns only

4.1.3 Report Layout

This section deals with the layout of a Pivot Table.

a. When we have multiple fields in the **Rows** area:

1. Show in Compact Form. This is the current layout of the Pivot Table as in Fig 4.7. All row fields are shown in one row rather than separate ones. In this layout if we want to filter by any of the fields in the **Rows** area we click on the drop-down button next to **Row Labels** and then by using **Select Field** we can select which field we want to filter by. See Fig 4.8.

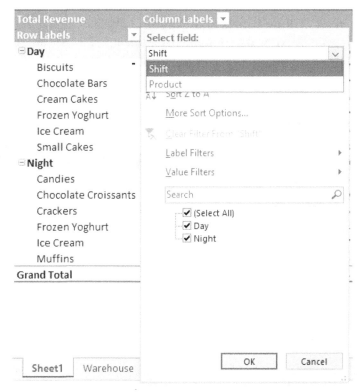

Fig 4.8: Selecting which field to filter by in **Compact Form**

Total Revenue		Year		
Shift	Product	2015	2016	Grand Total
Day		$7,754,976	$8,227,310	$15,982,286
	Biscuits	$538,395	$572,242	$1,110,637
	Chocolate Bars	$817,741	$894,926	$1,712,667
	Cream Cakes	$141,893	$177,936	$319,829
	Frozen Yoghurt	$2,394,360	$2,457,417	$4,851,777
	Ice Cream	$2,512,440	$2,708,699	$5,221,139
	Small Cakes	$1,350,148	$1,416,090	$2,766,238
Night		$7,474,735	$7,961,024	$15,435,759
	Candies	$1,153,840	$1,270,313	$2,424,153
	Chocolate Croissants	$494,613	$549,817	$1,044,430
	Crackers	$304,610	$321,556	$626,166
	Frozen Yoghurt	$2,226,200	$2,267,989	$4,494,188
	Ice Cream	$2,562,400	$2,740,257	$5,302,657
	Muffins	$733,072	$811,093	$1,544,165
Grand Total		$15,229,711	$16,188,334	$31,418,045

Fig 4.9: Outline form

2. Show in Outline Form. If we select this option instead of having all row fields displayed in one row, we have them displayed in one row per field as in Fig 4.9. In this layout, the first item of the next field is shown a row below and subtotals are shown in the first row of an item. Also note that with this option, instead of **Row Labels** and **Column Labels**, we have the actual field names displayed in the Labels area. If we want to manually filter a field, we can do it by clicking the drop-down button next to its name.

3. Show in Tabular Form. This form is similar to the **Outline form** with the difference that the subtotals appear at the bottom of a group and the first item of the next field appears in the same row as the item from the current field. See Fig 4.10.

Total Revenue		Year ▾			
Shift ▾	Product ▾	2015	2016	Grand Total	
⊟ Day	Biscuits	$538,395	$572,242	$1,110,637	
	Chocolate Bars	$817,741	$894,926	$1,712,667	
	Cream Cakes	$141,893	$177,936	$319,829	
	Frozen Yoghurt	$2,394,360	$2,457,417	$4,851,777	
	Ice Cream	$2,512,440	$2,708,699	$5,221,139	
	Small Cakes	$1,350,148	$1,416,090	$2,766,238	
Day Total		**$7,754,976**	**$8,227,310**	**$15,982,286**	
⊟ Night	Candies	$1,153,840	$1,270,313	$2,424,153	
	Chocolate Croissants	$494,613	$549,817	$1,044,430	
	Crackers	$304,610	$321,556	$626,166	
	Frozen Yoghurt	$2,226,200	$2,267,989	$4,494,188	
	Ice Cream	$2,562,400	$2,740,257	$5,302,657	
	Muffins	$733,072	$811,093	$1,544,165	
Night Total		**$7,474,735**	**$7,961,024**	**$15,435,759**	
Grand Total		**$15,229,711**	**$16,188,334**	**$31,418,045**	

Fig 4.10: Tabular Form

b. When we have multiple fields in the **Columns** area:

Note that the Pivot Table's columns design does not change much with each form, except that with **Outline** and **Tabular forms** we get each **Columns** field in a separate column whereas in **Compact form** we get it under one column labelled as **Column Labels**. If we want to manually filter a field in the **Outline** or **Tabular forms,** we would do this by clicking the drop-down button next to the field's name and then deselecting the items we want to filter. With **Compact form,** we click the drop-down button next to **Column Labels** and then by using **Select Field** we proceed with selecting the field we want to filter by.

Separately in **Report Layout** we have:

1. Repeat All Item Labels. This simply repeats the parent field's item for each item of the next row or column fields. In the example below *Product* is the last field in the **Rows** area following *Shift*. Therefore, each *Shift* item will be repeated for each *Product* item.

Total Revenue		Year ▼		
Shift ▼	Product ▼	2015	2016	Grand Total
⊟ Day		$7,754,976	$8,227,310	$15,982,286
Day	Biscuits	$538,395	$572,242	$1,110,637
Day	Chocolate Bars	$817,741	$894,926	$1,712,667
Day	Cream Cakes	$141,893	$177,936	$319,829
Day	Frozen Yoghurt	$2,394,360	$2,457,417	$4,851,777
Day	Ice Cream	$2,512,440	$2,708,699	$5,221,139
Day	Small Cakes	$1,350,148	$1,416,090	$2,766,238
⊟ Night		$7,474,735	$7,961,024	$15,435,759
Night	Candies	$1,153,840	$1,270,313	$2,424,153
Night	Chocolate Croissants	$494,613	$549,817	$1,044,430
Night	Crackers	$304,610	$321,556	$626,166
Night	Frozen Yoghurt	$2,226,200	$2,267,989	$4,494,188
Night	Ice Cream	$2,562,400	$2,740,257	$5,302,657
Night	Muffins	$733,072	$811,093	$1,544,165
Grand Total		$15,229,711	$16,188,334	$31,418,045

Fig 4.11: Repeating all item labels in a Pivot Table

2. Do Not Repeat All Item Labels. This simply removes the repetition from the above option.

4.1.4 Blank Rows

The **Blank Rows** button contains two options related to inserting blank lines. They are:

1. Insert Blank Line after Each Item. Inserts a blank row after each item as in Fig 4.12. Note that this is done only if there are two or more fields in **Rows** and not for the last field. In our example below the last field is *Product*.

Total Revenue		Year ▼		
Shift ▼	Product ▼	2015	2016	Grand Total
⊟ Day		$7,754,976	$8,227,310	$15,982,286
	Biscuits	$538,395	$572,242	$1,110,637
	Chocolate Bars	$817,741	$894,926	$1,712,667
	Cream Cakes	$141,893	$177,936	$319,829
	Frozen Yoghurt	$2,394,360	$2,457,417	$4,851,777
	Ice Cream	$2,512,440	$2,708,699	$5,221,139
	Small Cakes	$1,350,148	$1,416,090	$2,766,238
⊟ Night		$7,474,735	$7,961,024	$15,435,759
	Candies	$1,153,840	$1,270,313	$2,424,153
	Chocolate Croissants	$494,613	$549,817	$1,044,430
	Crackers	$304,610	$321,556	$626,166
	Frozen Yoghurt	$2,226,200	$2,267,989	$4,494,188
	Ice Cream	$2,562,400	$2,740,257	$5,302,657
	Muffins	$733,072	$811,093	$1,544,165
Grand Total		$15,229,711	$16,188,334	$31,418,045

Fig 4.12: One blank line added after each *Shift* item

2. Remove Blank Line after Each Item. Removes the blank row inserted with the option above.

4.2 PivotTable Style Options group

☑ Row Headers   ☐ Banded Rows

☑ Column Headers   ☐ Banded Columns

PivotTable Style Options   **Fig 4.13:** PivotTable Style Options

In **PivotTable Style Options** we get to choose whether we keep or remove formatted **Column Headers**, formatted **Row Headers**, **Banded Rows** or **Banded Columns**.

To illustrate the difference between using or not using these options in Fig 4.14 we have a Pivot Table with all options unchecked and in Fig 4.15 a Pivot Table with all options checked for comparison.

I encourage you to play with these options when building Pivot Tables to see which ones go best with your table.

Total Revenue		Year		
Shift	Product	2015	2016	Grand Total
Day		$7,754,976	$8,227,310	$15,982,286
	Biscuits	$538,395	$572,242	$1,110,637
	Chocolate Bars	$817,741	$894,926	$1,712,667
	Cream Cakes	$141,893	$177,936	$319,829
	Frozen Yoghurt	$2,394,360	$2,457,417	$4,851,777
	Ice Cream	$2,512,440	$2,708,699	$5,221,139
	Small Cakes	$1,350,148	$1,416,090	$2,766,238
Night		$7,474,735	$7,961,024	$15,435,759
	Candies	$1,153,840	$1,270,313	$2,424,153
	Chocolate Croissants	$494,613	$549,817	$1,044,430
	Crackers	$304,610	$321,556	$626,166
	Frozen Yoghurt	$2,226,200	$2,267,989	$4,494,188
	Ice Cream	$2,562,400	$2,740,257	$5,302,657
	Muffins	$733,072	$811,093	$1,544,165
Grand Total		**$15,229,711**	**$16,188,334**	**$31,418,045**

Fig 4.14: A Pivot Table with all style options unchecked

Total Revenue		Year		
Shift	Product	2015	2016	Grand Total
⊟ Day		$7,754,976	$8,227,310	$15,982,286
	Biscuits	$538,395	$572,242	$1,110,637
	Chocolate Bars	$817,741	$894,926	$1,712,667
	Cream Cakes	$141,893	$177,936	$319,829
	Frozen Yoghurt	$2,394,360	$2,457,417	$4,851,777
	Ice Cream	$2,512,440	$2,708,699	$5,221,139
	Small Cakes	$1,350,148	$1,416,090	$2,766,238
⊟ Night		$7,474,735	$7,961,024	$15,435,759
	Candies	$1,153,840	$1,270,313	$2,424,153
	Chocolate Croissants	$494,613	$549,817	$1,044,430
	Crackers	$304,610	$321,556	$626,166
	Frozen Yoghurt	$2,226,200	$2,267,989	$4,494,188
	Ice Cream	$2,562,400	$2,740,257	$5,302,657
	Muffins	$733,072	$811,093	$1,544,165
Grand Total		$15,229,711	$16,188,334	$31,418,045

Fig 4.15: The same Pivot Table with all style options checked

4.3 PivotTable Styles group

PivotTable Styles

Fig 4.16: PivotTable Styles

In **PivotTable Styles** group we get to choose the format of the Pivot Table namely the colours of the rows, columns and their borders. Excel comes with pre-built Pivot Table styles which are classified as Light, Medium or Dark.

If we click on the **More** button in the bottom right corner of the box (see Fig 4.17) we will be able to see each available style as in Fig 4.18.

PivotTable Styles

Fig 4.17: Accessing the **More** button

To find out how a style would look we simply point the mouse at it and it will automatically show in our Pivot Table. If we want to use it, we click it.

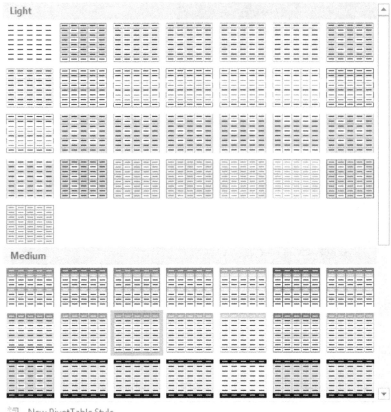

New PivotTable Style...

Clear

Fig 4.18: PivotTable Styles

Notice that at the end of the **PivotTables Styles** menu in Fig 4.18 we have two options:

1. New Pivot Table Style...

2. Clear

The **Clear** button removes all formatting from a Pivot Table.

The **New PivotTable Style...** button gives you the possibility to build your own Pivot Table styles. This can be very useful if for example you want a Pivot Table formatted with your organisation's colours or you are simply not happy with the styles available and want to use your own.

If you click this button the **New PivotTable Style** dialog box will appear where you can build your own style.

You can name your style by editing the **Name** box. You can change the format of many of your Pivot Table's elements. To do this select the ones you want to format under the **Table Element** section and then click on the **Format** button. For e.g. if you click on **Whole Table** and then on the **Format** button the **Format Cells** dialog box will pop up with the following tabs:

- Font
- Border
- Fill

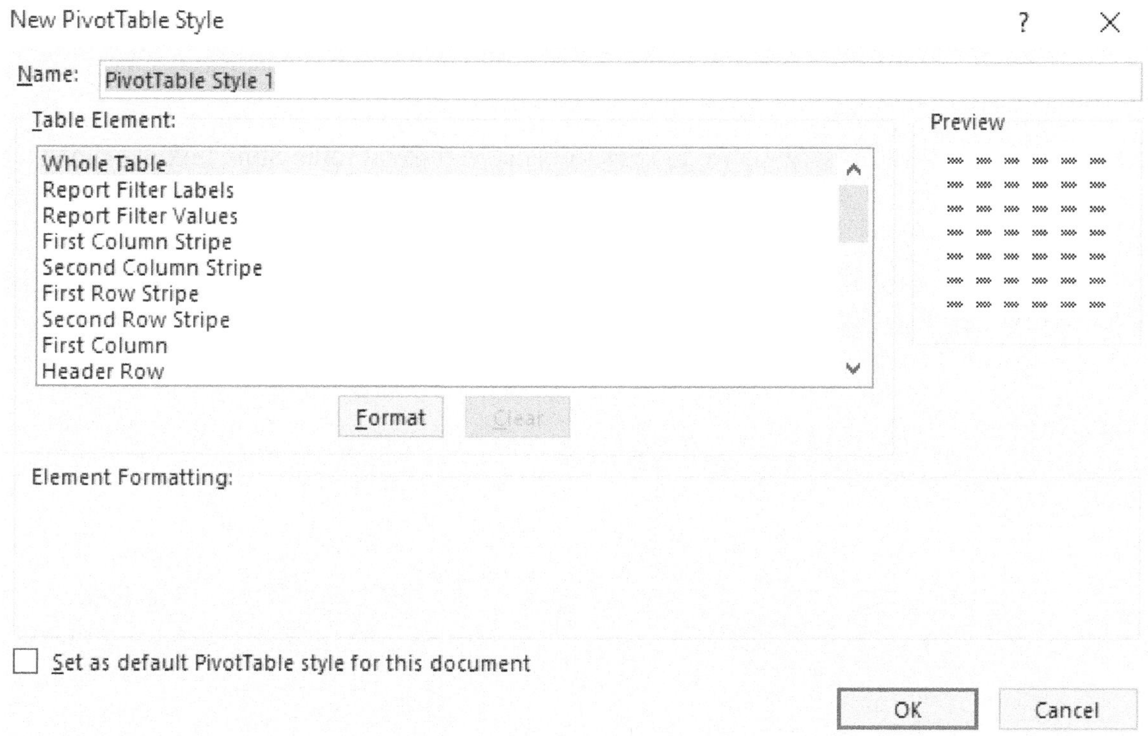

New PivotTable Style   ?   ✕

Name: PivotTable Style 1

Table Element: Preview

Whole Table
Report Filter Labels
Report Filter Values
First Column Stripe
Second Column Stripe
First Row Stripe
Second Row Stripe
First Column
Header Row

[Format]   [Clear]

Element Formatting:

☐ Set as default PivotTable style for this document

[OK]   [Cancel]

Fig 4.19: New **PivotTable Style** dialog box where you can build your own style

This dialog box is used to edit **Table Elements**.

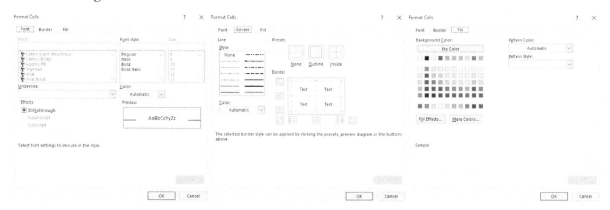

Fig 4.20: The three tabs of the **Format Cells** dialog box

Once you edit an element, changes are shown in the **Preview** box on the right. If you want to clear the formatting of a **Table Element** you select it and click the **Clear** button. A description of the formatting an element has is shown under the **Element Formatting** section.

When you are happy with your new custom style you can choose to **Set as default PivotTable style for this document** by clicking the checkbox in front of this statement.

After finishing all the formatting for your custom PivotTable style click the **OK** button and now you will have a new custom PivotTable style to use.

Once we have a custom style, if we look at the enlarged **PivotTable Style** box we can see a new category at the top called **Custom** which has our newly built **Pivot Table style** in it. Whenever we want to use this style we simply click on it.

If we want to modify, delete or duplicate this style we right click on it and then select the desired action (see Fig 4.22).

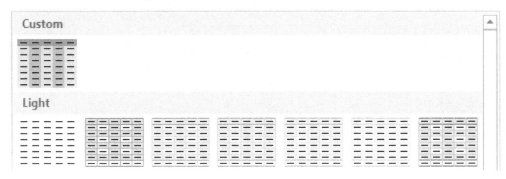

Fig 4.21: Custom Pivot Table Style

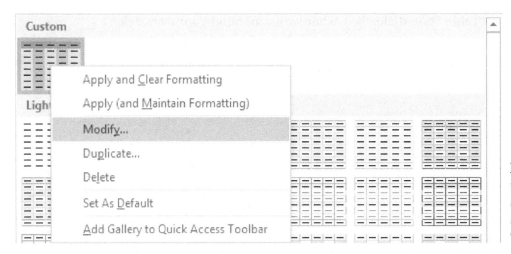

Fig 4.22: How to modify, duplicate or delete a Pivot Table Style

CHAPTER 5

Grouping items

Grouping items means grouping items within a field in a Pivot Table row or column and displaying the same calculations for this group as we do for each individual item.

Grouping items can be classified into 3 parts:

1. Grouping date & time items

2. Grouping number items

3. Grouping everything else

5.1 Grouping date & time items

Grouping date items requires a date field in a date format or a time field in a time format for e.g. 01/01/2017 or 02:45:23. In our data source, we have our *Date* field which is in a date format and shows the first day of a month.

Let's build a new Pivot Table where we have *Revenue* by *Date* and by *Production Line*. So, let's have *Date* in the **Rows** area, *Production Line* in the **Columns** area and *Revenue* in the Σ **Values** area. The Pivot Table should look like in Fig 5.1.

Sum of Revenue	Column Labels			
Row Labels	Line A	Line B	Line C	Grand Total
01/01/2015	$232,387	$224,730	$803,300	$1,260,417
01/02/2015	$212,988	$209,035	$760,800	$1,182,823
01/03/2015	$230,950	$221,905	$795,340	$1,248,195
01/04/2015	$228,750	$219,860	$788,400	$1,237,010
01/05/2015	$237,000	$223,002	$808,262	$1,268,263
01/06/2015	$232,637	$221,460	$794,201	$1,248,297
01/07/2015	$243,750	$234,550	$822,902	$1,301,202
01/08/2015	$237,100	$230,020	$810,805	$1,277,925
01/09/2015	$231,450	$224,994	$799,940	$1,256,384
01/10/2015	$240,750	$233,240	$819,900	$1,293,890
01/11/2015	$232,264	$234,835	$845,927	$1,313,026
01/12/2015	$254,560	$242,095	$845,624	$1,342,279
01/01/2016	$247,272	$242,021	$836,939	$1,326,231
01/02/2016	$235,353	$232,640	$781,322	$1,249,315
01/03/2016	$255,404	$244,532	$847,728	$1,347,664
01/04/2016	$252,147	$236,501	$816,234	$1,304,882
01/05/2016	$255,529	$236,200	$854,096	$1,345,825
01/06/2016	$248,934	$242,174	$849,224	$1,340,332
01/07/2016	$257,984	$248,663	$863,149	$1,369,796
01/08/2016	$258,606	$246,838	$841,173	$1,346,617
01/09/2016	$249,137	$242,340	$860,835	$1,352,311
01/10/2016	$264,844	$255,435	$861,536	$1,381,815
01/11/2016	$252,014	$258,195	$891,036	$1,401,244
01/12/2016	$281,813	$269,399	$871,090	$1,422,301
Grand Total	$5,873,623	$5,674,662	$19,869,760	$31,418,045

Fig 5.1: Pivot Table with numeric *Date* field in **Rows**

Click anywhere under **Row Labels** where the *Date* field is found, then go to the **Analyze** tab and click on **Group**.

Fig 5.2: Group list

In the list that appears as in Fig 5.2 click on either **Group Selection** or **Group Field**. In this case they both do the same thing. Once clicked the **Grouping** dialog box will appear which asks you to group items within the *Date* field into one or more of the options available.

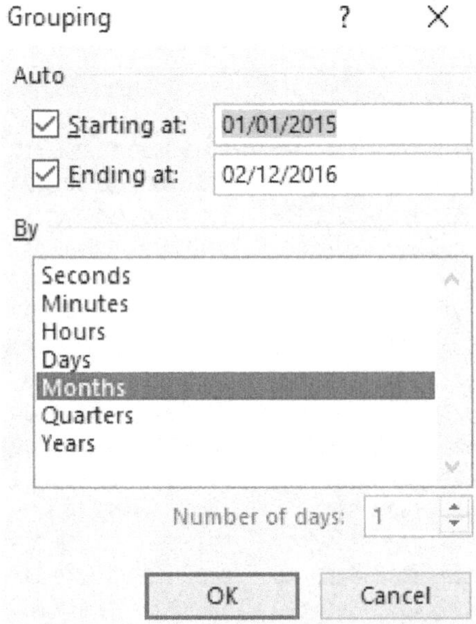

Fig 5.3: Grouping dialog box

As you can see Excel offers a few automatic groupings for date and time fields. For this exercise select *Months* and click **OK**. The Pivot Table will now look as in Fig 5.4.

We can group this a level further and instead of having only *Months* let's also group by *Quarters*. To do this right click anywhere under **Row Labels** and then click on **Group**.

In the **Grouping** dialog box select *Quarters* and press **OK**. Note that we could have done this in the beginning by selecting both *Months* and *Quarters* in the **Grouping** dialog box as in Fig 5.5.

Sum of Revenue	Column Labels			
Row Labels	Line A	Line B	Line C	Grand Total
Jan	$479,659	$466,751	$1,640,239	$2,586,649
Feb	$448,340	$441,675	$1,542,122	$2,432,138
Mar	$486,354	$466,437	$1,643,068	$2,595,859
Apr	$480,897	$456,361	$1,604,634	$2,541,892
May	$492,528	$459,201	$1,662,358	$2,614,088
Jun	$481,572	$463,634	$1,643,424	$2,588,629
Jul	$501,734	$483,213	$1,686,051	$2,670,998
Aug	$495,706	$476,858	$1,651,977	$2,624,541
Sep	$480,587	$467,334	$1,660,775	$2,608,695
Oct	$505,594	$488,675	$1,681,436	$2,675,704
Nov	$484,278	$493,030	$1,736,963	$2,714,270
Dec	$536,373	$511,494	$1,716,714	$2,764,581
Grand Total	$5,873,623	$5,674,662	$19,869,760	$31,418,045

Fig 5.4: Pivot Table with items in the date field grouped by *Month*

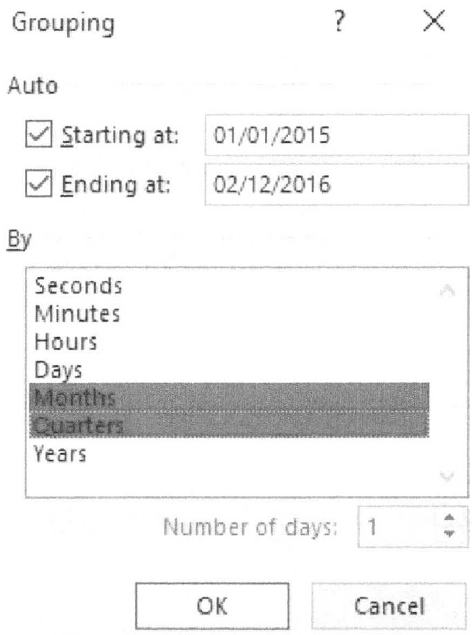

Grouping ? X

Auto

☑ Starting at: 01/01/2015

☑ Ending at: 02/12/2016

By

Seconds
Minutes
Hours
Days
Months
Quarters
Years

Number of days: 1

OK   Cancel

Fig 5.5: Grouping dialog box with two selections

The Pivot Table now includes a new group which is *Quarters*. Also note that when including more than one grouping level the latter ones appear as a field on the **PivotTable Fields List** as in this case does *Quarters* (see Fig 5.7). Just like normal fields they can change area or can be moved to the **Fields section**. If you ungroup to the original date, then these groups will be automatically removed from the **PivotTable Fields List**.

As an exercise repeat the above steps by adding *Years* to the Pivot Table.

If we want to go back to the original Pivot Table with the actual dates, we simply do a right click anywhere under **Row Labels** and then select **Ungroup**. We could also go to the **Analyze** tab click **Group** and then select **Ungroup**.

Sum of Revenue	Column Labels			
Row Labels	Line A	Line B	Line C	Grand Total
⊟ Qtr1				
Jan	$479,659	$466,751	$1,640,239	$2,586,649
Feb	$448,340	$441,675	$1,542,122	$2,432,138
Mar	$486,354	$466,437	$1,643,068	$2,595,859
⊟ Qtr2				
Apr	$480,897	$456,361	$1,604,634	$2,541,892
May	$492,528	$459,201	$1,662,358	$2,614,088
Jun	$481,572	$463,634	$1,643,424	$2,588,629
⊟ Qtr3				
Jul	$501,734	$483,213	$1,686,051	$2,670,998
Aug	$495,706	$476,858	$1,651,977	$2,624,541
Sep	$480,587	$467,334	$1,660,775	$2,608,695
⊟ Qtr4				
Oct	$505,594	$488,675	$1,681,436	$2,675,704
Nov	$484,278	$493,030	$1,736,963	$2,714,270
Dec	$536,373	$511,494	$1,716,714	$2,764,581
Grand Total	$5,873,623	$5,674,662	$19,869,760	$31,418,045

Fig 5.6: *Date* field grouped by *Months* and *Quarters*

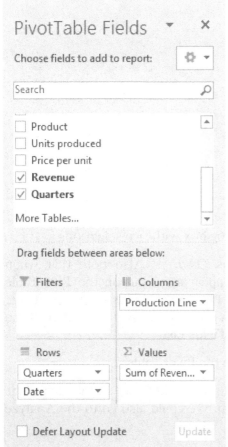

Fig 5.7: *Quarters* group automatically appearing as a field on the **PivotTable Fields List**

5.2 Grouping number items

Grouping number items is slightly different to grouping date and time items. To learn how to group number items, we will build a new Pivot Table in which we have *Price per unit* in **Rows**, *Shift* in **Columns** and *Units produced* in **∑ Values**. The new Pivot Table will look as in Fig 5.8.

Sum of Units produced	Column Labels		
Row Labels	Day	Night	Grand Total
$1.00	141,893		141,893
$1.25	796,542		796,542
$1.35	662,908		662,908
$1.75	307,654		307,654
$1.80		274,785	274,785
$1.85	309,320		309,320
$1.99		276,290	276,290
$2.00		152,305	152,305
$2.10		502,204	502,204
$2.30		352,649	352,649
$2.50	540,059	461,536	1,001,595
$2.60	544,650		544,650
$2.75		461,932	461,932
$4.00	628,110	640,600	1,268,710
$4.30	629,930	637,269	1,267,199
$4.50	532,080	494,711	1,026,791
$4.60	534,221	493,041	1,027,262
Grand Total	5,627,367	4,747,322	10,374,689

Fig 5.8: Pivot Table ready for number grouping

If we click anywhere under **Row Labels** and then do a right click and select **Group** or go to the **Analyze** tab, click on **Group** and then select **Group Selection** or **Group Field** the **Grouping** dialog box for number items will pop up as in Fig 5.9.

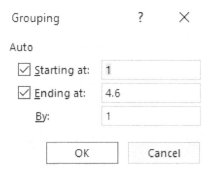

Fig 5.9: Grouping dialog box for number items

In this dialog box, we get the range of our number field and a **By** value which tells Excel what increment to use to group items in the field by. The increment, **starting at** or **ending at** values can be changed. For e.g. if we wanted only part of the range grouped by $1 increment and what is below the **Starting at** value in one group and what is above the **Ending at** value in another group, we would simply need to input the range in the **Starting at** and **Ending at** boxes and add the value of the increment in the **By** box.

If we use the automatic suggestions Excel provides in Fig 5.9 we should get the following groups:

- 1-2

- 2-3

- 3-4

- 4-5

Note that if there is no data in a group, this group won't appear in the Pivot Table. For e.g. if there is no data for the 3-4 group, this group won't appear in the Pivot Table. Let's click on the **OK** button and look at the new Pivot Table which now looks like in Fig 5.10.

Sum of Units produced	Column Labels		
Row Labels	Day	Night	Grand Total
1-2	2,218,317	551,075	2,769,392
2-3	1,084,709	1,930,626	3,015,335
4-5	2,324,341	2,265,621	4,589,962
Grand Total	5,627,367	4,747,322	10,374,689

Fig 5.10: Pivot Table with *Price per unit* field's items grouped

As already explained since there is no data for 3-4, this group won't appear in the Pivot Table.

This is how easy it is to group number items. Remember that this feature is quite flexible and you don't have to use the automatic grouping that Excel suggest. For e.g. we could group by 0.5 instead or we could choose to group up to 3.5 by 0.5 and have one single group above this. Pivot Tables in Fig 5.11 and Fig 5.12 show this respectively.

Sum of Units produced	Column Labels		
Row Labels	Day	Night	Grand Total
1-1.5	1,601,343		1,601,343
1.5-2	616,974	551,075	1,168,049
2-2.5		1,007,158	1,007,158
2.5-3	1,084,709	923,468	2,008,177
4-4.5	1,258,040	1,277,869	2,535,909
4.5-5	1,066,301	987,752	2,054,053
Grand Total	5,627,367	4,747,322	10,374,689

Fig 5.11: Grouping *Price per unit* by 0.5 increments

Sum of Units produced	Column Labels		
Row Labels	Day	Night	Grand Total
1-1.5	1,601,343		1,601,343
1.5-2	616,974	551,075	1,168,049
2-2.5		1,007,158	1,007,158
2.5-3	1,084,709	923,468	2,008,177
>3.5	2,324,341	2,265,621	4,589,962
Grand Total	5,627,367	4,747,322	10,374,689

Fig 5.12: Grouping by $0.5 increments up to a *Price per unit* of $3.5 and then grouping together anything above $3.5

Fig 5.13 shows the **Grouping** dialog box used to build the Pivot Table in Fig 5.12.

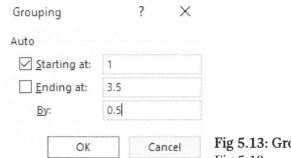

Fig 5.13: Grouping dialog box used to build Pivot Table in Fig 5.12

To ungroup right click under **Row Labels** and then select **Ungroup** or go to the **Analyze** tab, click on **Group** and then select **Ungroup**.

 With numeric items, you can only group one level.

5.3 Grouping everything else

We can group items even when we they are not part of numeric, date or time fields.

Let's go and build a new Pivot Table with *Month* in **Rows**, *Production Line* in **Columns** and *Revenue* in $\sum$ **Values**.

In this exercise we will group data in *Quarters*, however since *Month* is not a date field in the format we have mentioned previously then we must group items manually.

Select *January*, *February* & *March* and then right click and select **Group** or go to the **Analyze** tab and click on **Group** and then select **Group Selection**. (To select multiple items press and hold the *ctrl* button on your keyboard).

Excel will group these months and label them as *Group1* and put all the other months in a separate group. Next let's select the months for the 2nd quarter and group them. You can select the group version (coloured) or the normal item (uncoloured) or both. Proceed the same with the other quarters.

After manually grouping months into quarters our Pivot Table should look like in Fig 5.14.

Note that now we have a new field on the **PivotTable Fields List**, named as *Month2* (see Fig 5.15), found above *Month* in the **Rows** area. This is the new group that we just formed.

Sum of Revenue	Column Labels ▼			
Row Labels ▼	Line A	Line B	Line C	Grand Total
⊟Group1				
January	$479,659	$466,751	$1,640,239	$2,586,649
February	$448,340	$441,675	$1,542,122	$2,432,138
March	$486,354	$466,437	$1,643,068	$2,595,859
⊟Group2				
April	$480,897	$456,361	$1,604,634	$2,541,892
May	$492,528	$459,201	$1,662,358	$2,614,088
June	$481,572	$463,634	$1,643,424	$2,588,629
⊟Group3				
July	$501,734	$483,213	$1,686,051	$2,670,998
August	$495,706	$476,858	$1,651,977	$2,624,541
September	$480,587	$467,334	$1,660,775	$2,608,695
⊟Group4				
October	$505,594	$488,675	$1,681,436	$2,675,704
November	$484,278	$493,030	$1,736,963	$2,714,270
December	$536,373	$511,494	$1,716,714	$2,764,581
Grand Total	$5,873,623	$5,674,662	$19,869,760	$31,418,045

Fig 5.14: Manually grouping items within the *Month* field into *Quarters*

Fig 5.15: Group field appearing on the **PivotTable Fields List** both in **Fields** and **Area Sections**

Let's click on the name of this field in the **Rows** area and select **Field Settings**. Change the name of the field from *Month2* to *Quarter*. Note that this field can now be moved just like any other field, above or below *Month*, to the **Columns** area etc.

Since we changed the name of the group, we may also want to change the name of quarters from *Group1-4* to *Qtr1-4*. To do this we simply click on each cell with the group name in the Pivot Table and change the name in the **Formula Bar**. Now our Pivot Table will look the same as the one in Fig 5.6 when we grouped the *Date* field.

What is also important to know is that we can now group one level further. Let's group semi-annually. Let's select *Qtr1* and *Qtr2*, right click and select **Group**. Do the same for *Qtr3* and *Qtr4*.

Note that in this case it is important to select *Qtrs* and not the *Months*. If we select the latter, we won't have two levels of grouping, quarterly and semi-annually, but only one which is *semi-annually*. You can try both to see the difference.

After grouping another level, you should notice that we have a new field in the **Rows** area named as *Month2* which represents the new group (if you haven't already renamed *Month2* to *Quarters* the new field will be named *Month3* instead). Let's rename this in **Field Settings** to *Semi-Annual*. After you have done this, rename the groups in the Pivot Table from *Group1-2* to *HalfYear1-2*.

Now you should have a Pivot Table that looks like in Fig 5.16.

Sum of Revenue	Column Labels			
Row Labels	Line A	Line B	Line C	Grand Total
⊟ HalfYear1				
⊟ Qtr1				
January	$479,659	$466,751	$1,640,239	$2,586,649
February	$448,340	$441,675	$1,542,122	$2,432,138
March	$486,354	$466,437	$1,643,068	$2,595,859
⊟ Qtr2				
April	$480,897	$456,361	$1,604,634	$2,541,892
May	$492,528	$459,201	$1,662,358	$2,614,088
June	$481,572	$463,634	$1,643,424	$2,588,629
⊟ HalfYear2				
⊟ Qtr3				
July	$501,734	$483,213	$1,686,051	$2,670,998
August	$495,706	$476,858	$1,651,977	$2,624,541
September	$480,587	$467,334	$1,660,775	$2,608,695
⊟ Qtr4				
October	$505,594	$488,675	$1,681,436	$2,675,704
November	$484,278	$493,030	$1,736,963	$2,714,270
December	$536,373	$511,494	$1,716,714	$2,764,581
Grand Total	$5,873,623	$5,674,662	$19,869,760	$31,418,045

Fig 5.16: Pivot Table with two group levels

If we want to show subtotals for a group for e.g. *Quarter* we click on its name in the **Rows** area and select **Field Settings...** . In the **Field Settings** dialog box in the **Subtotals & Filters** tab select **Automatic** under **Subtotals** or if you want a custom calculation select the one you require under **Custom**. In this case let's go for an automatic calculation and click **OK**. The Pivot Table will now look like in Fig 5.17.

Sum of Revenue	Column Labels			
Row Labels	Line A	Line B	Line C	Grand Total
⊟HalfYear1				
⊟Qtr1	$1,414,353	$1,374,863	$4,825,430	$7,614,646
January	$479,659	$466,751	$1,640,239	$2,586,649
February	$448,340	$441,675	$1,542,122	$2,432,138
March	$486,354	$466,437	$1,643,068	$2,595,859
⊟Qtr2	$1,454,997	$1,379,196	$4,910,416	$7,744,610
April	$480,897	$456,361	$1,604,634	$2,541,892
May	$492,528	$459,201	$1,662,358	$2,614,088
June	$481,572	$463,634	$1,643,424	$2,588,629
⊟HalfYear2				
⊟Qtr3	$1,478,027	$1,427,404	$4,998,803	$7,904,234
July	$501,734	$483,213	$1,686,051	$2,670,998
August	$495,706	$476,858	$1,651,977	$2,624,541
September	$480,587	$467,334	$1,660,775	$2,608,695
⊟Qtr4	$1,526,245	$1,493,198	$5,135,112	$8,154,555
October	$505,594	$488,675	$1,681,436	$2,675,704
November	$484,278	$493,030	$1,736,963	$2,714,270
December	$536,373	$511,494	$1,716,714	$2,764,581
Grand Total	$5,873,623	$5,674,662	$19,869,760	$31,418,045

Fig 5.17: Pivot Table with *Quarter* group subtotals

If we want to ungroup we have three ways to go about it:

1. Remove *Quarter* and *Semi-Annual* from the **Rows** area as you would do with a normal field. They will continue to remain as fields and you can reuse them in the future if you want to.

2. Select a cell from the group (in this case *Quarter (Qtr1-4)* or *Semi-Annual (HalfYear1-2)*) and then right click and select **Ungroup** or go through the **Analyze** tab click on **Group** and then **Ungroup**. This option will remove *Quarter* or *Semi-Annual* from the **PivotTable Fields List**.

3. Click anywhere on the table and then go to the **Analyze** tab and then to **Actions, Clear** and finally click on **Clear All**. This will remove groupings and a few other things. Please read the dialog box that will pop up carefully before pressing **Clear PivotTable** as this method will affect all Pivot Tables built from the same data source.

CHAPTER 6
Calculated Fields & Calculated Items

6.1 Calculated Fields

A **Calculated Field** is essentially a new value field which is the result of a calculation involving the **Sum** of other value fields. The **Sum** value for each value field used in the calculation is dependent on which fields are in **Rows**, **Columns** or **Filters** areas and is also subject to any other filters applied to a Pivot Table.

For e.g. let's say that the Warehouse has an expected profit margin of 10%. We want a new value field in a Pivot Table that puts *Expected Profit* alongside *Revenue*. This can be done using a **Calculated Field**. If in our Pivot Table, we had *Month* in **Rows** and *Year* in **Columns** then the calculation for the *Expected Profit* in a given month of a given year would be:

Sum of Revenue for Month X in Year X * 10% = Expected Profit for Month X in Year X

A **Calculated Field** can be built using a value field, in the calculation, that is not in the **Σ Values** area.

Once calculated a **Calculated Field** appears on the **PivotTable Fields List** it can't be moved to **Rows**, **Columns** or **Filters** areas. It can only be moved in and out of the **Σ Values** area.

The new **Calculated Field** can also be used as an input for calculating another **Calculated Field**.

The calculation is always done on the **Sum** of a field and not on any other metric such as **Average** or **Max**. In fact, once a **Calculated Field** is calculated you can go to the **Value Field Settings** for this field and try and change the calculation from **Sum** to any other you like and you will find out that this won't affect the value.

Let's build a new Pivot Table where we have *Production Line* in **Rows**, *Shift* in **Columns** and *Price per unit* in **Σ Values**. Let's go to the *Price per unit* **Value Field Settings** and change the calculation from **Sum** to **Average**. Let's also change the number format to $ with two decimal places. Now you should have a Pivot Table like the one in Fig 6.1:

Average of Price per unit	Column Labels		
Row Labels	Day	Night	Grand Total
Line A	$1.55	$2.34	$1.94
Line B	$1.84	$2.05	$1.94
Line C	$4.35	$4.35	$4.35
Grand Total	$2.58	$2.91	$2.75

Fig 6.1: Pivot Table showing *Average Price per unit* by *Production Line* and *Shift*

The *Average Price per unit* in the Pivot Table above does not take into account the number of units produced of each product. Hence a better calculation would be the *Weighted Price per unit*.

To calculate this field, we will use the **Calculated Field** feature of the Pivot Table. Let's go to the **Analyze** tab and click on **Fields, Items & Sets** and then select **Calculated Field...** . The **Insert Calculated Field** dialog box will appear as in Fig 6.2:

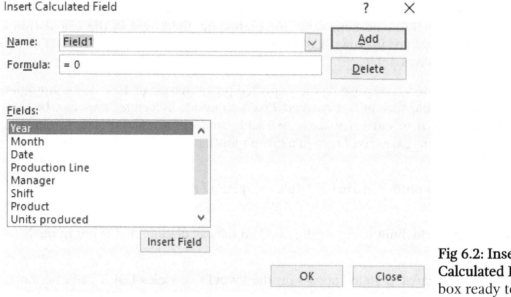

Fig 6.2: **Insert Calculated Field** dialog box ready to be filled

In the **Name box** write *Weighted Average Price Per Unit* and in the **Formula bar** write the formula *Revenue/'Units produced'* as in Fig 6.3. The **Formula bar** can be filled by writing the field names manually, by double clicking them in the **Fields** box or by clicking them in the **Fields** box and then clicking the **Insert Field** button.

I note again here that *Revenue* and *Units produced* are in fact *Sum of Revenue* and *Sum of Units produced* and not values of individual cells under *Revenue* and *Units produced* columns in the source data. When a *Weighted Average Price per Unit* value for e.g. for *January 2015* is placed in a Pivot Table cell (i.e. a Pivot Table with *Month* in **Rows** and *Year* in **Columns**), that value is calculated by Excel as *Sum of Revenue for January 2015/Sum of Units produced for January 2015*.

If you want to build another **Calculated Field** then click the **Add** button and then fill the **Name box** and **Formula bar** with what is required. Click **OK** to finish.

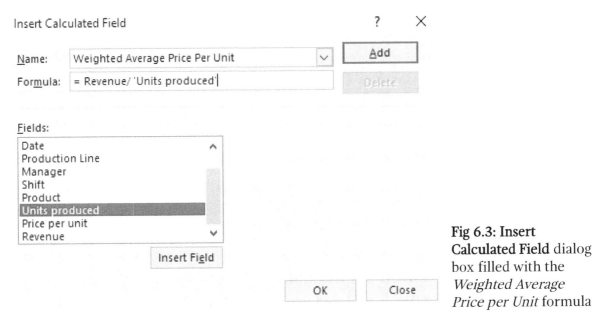

Fig 6.3: Insert Calculated Field dialog box filled with the *Weighted Average Price per Unit* formula

Now the *Weighted Average Price Per Unit* should appear in the $\sum$ **Values** area. Go to the **Value Field Settings** for this field and change the name to *Weighted PPU* and the number format to $ with two decimal places.

For ease of reading change the *Average of Price per unit* name to *Avg PPU*.

Now we have a new Pivot Table that looks like in Fig 6.4:

Column Labels						
	Day		Night		Total Avg PPU	Total Weighted PPU
Row Labels	Avg PPU	Weighted PPU	Avg PPU	Weighted PPU		
Line A	$1.55	$1.46	$2.34	$2.48	$1.94	$1.86
Line B	$1.84	$2.25	$2.05	$2.07	$1.94	$2.16
Line C	$4.35	$4.33	$4.35	$4.32	$4.35	$4.33
Grand Total	$2.58	$2.84	$2.91	$3.25	$2.75	$3.03

Fig 6.4: Pivot Table with **Calculated Field**

Taking into account *Units produced* when calculating *Average Price Per Unit* produces quite different results.

You must have noticed that in the **Columns** area we have a field named as $\sum$ *Value*. This field appears when we have more than one value field in $\sum$ **Values** and is used to control whether value fields are displayed in rows or columns. If we move $\sum$ *Value* to the **Rows** area the format of the Pivot Table will change as in Fig 6.5. In Fig 6.4 value fields are displayed in columns whereas in Fig 6.5 they are displayed in rows.

Row Labels	Column Labels		
	Day	Night	Grand Total
Line A			
Avg PPU	$1.55	$2.34	$1.94
Weighted PPU	$1.46	$2.48	$1.86
Line B			
Avg PPU	$1.84	$2.05	$1.94
Weighted PPU	$2.25	$2.07	$2.16
Line C			
Avg PPU	$4.35	$4.35	$4.35
Weighted PPU	$4.33	$4.32	$4.33
Total Avg PPU	$2.58	$2.91	$2.75
Total Weighted PPU	$2.84	$3.25	$3.03

Fig 6.5: Pivot Table with value fields in rows

6.1.1 Building Calculated Fields using worksheet functions

The formula for **Calculated Fields** that is input in the **Formula bar** can use worksheet functions, however these cannot refer to cells or named ranges.

Let's build a new Pivot Table where we have *Month* in **Rows**, *Year* in **Columns** and Revenue in Σ **Values**.

Let's also build *Expected Profit* as a **Calculated Field** for this Pivot Table. The formula for *Expected Profit* is:

If Monthly Revenue > 1,200,000

then Expected Profit margin is 12%

Else Expected Profit margin is 10%

Let's put this formula into the **Insert Calculated Field** dialog box. The dialog box should look like in Fig 6.6:

Insert Calculated Field   ?   ×

Name: Expected Profit   [Add]

Formula: =IF(Revenue>1200000,Revenue*0.12,Revenue*0.10)   [Delete]

Fields:
Year
Month
Date
Production Line
Manager
Shift
Product
Units produced

[Insert Field]

[OK]   [Close]

Fig 6.6: Insert Calculated Field dialog box with **IF** function

The Pivot Table with calculated *Expected Profit* will look like in Fig 6.7:

Column Labels						
	2015		2016		Total Revenue	Total Expected Profit
Row Labels	Revenue	Expected Profit	Revenue	Expected Profit		
January	$1,260,417	$151,250	$1,326,231	$159,148	$2,586,649	$310,398
February	$1,182,823	$118,282	$1,249,315	$149,918	$2,432,138	$291,857
March	$1,248,195	$149,783	$1,347,664	$161,720	$2,595,859	$311,503
April	$1,237,010	$148,441	$1,304,882	$156,586	$2,541,892	$305,027
May	$1,268,263	$152,192	$1,345,825	$161,499	$2,614,088	$313,691
June	$1,248,297	$149,796	$1,340,332	$160,840	$2,588,629	$310,636
July	$1,301,202	$156,144	$1,369,796	$164,376	$2,670,998	$320,520
August	$1,277,925	$153,351	$1,346,617	$161,594	$2,624,541	$314,945
September	$1,256,384	$150,766	$1,352,311	$162,277	$2,608,695	$313,043
October	$1,293,890	$155,267	$1,381,815	$165,818	$2,675,704	$321,085
November	$1,313,026	$157,563	$1,401,244	$168,149	$2,714,270	$325,712
December	$1,342,279	$161,074	$1,422,301	$170,676	$2,764,581	$331,750
Grand Total	$15,229,711	$1,827,565	$16,188,334	$1,942,600	$31,418,045	$3,770,165

Fig 6.7: Pivot Table with *Expected Profit* as a **Calculated Field**

The **Grand Total** and **Subtotals** for a **Calculated Field** are calculated using the same formula as the **Calculated Field**. When we use conditional functions this calculation can be incorrect. In our case since the **Grand Total** for *Revenue* in 2015 is greater than $1,200,000 the 12% margin is applied when calculating the **Grand Total** for *Expected Profit* instead of summing all the monthly values for the year. If we sum all the values, the actual correct **Grand Total** is $1,803,909. The same issue is valid for *Expected Profit* in 2016 and *Total Expected Profit*. In such a case it might be better to remove **Subtotals** and **Grand Totals** from the Pivot Table and calculate them separately if necessary.

6.1.2 Modifying and Deleting Calculated Fields

If we don't want to use a **Calculated Field** but we don't want to delete it either we can simply untick it in the **PivotTable Fields List** or move it out of the Σ **Values** area into the fields section or into the spreadsheet area as you would do with a normal field.

Once built a **Calculated Field** will keep appearing on the **PivotTable Fields List** unless we delete it or clear the Pivot Table by going to the **Analyze** tab and then clicking **Actions**, **Clear** and finally **Clear All**.

To delete a **Calculated Field** we click anywhere in the Pivot Table and then go to the **Analyze** tab, click on **Fields, Items & Sets** and then click on **Calculated Field....** In the **Insert Calculated Field** dialog box that appears at the end of the **Name box** click on the drop-down button. The **Insert Calculated Field** dialog box will look as in Fig 6.8.

Select the **Calculated Field** you want to delete and then press the **Delete** button.

If you want to modify a **Calculated Field** then after selecting it as above, update the formula in the **Formula bar** and click the **Modify** button. See Fig 6.9.

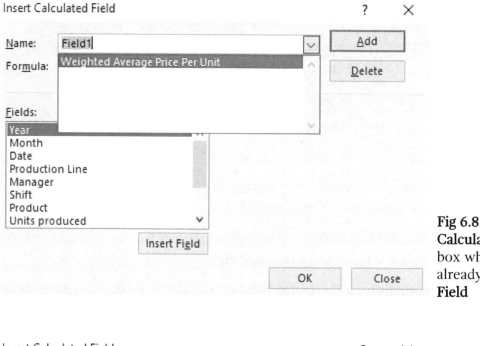

Fig 6.8: Insert **Calculated Field** dialog box when selecting an already built **Calculated Field**

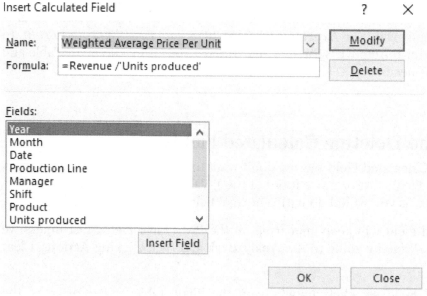

Fig 6.9: How to modify a **Calculated Field**

6.2 Calculated Items

Calculated Items are new items added to a field which are calculated from other items of the same field. A **Calculated Item** is calculated based on the **Sum** of the other items. First the **Sum** for items in a field is calculated then the value of the **Calculated Item** based on these sums is calculated.

Calculated Items can be seen as another way of grouping items.

Calculated Items are listed together with other items in the rows or columns of a Pivot Table.

Let's understand this feature better through an example. Let's build a Pivot Table where we have *Month* in **Rows**, *Shift* in **Columns** and *Revenue* in ∑ **Values**.

Let's click under **Row Labels** in the Pivot Table and then go to the **Analyze** tab, select **Fields, Items & Sets** and then **Calculated Item...** . A dialog box like the one in Fig 6.10 will appear where you will be asked to build a **Calculated Item**.

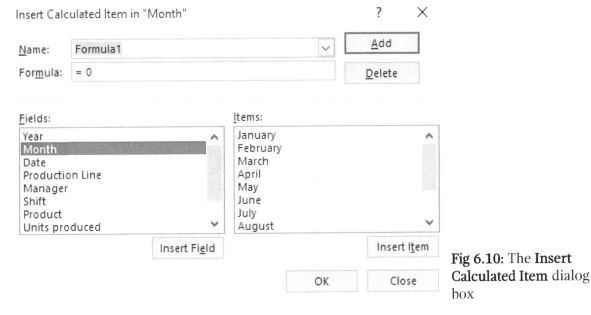

Fig 6.10: The **Insert Calculated Item** dialog box

Let's build our first item:

- In the **Name box** add the name of the new item. Let's call it *Qtr1*.

- From the **Fields** list click on *Month* (This should be automatically selected since we clicked an item of the *Month* field under **Row Labels**).

- In the **Formula bar**, we will add the following: =*January + February + March*. To add an item from *Month* double click on it or click once and then click on the **Insert Item** button or simply type it in the **Formula bar**.

- Now click **Add**.

- Do the same for the other quarters *Qtr2-4*.

Once you have done this the Pivot Table will look like in Fig 6.11 with *Qtr1-4* added to the bottom of the table.

Sum of Revenue	Column Labels		
Row Labels	Day	Night	Grand Total
January	$1,310,267	$1,276,382	$2,586,649
February	$1,243,588	$1,188,550	$2,432,138
March	$1,322,313	$1,273,546	$2,595,859
April	$1,280,220	$1,261,672	$2,541,892
May	$1,312,390	$1,301,698	$2,614,088
June	$1,307,560	$1,281,070	$2,588,629
July	$1,359,921	$1,311,077	$2,670,998
August	$1,345,268	$1,279,274	$2,624,541
September	$1,317,572	$1,291,122	$2,608,695
October	$1,358,218	$1,317,487	$2,675,704
November	$1,417,931	$1,296,340	$2,714,270
December	$1,407,039	$1,357,541	$2,764,581
Qtr1	$3,876,168	$3,738,478	$7,614,646
Qtr2	$3,900,170	$3,844,440	$7,744,610
Qtr3	$4,022,761	$3,881,473	$7,904,234
Qtr4	$4,183,187	$3,971,368	$8,154,555
Grand Total	$31,964,572	$30,871,518	$62,836,090

Fig 6.11: Pivot Table with **Calculated Items** for the *Month* field

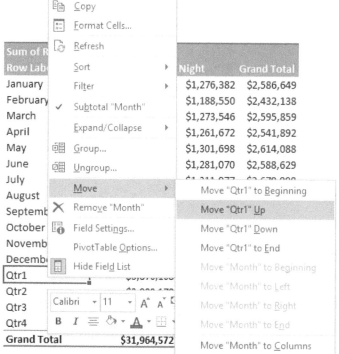

To move **Calculated Items** to a more suitable position let's use the **Move** functionality as in Fig 6.12. Select the cell with *Qtr1* and then right click and go to **Move** and then select **Move "Qtr1" Up**. Repeat until you reach the desired row. Do the same with the other **Calculated Items**.

Note that when using **Calculated Items** it is advisable to remove **Column Totals** when **Calculated Items** are in rows and **Row Totals** when **Calculated Items** are in columns as there will be double counting. The same is also valid for **subtotals** when **Calculated Items** have a parent field.

Fig 6.12: How to move **Calculated Items** up or down a Pivot Table

Once you have placed the quarters in the right position the Pivot Table will look like in Fig 6.13.

Sum of Revenue	Column Labels	
Row Labels	Day	Night
January	$1,310,267	$1,276,382
February	$1,243,588	$1,188,550
March	$1,322,313	$1,273,546
Qtr1	**$3,876,168**	**$3,738,478**
April	$1,280,220	$1,261,672
May	$1,312,390	$1,301,698
June	$1,307,560	$1,281,070
Qtr2	**$3,900,170**	**$3,844,440**
July	$1,359,921	$1,311,077
August	$1,345,268	$1,279,274
September	$1,317,572	$1,291,122
Qtr3	**$4,022,761**	**$3,881,473**
October	$1,358,218	$1,317,487
November	$1,417,931	$1,296,340
December	$1,407,039	$1,357,541
Qtr4	**$4,183,187**	**$3,971,368**

Fig 6.13: Pivot Table with **Calculated Items** moved to a better position

Note that in Fig 6.13 the highlighting and the bolding is done using Excel formatting and is not automatic.

A **Calculated Item** appears only when the field it is built upon is in the Pivot Table. If this field is removed so is the **Calculated Item**.

Now let's suppose that we add another field to the **Rows** area either above or below *Month*. What will happen? The **Calculated Items** will be there and will behave exactly like the other items of the *Month* field i.e. be split by the new field. To see this clearly let's add *Production line* above *Month* in the **Rows** area. Now the Pivot Table will look like in Fig 6.14 and *Qtr1-4* will split for each *Production line*.

The same can be achieved by grouping items as we saw in chapter 5, however **Calculated Items** do give a neater look to the Pivot Table, and you can have as many items as you like in the same row whereas with groups the more levels you add the messier the Pivot Table gets.

Note that in Fig 6.14 subtotals have been removed as these contained double counting.

To remove a **Calculated Item** click either under **Row Labels** or under **Column Labels** depending on where the field it is built upon is located and then go to the **Analyze** tab, select **Fields, Items & Sets** and then click on **Calculated Item...** . On the **Insert Calculated Item** dialog box click on the drop-down button that appears at the end of the **Name box**. The **Insert Calculated Item** dialog box will look as in Fig 6.15.

Sum of Revenue	Column Labels	
Row Labels	Day	Night
Line A		
January	$233,649	$246,010
February	$213,539	$234,801
March	$230,515	$255,840
Qtr1	**$677,702**	**$736,651**
April	$230,040	$250,857
May	$237,408	$255,120
June	$226,264	$255,308
Qtr2	**$693,713**	**$761,285**
July	$242,527	$259,208
August	$240,499	$255,207
September	$232,366	$248,221
Qtr3	**$715,392**	**$762,636**
October	$242,232	$263,362
November	$233,860	$250,418
December	$260,404	$275,968
Qtr4	**$736,497**	**$789,748**
Line B		
January	$255,996	$210,755
February	$242,257	$199,418
March	$253,674	$212,763
Qtr1	**$751,927**	**$622,936**

Fig 6.14: Calculated Items split by *Production Line*

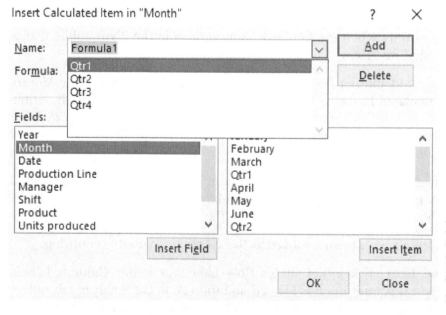

Fig 6.15: The **Insert Calculated Item** dialog box when selecting a **Calculated Item** to modify or delete

Select the **Calculated Item** you want to delete and then press the **Delete** button.

If you want to modify a **Calculated Item**, after selecting it as above, update the formula in the **Formula bar** and click the **Modify** button. See Fig 6.16.

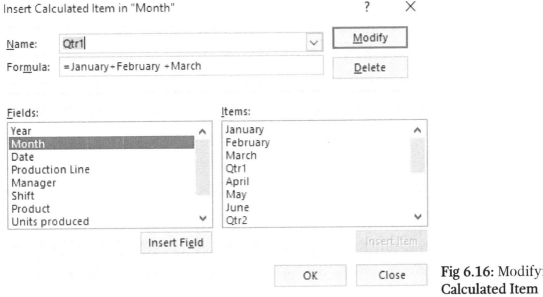

Fig 6.16: Modifying a Calculated Item

 If a field uses **Calculated Items** it can't be moved to the **Filters** area and it can't be placed multiple times into the Σ **Values** area.

6.3 Solve Order and List Formulas

6.3.1 Solve Order

The **Solve Order** is very important if you are using multiple **Calculated Items** in both rows and columns because some Pivot Table cells are affected by more than one **Calculated Item**. To understand exactly how the solve order works we will proceed with an example.

Let's build a Pivot Table where we have *Month* in **Rows**, *Production Line* in **Columns** and *Revenue* in Σ **Values**. We should already have *Qtr1-4* as **Calculated Items** for *Month*, if not re-calculate them as described earlier in this chapter.

Let's calculate a new item called *'Qtr1 % of Total'* whose formula is shown in Fig 6.17. To do this click under **Row Labels** and then go to the **Analyze** tab, **Fields, Items & Sets** and then click on **Calculated Item....** Fill the **Insert Calculated Item** dialog box as in Fig 6.17 and click **OK.**

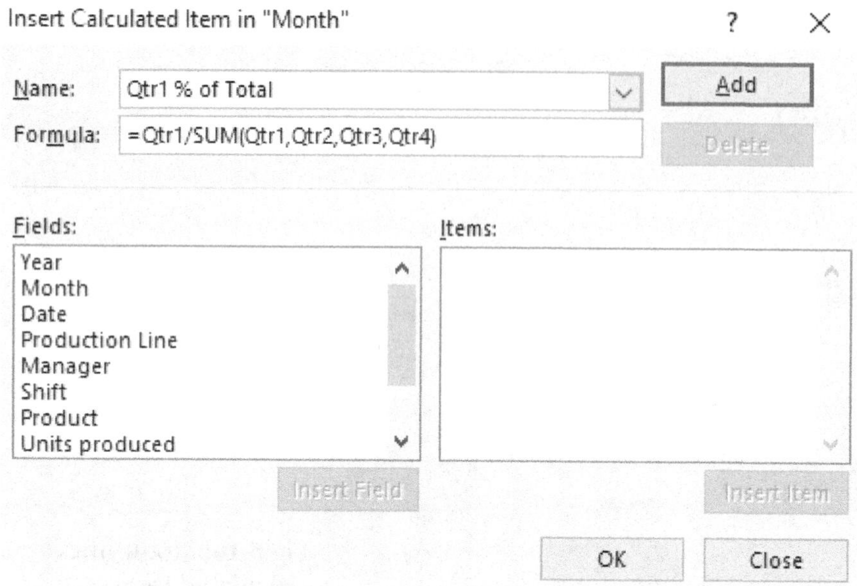

Fig 6.17: Insert **Calculated Item** dialog box with *Qtr1 % of Total* calculation

Select the value row for *'Qtr1 % of Total'* and then go to the **Home** tab and in the **Number** group select **Percentage** from the drop-down list. This will change the number format for the selected cells only.

Move *'Qtr1 % of Total'* under *Qtr1*. To do this right click on *Qtr1 % of Total* and then select **Move** and then **Move "Qtr1 % of Total" Up**. Repeat until desired position is reached.

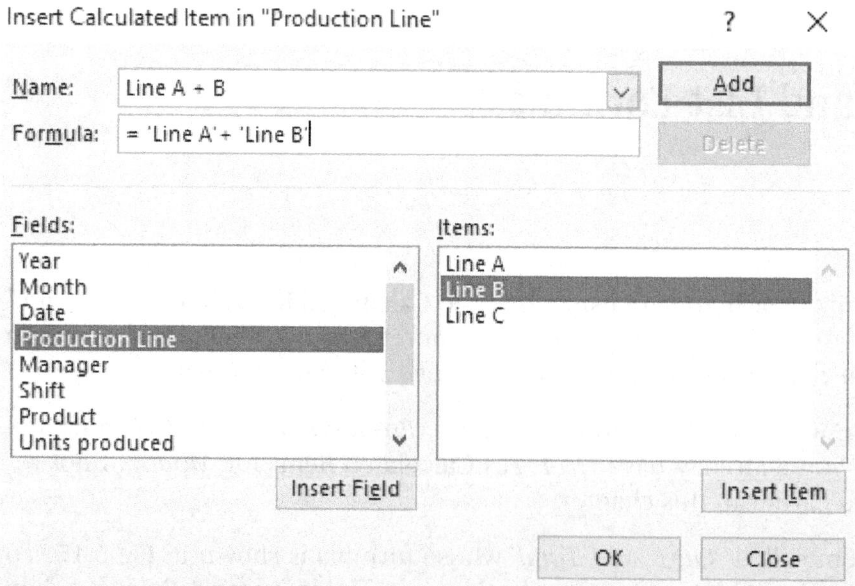

Fig 6.18: New **Calculated Item** being added to the *Production Line* field

Let's click on any item of the column field that we want the **Calculated Item** built on, in this case *Production Line*, and then go to **Calculated Item...** as we did above, and add a new **Calculated Item** and name it *Line A + B* as in Fig 6.18.

After clicking **OK** we will have a new **Calculated Item** in columns. Let's remove **Grand Totals** if we have them displayed since there will be double counting. To do this click anywhere in the Pivot Table and then go to the **Design** tab. In the **Layout** group click on **Grand Totals** and then click on **Off for Rows and Columns**.

The Pivot Table should now look as in Fig 6.19.

| Sum of Revenue | Column Labels | | | |
Row Labels	Line A	Line B	Line C	Line A + B
January	$479,659	$466,751	$1,640,239	$946,410
February	$448,340	$441,675	$1,542,122	$890,015
March	$486,354	$466,437	$1,643,068	$952,791
Qtr1	$1,414,353	$1,374,863	$4,825,430	$2,789,216
Qtr1 % of Total	24.08%	24.23%	24.29%	48.31%
April	$480,897	$456,361	$1,604,634	$937,259
May	$492,528	$459,201	$1,662,358	$951,730
June	$481,572	$463,634	$1,643,424	$945,205
Qtr2	$1,454,997	$1,379,196	$4,910,416	$2,834,193
July	$501,734	$483,213	$1,686,051	$984,948
August	$495,706	$476,858	$1,651,977	$972,564
September	$480,587	$467,334	$1,660,775	$947,920
Qtr3	$1,478,027	$1,427,404	$4,998,803	$2,905,432
October	$505,594	$488,675	$1,681,436	$994,269
November	$484,278	$493,030	$1,736,963	$977,308
December	$536,373	$511,494	$1,716,714	$1,047,867
Qtr4	$1,526,245	$1,493,198	$5,135,112	$3,019,443

Fig 6.19: Pivot Table showing incorrect calculation for *Qtr1 % of Total* under *Line A + B*

 If you still would like to use **Grand Totals** in your Pivot Table you can build these as **Calculated Items** for both **Rows** and **Columns**.

If we look at the *'Qtr1 % of Total'* row we will notice that under the *'Line A + B'* column the % does not look quite right. We should be expecting this to be around half the current value.

If we click on the cell where *'Qtr1 % of Total'* crosses with *'Line A'* we can see the last formula that applies to this cell in the **Formula bar.** See Fig 6.20.

If we click on the cell where *'Qrt1 % of Total'* crosses with *'Line A+B'*, see Fig 6.21, we can see that the last formula that applies to this cell is different from the one in Fig 6.20.

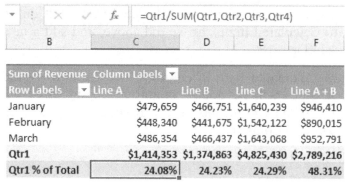

Fig 6.20: Calculation formula when we have only one **Calculated Item** in cell

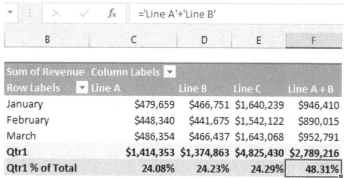

Fig 6.21: Calculation formula for cell where two **Calculated Items** cross

To investigate this problem further and then solve it let's go to the **Analyze** tab and click on **Fields, Items & Sets** and then on **Solve Order....** In the dialog box that appears we can see the **Solve Order** of **Calculated Items**.

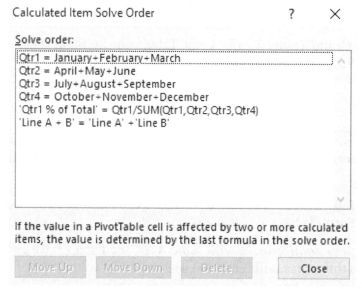

Fig 6.22: Calculated Item Solve Order dialog box

As you can see from the **Solve Order**, at first *Qtr1-4* are calculated then *'Qtr1 % of Total'* and finally *'Line A + B'*.

With the current **Solve Order** at the point that *'Qtr1 % of Total'* is calculated *'Line A + B'* does not exist since we haven't calculated it yet therefore the *'Qtr1 % of Total'* calculation is done only from *Line A* to *Line C*. When *'Line A + B'* is calculated then this calculation is also done for *'Qtr1 % of Total'*. In Fig 6.21 48.31% is simply 24.08% + 24.23% i.e. *Line A + Line B*.

To solve this problem we need to move the *'Line A+B'* calculation above *'Qtr1 % of Total'* calculation so that the *'Line A+B'* calculation is done first.

To do this simply select the *'Line A+B'* calculation and click on the **Move Up** button and then click **Close**. Now the Pivot Table displays the correct figure. If we click on the Pivot Table cell where *'Qtr1 % of Total'* and *'Line A + B'* cross, we can see as in Fig 6.23 that the formula in the **Formula bar** is now the same as for the other cells in the same row.

	f_x	=Qtr1/SUM(Qtr1,Qtr2,Qtr3,Qtr4)			
B	C		D	E	F

Sum of Revenue	Column Labels			
Row Labels	Line A	Line B	Line C	Line A + B
January	$479,659	$466,751	$1,640,239	$946,410
February	$448,340	$441,675	$1,542,122	$890,015
March	$486,354	$466,437	$1,643,068	$952,791
Qtr1	$1,414,353	$1,374,863	$4,825,430	$2,789,216
Qtr1 % of Total	24.08%	24.23%	24.29%	24.15%

Fig 6.23: Pivot Table with correct calculation in the cell where two **Calculated Items** cross

6.3.2 List Formulas

This feature can be accessed by clicking anywhere on a Pivot Table and then going to the **Analyze** tab, **Fields, Items and Sets** and then **List Formulas**. Upon doing this details on **Calculated Fields** and **Calculated Items**, respective formulas and **Solve Order** are displayed on a new sheet as in Fig 6.24:

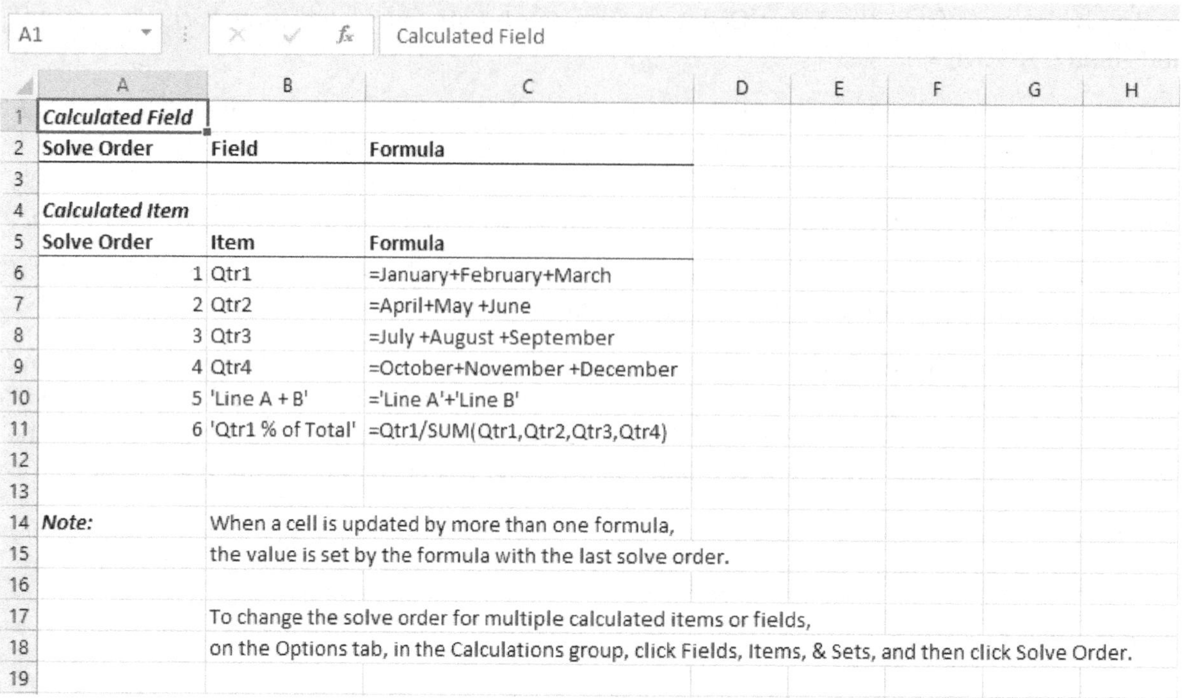

	A	B	C	D	E	F	G	H
	A1	▾ : × ✓ *fx*	Calculated Field					
1	*Calculated Field*							
2	Solve Order	Field	Formula					
3								
4	*Calculated Item*							
5	Solve Order	Item	Formula					
6		1 Qtr1	=January+February+March					
7		2 Qtr2	=April+May +June					
8		3 Qtr3	=July +August +September					
9		4 Qtr4	=October+November +December					
10		5 'Line A + B'	='Line A'+'Line B'					
11		6 'Qtr1 % of Total'	=Qtr1/SUM(Qtr1,Qtr2,Qtr3,Qtr4)					
12								
13								
14	*Note:*		When a cell is updated by more than one formula,					
15			the value is set by the formula with the last solve order.					
16								
17			To change the solve order for multiple calculated items or fields,					
18			on the Options tab, in the Calculations group, click Fields, Items, & Sets, and then click Solve Order.					
19								

Fig 6.24: Formulas for **Calculated Fields** and **Calculated Items** listed in a new sheet

CHAPTER 7
Pivot Table Options

Pivot Table options are accessible through the **Analyze** tab.

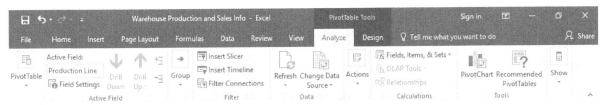

Fig 7.1: The **Analyze** tab

If we click the **PivotTable** button in the **PivotTable** group as in Fig 7.2 we will access the following options:

- The **PivotTable Name** box where we can change the name of the Pivot Table

- An **Options** button with a drop-down button next to it.

Fig 7.2: Accessing options within the **PivotTable** group

If we click on the drop-down button next to **Options** we can access:

- **PivotTable Options** dialog box by clicking on the **Options** button

- **Show Report Filter Pages...** which generates a new Pivot Table for each filter

- the option on whether to generate the **GetPivotData** formula or not when referencing to a cell in a Pivot Table. If this option is not selected, you can reference to a cell within a Pivot Table as you would do to a normal table

 Try switching **GetPivotData** on and off and then do a simple referencing to a cell in a Pivot Table from a cell outside it, for e.g. =C13 where C13 is a cell within the Pivot Table, to see the difference.

7.1 Show Report Filter Pages

When we have one or more fields in the **Filters** area and we want to generate a Pivot Table for each filter in a new worksheet then we use the **Report Filter Pages** feature. Let's illustrate this with an example.

Let's use one of our previous Pivot Tables where we had *Month* in **Rows**, *Production Line* in **Columns** and *Revenue* in **∑ Values**. To be able to use the **Report Filter Pages** feature we need at least one field in the **Filters** area so let's add *Year*.

The Pivot Table will look like in Fig 7.3.

Year	(All)			

Sum of Revenue	Column Labels			
Row Labels	Line A	Line B	Line C	Grand Total
January	$479,659	$466,751	$1,640,239	$2,586,649
February	$448,340	$441,675	$1,542,122	$2,432,138
March	$486,354	$466,437	$1,643,068	$2,595,859
April	$480,897	$456,361	$1,604,634	$2,541,892
May	$492,528	$459,201	$1,662,358	$2,614,088
June	$481,572	$463,634	$1,643,424	$2,588,629
July	$501,734	$483,213	$1,686,051	$2,670,998
August	$495,706	$476,858	$1,651,977	$2,624,541
September	$480,587	$467,334	$1,660,775	$2,608,695
October	$505,594	$488,675	$1,681,436	$2,675,704
November	$484,278	$493,030	$1,736,963	$2,714,270
December	$536,373	$511,494	$1,716,714	$2,764,581
Grand Total	$5,873,623	$5,674,662	$19,869,760	$31,418,045

Fig 7.3: Pivot Table with *Year* as filter

Now go to the **Analyze** tab and click on **PivotTable** and then click on the **Options** dropdown button and finally click on **Report Filter Pages...** . The **Show Report Filter Pages** dialog box will appear as in Fig 7.4:

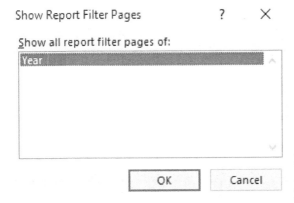

Fig 7.4: Show Report Filter Pages dialog box activated when we have at least one field in the **Filters** area

Select *Year* and click **OK**. Once you click **OK** you will get a new worksheet for each *Year* with the filter applied and the worksheet named with each *Year*'s name. In our case you will get two new worksheets named 2015 and 2016 with a filtered Pivot Table in each. See Fig 7.5.

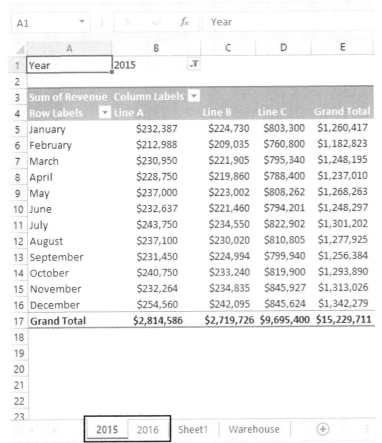

Fig 7.5: Two worksheets with a filtered Pivot Table in them and named as per filtered item

7.2 PivotTable Options dialog box

To access the **PivotTable Options** dialog box go to the **Analyze** tab, then click on **PivotTable** and select **Options**. Alternatively you can right click anywhere on the Pivot Table and select **PivotTable Options...** . A dialog box like the one in Fig 7.6 will appear.

PivotTable Options	? ✕

PivotTable **N**ame: PivotTable1

Layout & Format	Totals & Filters	Display	Printing	Data	Alt Text

Layout

☐ **M**erge and center cells with labels

When in **c**ompact form indent row labels: 1 ⬍ character(s)

Display fields in report filter area: Down, Then Over ⌄

Report filter **f**ields per column: 0 ⬍

Format

☐ For **e**rror values show: [   ]

☑ For empty cells s**h**ow: [   ]

☑ **A**utofit column widths on update
☑ **P**reserve cell formatting on update

[OK   ]   [Cancel]   **Fig 7.6:** PivotTable
Options dialog box

On the top of this dialog box you can change the name of the Pivot Table. Slightly below that there are several tabs. We will go through each of them to see the options available in detail.

7.2.1 Layout & Format tab

This is the first tab of the **PivotTable Options** dialog box and it is separated into two sections **Layout** and **Format**.

Layout

☐ Merge and center cells with labels

This option is not selected by default.

If you tick this checkbox all label cells will be centered and on occasions where you have more than one field in the **Columns** area the top fields' cells will be merged and centered. Fig 7.7 shows a table with this option enabled.

Sum of Revenue	Year	Production Line		
		2015		Grand Total
Month	Line A	Line B	Line C	
January	$232,387	$224,730	$803,300	$1,260,417
February	$212,988	$209,035	$760,800	$1,182,823
March	$230,950	$221,905	$795,340	$1,248,195
April	$228,750	$219,860	$788,400	$1,237,010
May	$237,000	$223,002	$808,262	$1,268,263
June	$232,637	$221,460	$794,201	$1,248,297
July	$243,750	$234,550	$822,902	$1,301,202
August	$237,100	$230,020	$810,805	$1,277,925
September	$231,450	$224,994	$799,940	$1,256,384
October	$240,750	$233,240	$819,900	$1,293,890
November	$232,264	$234,835	$845,927	$1,313,026
December	$254,560	$242,095	$845,624	$1,342,279
Grand Total	$2,814,586	$2,719,726	$9,695,400	$15,229,711

Fig 7.7: Notice all **Column** and **Row Labels** have been centered and where required merged

When in compact form indent row labels *(X)* character(s):

The default is 1 character. If you have your Pivot Table in compact form and you have more than one field in the **Rows** area then each sub field will be indented by **1** character unless this is changed in the option above.

Fig 7.8 shows an example with a sub field indented by 5 characters and for comparison Fig 7.9 shows an example with a sub field indented by 1 character.

Sum of Revenue	Column Labels		
Row Labels	2015	2016	Grand Total
⊟ Line A			
Day	$1,356,136	$1,467,168	$2,823,304
Night	$1,458,450	$1,591,869	$3,050,319
⊟ Line B			
Day	$1,492,041	$1,594,026	$3,086,067
Night	$1,227,685	$1,360,910	$2,588,595
⊟ Line C			
Day	$4,906,800	$5,166,116	$10,072,916
Night	$4,788,600	$5,008,245	$9,796,845
Grand Total	$15,229,711	$16,188,334	$31,418,045

Fig 7.8: *Shift* indented by 5 characters

Sum of Revenue	Column Labels ▼		
Row Labels ▼	2015	2016	Grand Total
⊟ Line A			
Day	$1,356,136	$1,467,168	$2,823,304
Night	$1,458,450	$1,591,869	$3,050,319
⊟ Line B			
Day	$1,492,041	$1,594,026	$3,086,067
Night	$1,227,685	$1,360,910	$2,588,595
⊟ Line C			
Day	$4,906,800	$5,166,116	$10,072,916
Night	$4,788,600	$5,008,245	$9,796,845
Grand Total	$15,229,711	$16,188,334	$31,418,045

Fig 7.9: *Shift* indented by 1 character

Display fields in report filter area: [Down, Then Over] or [Over, Then Down]

& Report filter fields per column/row: [0]

These options relate to the way **Filters** are displayed on top of a Pivot Table when there are more than one filters in the **Filters** area.

Down, Then Over: With this option **Filters** get listed on the next row first depending on how many **Report filter fields per column** we have set.

- If set to 0 the following **Filters** will be listed in rows.

- If set to 1 the following **Filters** will be listed in the same row but different columns.

- If set to 2+ then we will have 2+ **Filters** in 2+ rows and then the next 2+ **Filters** in 2+ rows but in a different column and so on.

Over, Then Down: Using this option **Filters** get listed in columns depending on how many **Report filter fields per row** we have set.

- If set to 0 the following **Filters** will be listed in columns.

- If set to 1 the following **Filters** will be listed in the same column but the rows below.

- If set to 2+ then we will have 2+ **Filters** in 2+ columns and then the next 2+ **Filters** will be listed in the next row under the same columns and so on.

This is better understood by a few examples.

Let's build a Pivot Table with three **Filters**. These will be *Production Line, Shift* and *Month*. In **Columns** we will put *Year* whereas in **Rows** we will put *Product* and in ∑ **Values** *Revenue*.

With the standard option which is **Down, Then Over** and **Report filter fields per column** set to 0, **Filters** will be listed as in Fig 7.10.

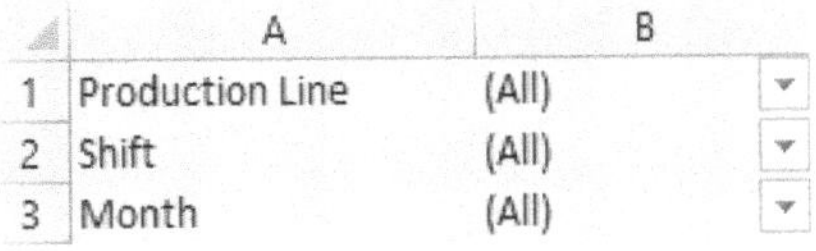
A
B
1 Production Line (All)
2 Shift (All)
3 Month (All)

Fig 7.10: The standard way filters are listed above a Pivot Table

If we change from **Down, Then Over** to **Over, Then Down** and leave **Report filter fields per row** set to 0 then **Filters** will be listed as in Fig 7.11:

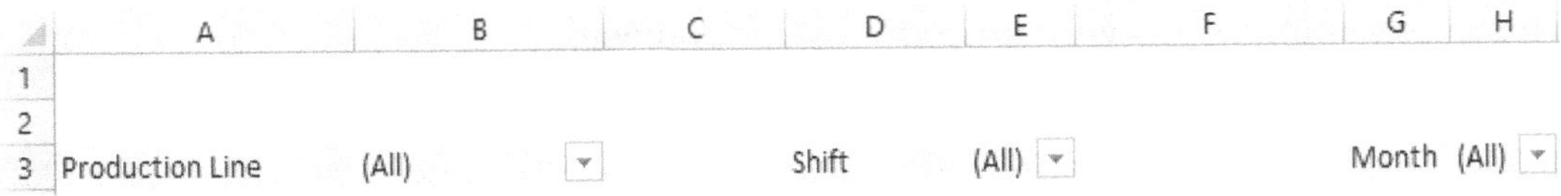
A B C D E F G H
1
2
3 Production Line (All) Shift (All) Month (All)

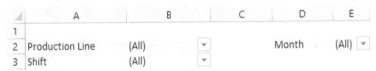

Fig 7.11: All filters listed in a single row

If we change back to **Down, Then Over** and set **Report filter fields per column** to 2 then we will get the **Filters** listed as in Fig 7.12:

A B C D E
1
2 Production Line (All) Month (All)
3 Shift (All)

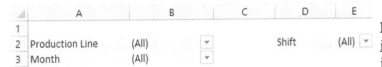

Fig 7.12: The first two filters listed in the same column and the next one in another

If we change from **Down, Then Over** to **Over, Then Down** and leave **Report filter fields per row** set to 2 then we will get the **Filters** listed as in Fig 7.13:

A B C D E
1
2 Production Line (All) Shift (All)
3 Month (All)

Fig 7.13: The first two filters listed in the same row and the next one in another

Note that while the format of the **Filters** appears the same in figures 7.12 and 7.13 the order is different.

Format

In the **Format** section of the **Layout & Format** tab we have the option to deal with error display and empty cells display.

☐ **For error values show:** [ ]

- If we leave this checkbox unticked then whenever an error occurs standard error warnings will be displayed in a cell depending on the error such as #DIV/0!, #NULL!, #N/A, #REF! etc.

- If we tick this checkbox and if we leave the box empty then errors will be displayed as blank otherwise we can type anything we like in the box.

⊠ **For empty cells show:** [   ]

This checkbox is ticked by default.

- If we untick this checkbox, instead of empty cells Excel will display zero values.

- If we leave this checkbox ticked then, to show blanks whenever there are empty cells leave the box empty, otherwise type any values you want.

⊠ **Autofit column widths on update**

This checkbox is ticked by default.

If this checkbox is ticked, when updating a Pivot Table, Excel will change column widths automatically depending on the length of your longest field or item. If you untick it then column widths will be fixed.

⊠ **Preserve cell formatting on update**

This checkbox is ticked by default.

If you format a Pivot Table and then update it, if **Preserve cell formatting on update** is ticked your formatting will be preserved. If it is not ticked then your formatting will be lost.

Note that if **Preserve cell formatting on update** is selected, any update generated new rows or columns will need to be formatted manually.

7.2.2 Totals & Filters tab

In the **Totals & Filters** tab, see Fig 7.14, we have three sections: Grand Totals, Filters and Sorting.

Grand Totals

⊠ **Show grand totals for rows**

⊠ **Show grand totals for columns**

Both checkboxes are ticked by default.

If you untick either of them, then depending on which you unticked the grand totals for rows or columns or both will not show in the Pivot Table. These are the same options as the **Grand Totals** options in the **Layout** group of the **Design** tab.

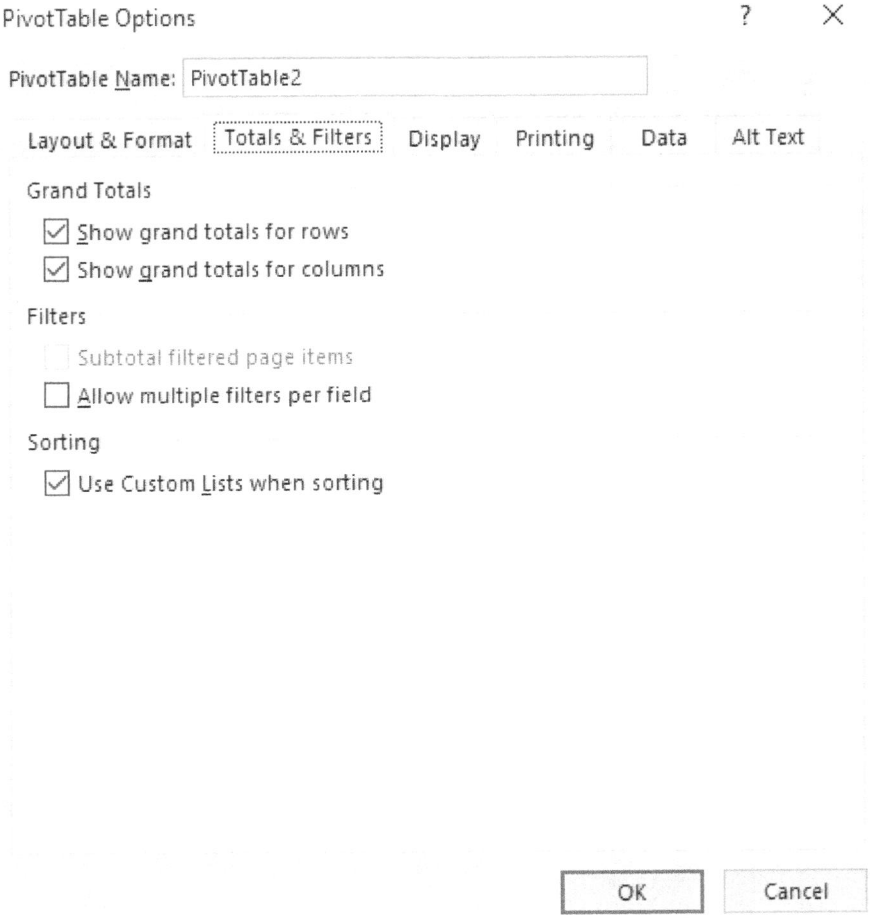

Fig 7.14: Totals & **Filters** tab with default options

Filters

☐ Subtotal filtered page items

This option is greyed out unless using an OLAP (Online Analytical Processing) data source. Check out chapter 10 for more information on this.

☐ Allow multiple filters per field

This option in unticked by default.

If ticked it will allow us to filter using both label and value filters on a single field at the same time.

To better understand the implications of this option let's look at a couple of examples.

Let's build a simple Pivot Table where we have *Product* in **Rows**, *Year* in **Columns** and *Revenue* in Σ **Values**.

In the **Totals & Filters** tab keep **Allow multiple filters per field** unchecked.

Now let's go and filter out all *Products* which don't have the word *'Chocolate'*. To do this click on the drop-down button next to **Row Labels** and then move your mouse to **Label Filters** and then click on **Contains...** .

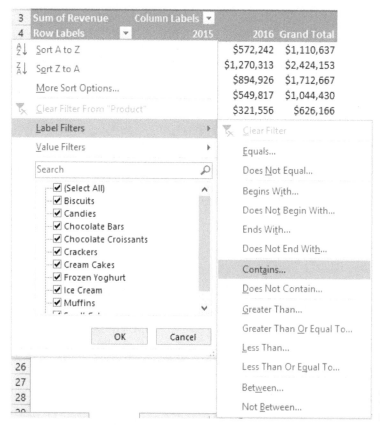

Fig 7.15: Accessing the **Contains...** condition for filtering

In the **Label Filter** dialog box that opens write *Chocolate* and click **OK**. The Pivot Table will now look like in Fig 7.16.

Sum of Revenue	Column Labels		
Row Labels	2015	2016	Grand Total
Chocolate Bars	$817,741	$894,926	$1,712,667
Chocolate Croissants	$494,613	$549,817	$1,044,430
Grand Total	$1,312,354	$1,444,743	$2,757,097

Fig 7.16: Pivot Table with *Chocolate* filter applied to *Product*

Now let's suppose that we want to show the top selling chocolate product only. To do this we need to add a new filter to the field. Let's click again on the drop-down button next to **Row Labels**, then click on **Value Filter** and then **Top 10...** .

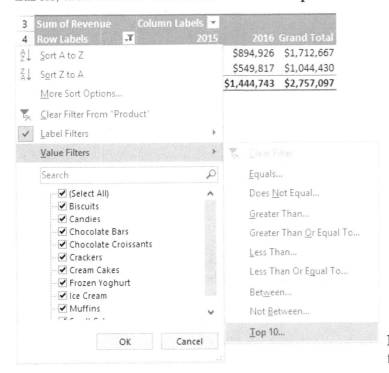

Fig 7.17: Accessing the top 10 filtering condition

In the **Top 10 Filter** dialog box instead of **Top 10 items** let's do **Top 1 items** and click **OK**. The Pivot Table will now look like in Fig 7.18:

Sum of Revenue	Column Labels		
Row Labels	2015	2016	Grand Total
Ice Cream	$5,074,840	$5,448,956	$10,523,796
Grand Total	$5,074,840	$5,448,956	$10,523,796

Fig 7.18: Top 1 item turns out to be *Ice Cream* when in fact we wanted the top *Chocolate* product

Notice that now we don't have a *Chocolate* product in the Pivot Table. What has happened is that the **Label Filter** has been disabled and only the **Value Filter** has been applied. This can be seen in Fig 7.19 where now the tick is next to the **Value Filter** only.

Now let's do a right click anywhere on the Pivot Table and then select **PivotTable Options....** In the **Totals & Filters** tab tick the checkbox before **Allow multiple filters per field** and then click **OK**.

Click the drop-down button next to **Row Labels** and go to **Label Filters**, then click on **Contains...** . Type *Chocolate* in the **Label Filter** dialog box and click **OK**. Now the Pivot Table shows *Chocolate Bars* instead of *Ice Cream* which is the result we expect to see (See Fig 7.20).

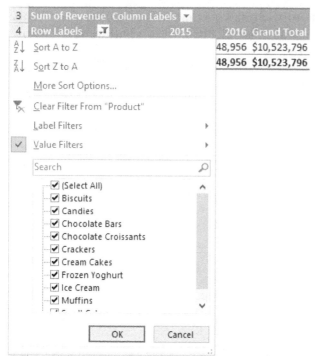

Fig 7.19: Label Filter has been disabled since the Pivot Table does not accept multiple filters per field

Sum of Revenue	Column Labels		
Row Labels	2015	2016	Grand Total
Chocolate Bars	$817,741	$894,926	$1,712,667
Grand Total	$817,741	$894,926	$1,712,667

Fig 7.20: Pivot Table showing expected item after accepting multiple filters per field

If we click on the button next to **Row Labels** we should see that both **Label** and **Value Filters** are ticked (Fig 7.21).

Sorting

☒ Use Custom Lists when sorting

This option is ticked by default.

It allows the sorting of a Pivot Table automatically with a custom sort list. What custom sort lists are and how to build them is explained in the Appendix.

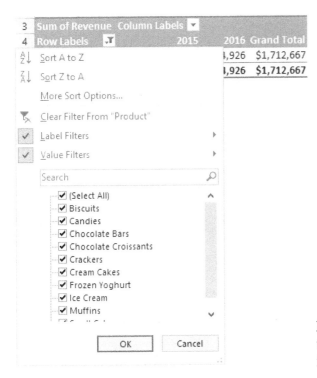

Fig 7.21: Both **Label** and **Value Filters** working together once the option for allowing multiple filters per field has been enabled

7.2.3 Display tab

The **Display** tab with default options is shown in Fig 7.22. It is composed of two sections: display and field list.

Display

☒ **Show expand/collapse buttons**

This option is selected by default.

When we have more than one field in the **Rows** area **expand/collapse buttons** are added automatically next to each parent field's item. If this option is selected **expand/collapse buttons** are shown in the Pivot Table, if not they aren't. If this option is not selected beware that you may not be able to **expand/collapse** fields. Fig 7.23 and Fig 7.24 show this clearly.

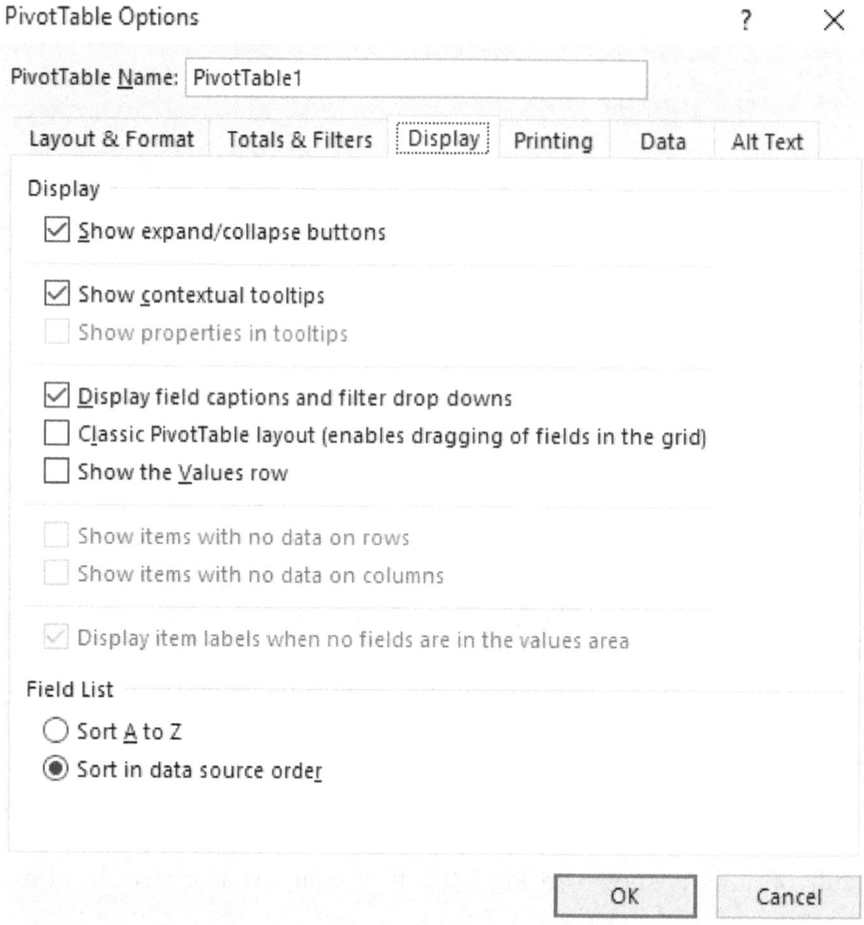

Fig 7.22: Display tab with default options

Fig 7.23: A Pivot Table showing expand/collapse buttons

⊠ Show contextual tooltips

This option is ticked by default.

When pointing your mouse to any cell in a Pivot Table, except for header cells, and leaving it in that position for a couple of seconds a small box appears as in Fig 7.25 with details about that cell. The level of detail shown depends on the cell selected. This box is the **contextual tooltips**. If you don't want it shown, then untick the checkbox.

Sum of Revenue	Column Labels ▼		
Row Labels ▼	2015	2016	Grand Total
Line A			
Day	$1,356,136	$1,467,168	$2,823,304
Night	$1,458,450	$1,591,869	$3,050,319
Line B			
Day	$1,492,041	$1,594,026	$3,086,067
Night	$1,227,685	$1,360,910	$2,588,595
Line C			
Day	$4,906,800	$5,166,116	$10,072,916
Night	$4,788,600	$5,008,245	$9,796,845
Grand Total	$15,229,711	$16,188,334	$31,418,045

Fig 7.24: The same table as in Fig 7.23 but **NOT** showing **expand/collapse buttons**

Sum of Revenue
Value: $1,591,869
Row: Line A - Night
Column: 2016   **Fig 7.25:** Contextual tooltips

☐ Show properties in tooltips

This option is greyed out unless the Pivot Table is connected to an OLAP cube and the cube administrator has enabled the display of member property information. If so by ticking this checkbox you can display properties in a tooltip when moving the mouse pointer to a cell.

☒ Display field captions and filter drop downs

This option is ticked by default.

If unticked and the Pivot Table is in compact form then **Row** & **Column Labels** and drop-down buttons will be removed from the Pivot Table. If unticked and the Pivot Table is in outline or tabular form then **field captions** and drop-down buttons will be removed from the Pivot Table. Fig 7.26 illustrates what happens when a Pivot Table is in compact form.

☐ Classic PivotTable layout (enables dragging of fields in the grid)

By default this option is not ticked.

If ticked it will enable the dragging of fields in the grid, just like old versions of Excel. This option does not work with the compact form and when a Pivot Table is in this form it automatically changes it's layout.

Sum of Revenue	2015	2016	Grand Total
Line A			
Day	$1,356,136	$1,467,168	$2,823,304
Night	$1,458,450	$1,591,869	$3,050,319
Line B			
Day	$1,492,041	$1,594,026	$3,086,067
Night	$1,227,685	$1,360,910	$2,588,595
Line C			
Day	$4,906,800	$5,166,116	$10,072,916
Night	$4,788,600	$5,008,245	$9,796,845
Grand Total	$15,229,711	$16,188,334	$31,418,045

Fig 7.26: Pivot Table without field captions and drop downs

When a Pivot Table is empty the **Classic Layout** looks like in Fig 7.27.

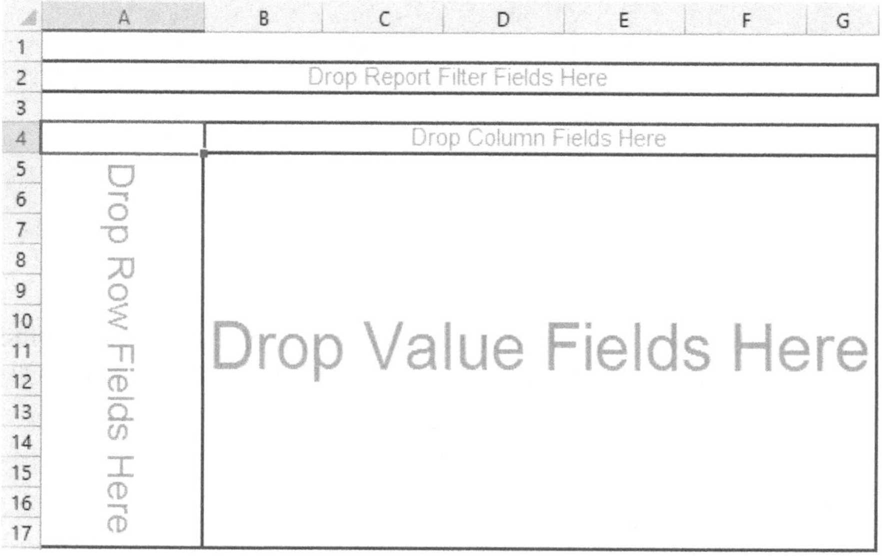

Fig 7.27: An empty Pivot Table in **Classic Layout**

The classic layout is intuitive. Just select a cell belonging to the field you want to move and change its position by dragging it to any area you like such as **Rows, Columns, Filters** or ∑ **Values** or drag it out of the table to completely remove it.

You can add a new field by dragging it from the **PivotTable Fields List** to the required area in the Pivot Table. Also, remember that you can still work in the **PivotTable Fields List** as normal in addition to using the classic Pivot Table feature.

Fig 7.28 shows how a simple Pivot Table with *Production Line* and *Shift* in **Rows**, *Year* in **Columns** and *Revenue* in ∑ **Values** looks like when trying to drop a third field before *Production Line* in the grid.

Fig 7.28: Classic Pivot Table layout. The green line before *Production Line* indicates an attempt to drop a new field before it

☐ Show items with no data on rows

This option is available only with an OLAP data source.

☐ Show items with no data on columns

This option is available only with an OLAP data source.

☐ Display item labels when no fields are in the values area

This option applies to Pivot Table reports built prior to Excel 2007 i.e. in .xls files. If this option is selected, row and column field items will be displayed on a Pivot Table even when there are no fields in the **Σ Values** area.

Field List

The following two options are mutually exclusive:

☐ **Sort A to Z**

This option is not selected by default.

Select to sort fields in the **Fields Section** of the **PivotTable Fields List** in alphabetical order.

☒ **Sort in data source order**

This option is selected by default.

Select to sort fields in the **Fields Section** of the **PivotTable Fields List** in the order found in the data source.

In Fig 7.29 the fields are sorted in data source order.

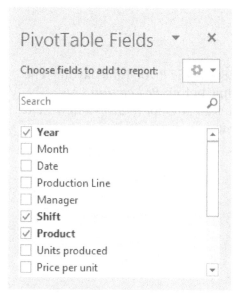

Fig 7.29: Fields list sorted in data source order

If we go to the **Display** tab in the **PivotTable Options** dialog box and select **Sort A to Z** instead the fields list will now look as in Fig 7.30.

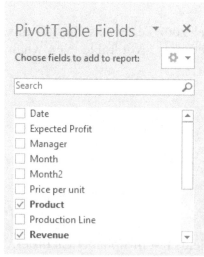

Fig 7.30: Fields sorted in A to Z order

These two options are also accessible from the **PivotTable Fields List**'s settings button. For details check chapter 9.

7.2.4 Printing tab

Fig 7.31 shows the **Printing** tab in the **PivotTable Options** dialog box with default options selected.

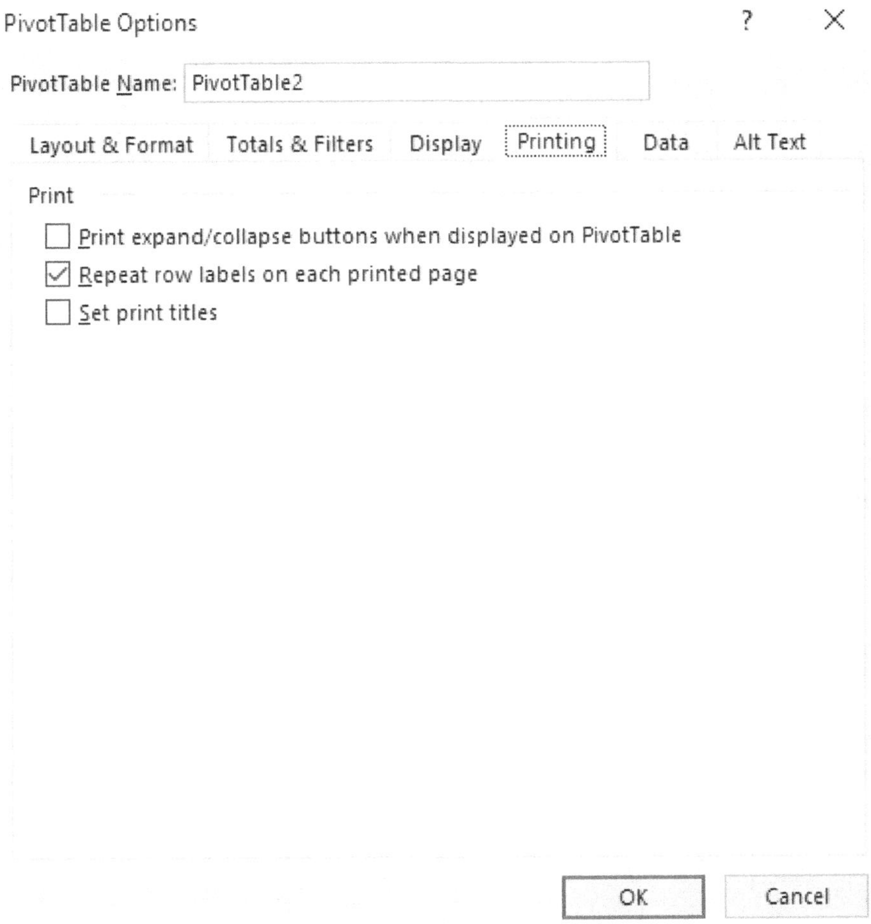

PivotTable Options   ?   ✕

PivotTable <u>N</u>ame: PivotTable2

| Layout & Format | Totals & Filters | Display | Printing | Data | Alt Text |

Print

☐ <u>P</u>rint expand/collapse buttons when displayed on PivotTable
☑ <u>R</u>epeat row labels on each printed page
☐ <u>S</u>et print titles

OK   Cancel

Fig 7.31: Printing tab in **PivotTable Options** dialog box

☐ **Print expand/collapse buttons when displayed on PivotTable**

This option is not selected by default.

When printing a Pivot Table if you would like to print **expand/collapse buttons** then tick this checkbox. Note that if **expand/collapse buttons** are not displayed because **Show expand/collapse buttons** is not selected in the **Display** tab, then **expand/collapse buttons** won't be printed even if this option is selected.

Fig 7.32 shows the print preview of a Pivot Table when this option is selected.

Sum of Revenue		Year		
Shift	Product	2015	2016	Grand Total
⊟ Day	Biscuits	$538,595	$573,342	$1,110,857
	Chocolate Bars	$817,741	$894,926	$1,712,667
	Cream Cakes	$141,593	$177,926	$319,529
	Frozen Yoghurt	$2,394,360	$2,457,417	$4,851,777
	Ice Cream	$2,512,440	$2,708,699	$5,221,139
	Small Cakes	$1,350,148	$1,416,090	$2,766,238
Day Total		$7,754,976	$8,227,310	$15,982,286
⊟ Night	Candies	$1,153,540	$1,270,615	$2,424,155
	Chocolate Croissants	$494,613	$549,817	$1,044,430
	Crackers	$304,610	$321,556	$626,166
	Frozen Yoghurt	$2,236,200	$2,267,989	$4,504,189
	Ice Cream	$2,562,400	$2,740,257	$5,302,657
	Muffins	$733,072	$811,093	$1,544,165
Night Total		$7,474,733	$7,961,024	$15,435,759
Grand Total		$15,229,711	$16,188,334	$31,418,045

Fig 7.32: Print preview of Pivot Table with **Print expand/collapse buttons** option ticked

☒ Repeat row labels on each printed page

This option is selected by default.

If a Pivot Table has more than one field in **Rows** and it is in either outline or tabular form and you want to display the current item from each row field in the first row of each printed page, tick this checkbox otherwise leave it cleared.

This is better understood by an example. Let's build a Pivot Table where we have *Month*, *Shift* and *Product* in **Rows** and *Revenue* in ∑ **Values**.

Click anywhere on the Pivot Table and go to the **Analyze** tab, **PivotTable** group and then **Options**. In the **Printing** tab clear the checkbox before **Repeat row labels on each printed page**.

Now go to **File** and then **Print** and look at the second page of the **Print Preview**. The top of this page should look like Fig 7.33.

	Cream Cakes	$26,164	
	Frozen Yoghurt	$581,891	
	Ice Cream	$421,766	
	Small Cakes	$230,559	
Night		$1,261,672	
	Candies	$200,468	
	Chocolate Croissants	$84,112	
	Crackers	$60,591	
	Frozen Yoghurt	$372,145	
	Ice Cream	$428,818	
	Muffins	$125,746	
May		$2,614,088	
Day		$1,312,390	
	Biscuits	$92,591	
	Chocolate Bars	$144,817	
	Cream Cakes	$26,900	
	Frozen Yoghurt	$395,958	
	Ice Cream	$433,146	
	Small Cakes	$219,000	
Night		$1,301,698	
	Candies	$203,002	
	Chocolate Croissants	$83,987	
	Crackers	$85,117	
	Frozen Yoghurt	$386,036	
	Ice Cream	$447,240	
	Muffins	$129,314	

Fig 7.33: Top section of 2ⁿᵈ page of **Print Preview**

Let's go again to the **Printing** tab in the **PivotTable Options** dialog box and tick the checkbox before **Repeat row labels on each printed page**.

Go back again and have a look at the second page of the **Print Preview**. It should now look like Fig 7.34 with the current item from each row field repeated on the first row.

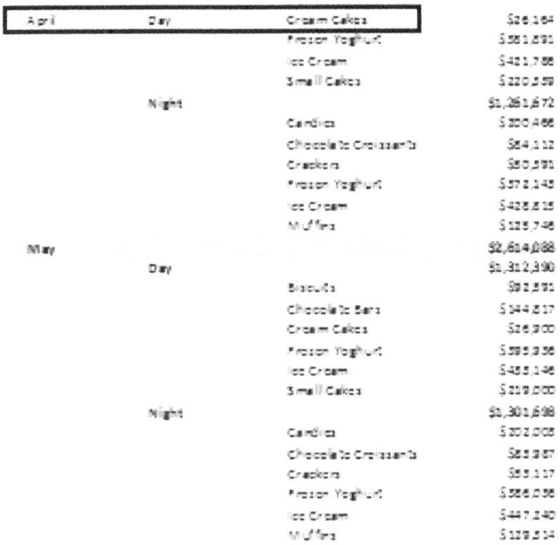

Fig 7.34: The current item from each row field is repeated on the first row

☐ **Set print titles**

This option is not selected by default.

If you select it Excel will print row and column labels on each printed page of a Pivot Table report.

Let's look at an example to understand this better. Using the same Pivot Table as the above example if we leave **Set print titles** cleared then the top of the second page will look like Fig 7.34 or Fig 7.33 depending on whether we have selected **Repeat row labels on each printed page** or not.

Now click anywhere on the Pivot Table and select **Options** from the **PivotTable** group in the **Analyze** tab. Go to the **Printing** tab and tick the checkbox before **Set print titles** and then click **OK**.

After you have done this go to the **File** tab and then **Print** and look at the second page of the **Print Preview**. It will look as in Fig 7.35 with row and column labels printed.

Month	Shift	Product	Sum of Revenue
April	Day	Cream Cakes	$26,164
		Frozen Yoghurt	$581,891
		Ice Cream	$421,766
		Small Cakes	$230,559
	Night		$1,261,672
		Candies	$200,466
		Chocolate Croissants	$64,112
		Crackers	$50,591
		Frozen Yoghurt	$572,143
		Ice Cream	$426,833
		Muffins	$125,746
May			$2,614,088
	Day		$1,312,390
		Biscuits	$92,591
		Chocolate Bars	$344,817
		Cream Cakes	$26,900
		Frozen Yoghurt	$595,936
		Ice Cream	$435,146
		Small Cakes	$219,000
	Night		$1,301,698
		Candies	$203,008
		Chocolate Croissants	$65,987
		Crackers	$65,117
		Frozen Yoghurt	$596,056
		Ice Cream	$447,240
		Muffins	$129,514

Fig 7.35: Row and column labels printed on 2nd page with **Set print titles** option selected

To print titles you must enter values in **Rows to repeat at top** and **Columns to repeat at left** in the **Sheet** tab of the **Page Setup** dialog box that pops up after clicking **Print Titles** under **Page Setup** group in the **Page Layout** tab. It seems that ticking and unticking **Set print titles** automatically adds or removes values from **Rows to repeat at top** and **Columns to repeat at left**. If you are having problems with this option do check this out.

7.2.5 Data tab

The **Data** tab with default options selected looks as in Fig 7.36. It is composed of three sections: PivotTable Data, Retain items deleted from the data source and What-If analysis.

PivotTable Data

☒ **Save source data with file**

This option is selected by default.

When a Pivot Table is built, Excel saves the source data in a special memory called a **Pivot Cache**. This has the advantage of opening the file quickly without the need to refresh the table. With large datasets however, it can take up significantly more space. If you clear this option then it can be a good idea to select the third option in the **Data** tab, **Refresh data when opening the file**, otherwise you will have to do this manually each time you open your file and try to make changes to the table.

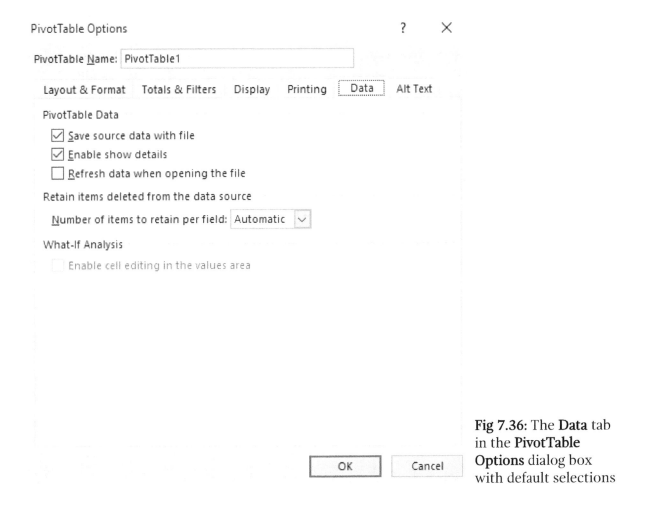

Fig 7.36: The **Data** tab in the **PivotTable Options** dialog box with default selections

☒ Enable show of detail

This option is selected by default.

When selected this option enables two features:

1. If you double click on a value cell in a Pivot Table, Excel will show the rows that were used to calculate that cell in a new worksheet. For e.g. in the Pivot Table we used above let's double click on the **Sum of Revenue** ($90,312) that corresponds to *Biscuits* on the *Day Shift* in *January*.

	A	B	C	D	E	F	G	H	I	J
1	Year	Month	Date	Production Line	Manager	Shift	Product	Units produced	Price per unit	Revenue
2	2016	January	########	Line A	Steven Robe	Day	Biscuits	24601	1.85	45511.85
3	2015	January	########	Line A	Steven Robe	Day	Biscuits	25600	1.75	44800

Fig 7.37: Details on the double-clicked Pivot Table cell

If you add the two cells from the *Revenue* column you will get the value $90,312.

2. Going back to the same Pivot Table let's double click on any item in the last row field. Continuing with the example above double click on *Biscuits* on the *Day Shift* in *January* or alternatively click on *Biscuits* on the *Day Shift* in *January* and then in the **Analyze** tab go to the **Active Field** group and click on the **Expand Field** button (see Fig 7.38).

Fig 7.38: Expand Field button encircled

Both ways will result in the **Show Detail** dialog box showing as in Fig 7.39:

Show Detail	?	✕

Choose the field containing the detail you want to show:

Year
Date
Production Line
Manager
Units produced
Price per unit
Revenue
Month2

OK   Cancel

Fig 7.39: Show Detail dialog box

In this dialog box let's select the field that we want to show detail on. In here you will find all fields except the ones already showing in **Rows** or **Columns**. In this case let's select *Production Line* and click **OK**.

Once selected *Production Line* will appear as a new field after *Product* as in Fig 7.40.

Month ▼	Shift ▼	Product ▼	Production Line ▼	Sum of Revenue
⊟January				$2,586,649
	⊟Day			$1,310,267
		⊟Biscuits		$90,312
			Line A	$90,312
		⊞Chocolate Bars		$143,337
		⊞Cream Cakes		$25,191
		⊞Frozen Yoghurt		$393,859
		⊞Ice Cream		$426,763
		⊞Small Cakes		$230,805

Fig 7.40: A new field added to the Pivot Table by using the **Show Detail** dialog box

☐ **Refresh data when opening the file**

This option is not selected by default.

If selected it will automatically refresh data when opening the file. Can be useful if **Save source data with file** is not selected or if using external data.

Retain items deleted from the data source

Number of items to retain per field: | Automatic |

This option specifies the number of items for each field to temporarily cache with the workbook. There are three options to select from.

- **Automatic:** The default number of unique items for each field

- **None**

- **Max:** The maximum number which is up to 1,048,576 items

To understand this option through an example let's build a simple Pivot Table with *Month* in **Rows** and *Revenue* in **Σ Values**. If we click on the drop-down button next to *Month* we can see the list of months we can filter by as in Fig 7.41.

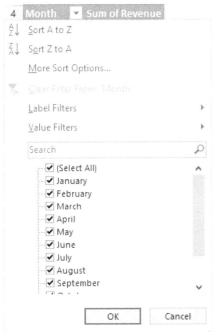

Fig 7.41: List of months we can manually filter by

Now let's go to the data source and change each month from the full name to a three-lettered name and then right click on any Pivot Table cell and click **Refresh**. This will be the equivalent of deleting the data. If we click on the drop-down button next to *Month* we can see that the old names are still there together with the new ones as in Fig 7.42.

This is because we have set the **Number of items to retain per field** to **Automatic**. If we set this to **None**, click **OK** and then **Refresh** the Pivot Table we will see only the new names in the filter as in Fig 7.43.

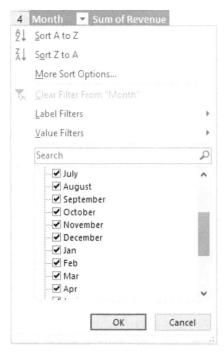

Fig 7.42: Old names together with new names in the manual filter section

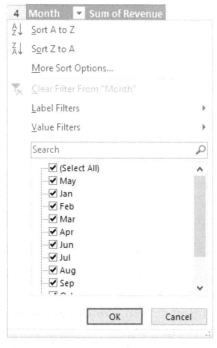

Fig 7.43: Only new names in the manual filter section after **Number of items to retain per field** set to **None**

What-If Analysis

☐ Enable cell editing in the values area

This option is greyed out unless connected to an OLAP data source that allows for this type of analysis.

7.2.6 Alt Text tab

The last tab in the **PivotTable Options** dialog box is the **Alt Text** tab (Fig 7.44).

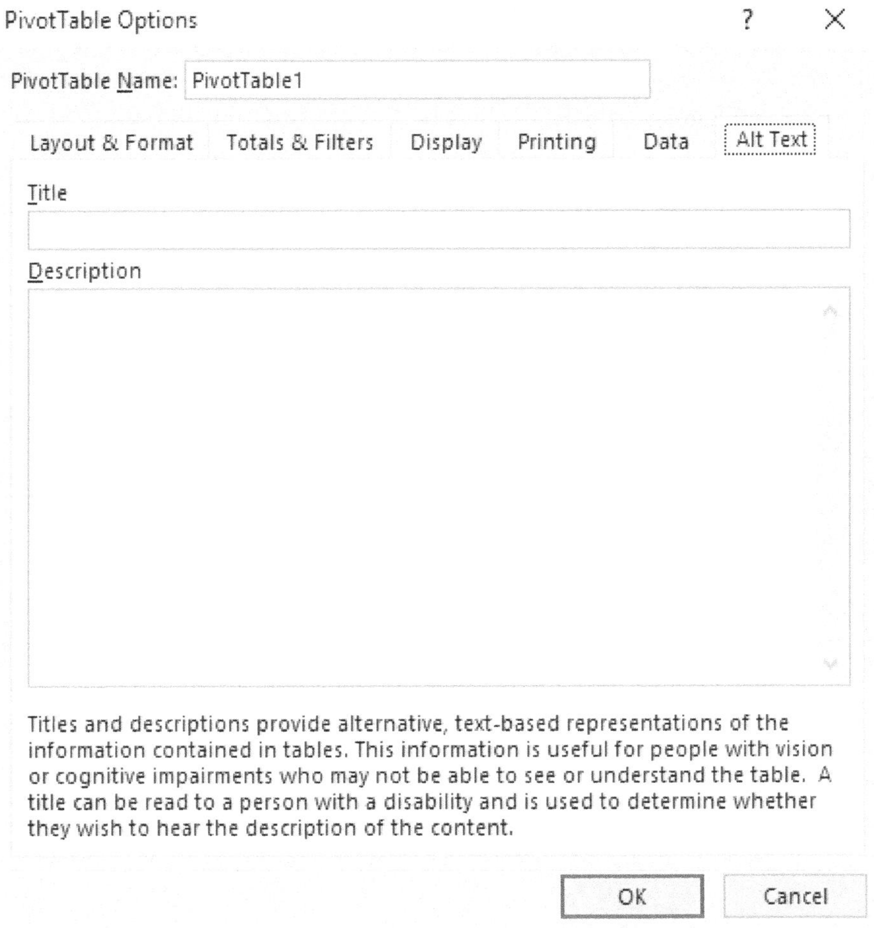

Fig 7.44: The **Alt Text** tab

In this tab, you can write a title for the Pivot Table and a description of its contents which will be useful for people with vision or cognitive problems.

CHAPTER 8

Pivot Charts

A **Pivot Chart** is essentially the same as an **Excel Chart** except that it is based on a Pivot Table and can only be built using a Pivot Table. **Pivot Charts** can be very useful and can give a visual perspective to your data. Moreover, they get updated automatically with your Pivot Table. Any filtering done to it automatically gets updated in the **Pivot Chart** and vice versa.

To build a **Pivot Chart** click anywhere on the Pivot Table you wish to chart and then go to the **Analyze** tab, **Tools** group and click on **PivotChart** (Fig 8.1).

PivotChart Recommended
            PivotTables

Tools

Fig 8.1: PivotChart in **Tools** group

Let's build a **Pivot Chart** based on a new Pivot Table. In this Pivot Table let's have *Product* in **Rows**, *Year* in **Columns** and *Revenue, Units Produced* and *Weighted Average Price per Unit* in ∑ **Values**.

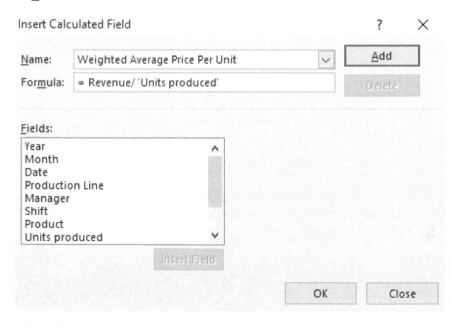

Fig 8.2: Re-calculating **Weighted Average Price Per Unit**

Weighted Average Price per Unit is a **Calculated Field** that we have previously calculated. If you have removed it from the **PivotTable Fields List** then go to the **Analyze** tab, **Fields, Items & Sets** and then click on **Calculated Field....** Fill the **Insert Calculated Field** dialog box as in Fig 8.2 and click **OK**. Now it should appear on your **PivotTable Fields List**.

In this new Pivot Table we want value fields to appear in columns rather than in rows therefore let's keep *∑ Values* (This appears when we have more than one value field in ∑ **Values**) in the **Columns** area (or move it to **Columns** if it appears in **Rows**) in the PivotTable Fields List.

Now let's edit the names of value fields in their respective **Value Field Settings**:

- Sum of Revenue - *Revenues*

- Sum of Units Produced - *Units*

- Sum of Weighted Average Price Per Unit - *Weighted Avg PPU*

and also edit number formats:

- *Revenues* in $ (US) with no decimal places

- *Units* in Number with thousandths separator

- *Weighted Avg PPU* in $ (US) with 2 decimal places

The updated Pivot Table should look like the one in Fig 8.3:

Product	Year ▾ Values 2015 Revenues	Units	Weighted Avg PPU	2016 Revenues	Units	Weighted Avg PPU	Total Revenues	Total Units	Total Weighted Avg PPU
Biscuits	$538,395	307,654	$1.75	$572,242	309,320	$1.85	$1,110,637	616,974	$1.80
Candies	$1,153,840	461,536	$2.50	$1,270,313	461,932	$2.75	$2,424,153	923,468	$2.63
Chocolate Bars	$817,741	654,193	$1.25	$894,926	662,908	$1.35	$1,712,667	1,317,101	$1.30
Chocolate Croissants	$494,613	274,785	$1.80	$549,817	276,290	$1.99	$1,044,430	551,075	$1.90
Crackers	$304,610	152,305	$2.00	$321,556	153,122	$2.10	$626,166	305,427	$2.05
Cream Cakes	$141,893	141,893	$1.00	$177,936	142,349	$1.25	$319,829	284,242	$1.13
Frozen Yoghurt	$4,620,560	1,026,791	$4.50	$4,725,405	1,027,262	$4.60	$9,345,965	2,054,053	$4.55
Ice Cream	$5,074,840	1,268,710	$4.00	$5,448,956	1,267,199	$4.30	$10,523,796	2,535,909	$4.15
Muffins	$733,072	349,082	$2.10	$811,093	352,649	$2.30	$1,544,165	701,731	$2.20
Small Cakes	$1,350,148	540,059	$2.50	$1,416,090	544,650	$2.60	$2,766,238	1,084,709	$2.55
Grand Total	$15,229,711	5,177,008	$2.94	$16,188,334	5,197,681	$3.11	$31,418,045	10,374,689	$3.03

Fig 8.3: Completed Pivot Table ready for building a **Pivot Chart**

Now that we have completed our Pivot Table we can build a **Pivot Chart** based on it.

Click anywhere on the Pivot Table and go to the **Analyze** tab, **Tools** group and click on PivotChart. The **Insert Chart** dialog box will appear as in Fig 8.4.

The next step is to choose the right **Chart Type** for our Pivot Table.

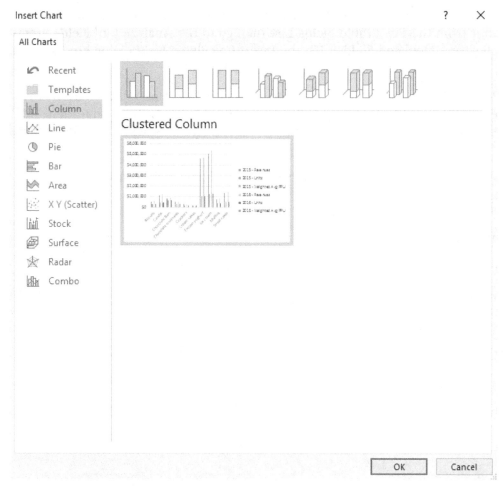

Fig 8.4: The **Insert Chart** dialog box

Let's go to **Combo** and select **Custom Combination** and then put *Year-Weighted Avg PPU* in the **Secondary Axis** by ticking the checkbox next to **Chart Type.** For the same series (*Year – Weighted Avg PPU*) set **Chart Type** to **Line** whereas for the other series **Chart Type** should be set to **Clustered Column**. See Fig 8.5.

After finishing click **OK** and a **Pivot Chart** will be built that looks like in Fig 8.6.

Let's note the similarities of the **Pivot Chart** to the Pivot Table it's built upon. *Product* and *Year* are in different axes in the **Pivot Chart**, *Product* in **Axis Fields** whereas *Year* in **Legend Fields**, as they are in **Rows** and **Columns** respectively in the Pivot Table. *Revenues, Units* and *Weighted Avg PPU* are in the same order as in the Σ **Values** area.

Values button is in the **Legend Fields** which corresponds to Σ *Values* being in the **Columns** area. If Σ *Values* was in the **Rows** area the **Values** button would have been next to *Product*.

If we right click on each field button there are a few things we can do with each:

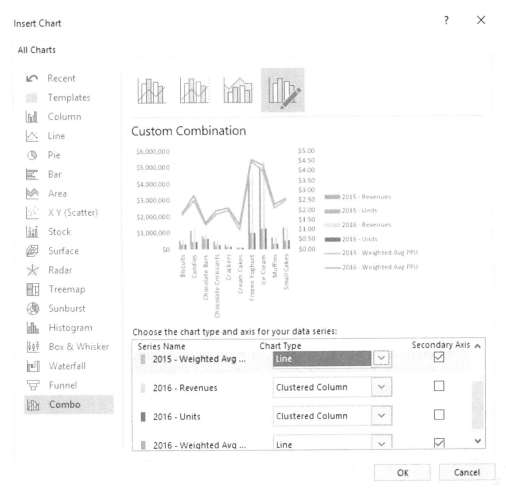

Fig 8.5: Setting up a **Combination Combo Pivot Chart**

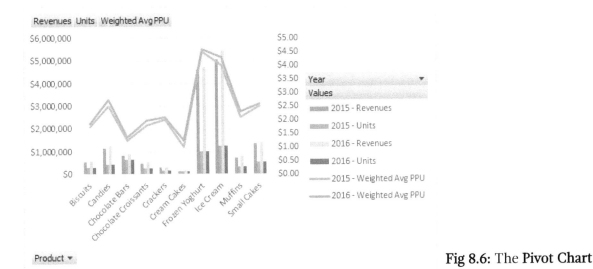

Fig 8.6: The **Pivot Chart**

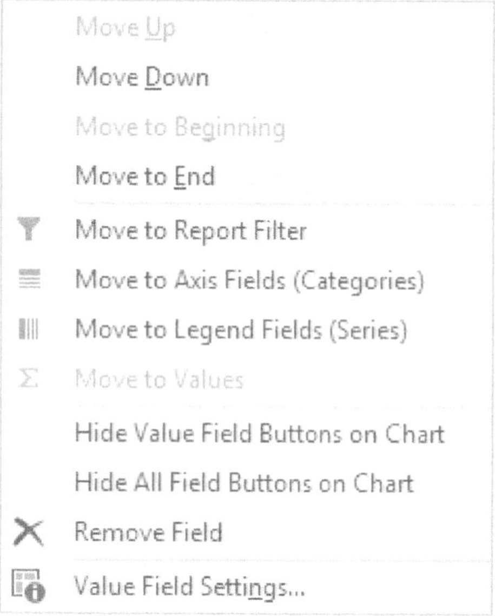

Move <u>U</u>p

Move <u>D</u>own

Move to Beginning

Move to <u>E</u>nd

Move to Report Filter

Move to Axis Fields (Categories)

Move to Legend Fields (Series)

Move to Values

Hide Value Field Buttons on Chart

Hide All Field Buttons on Chart

Remove Field

Value Field Set<u>t</u>ings...

Fig 8.7: What can be done with fields in a **Pivot Chart**

We can move a field up and down its area (i.e. if in the **Rows** area up and down **Rows**) using the top 4 buttons in Fig 8.7. We can turn it into a filter by moving it to the **Report Filter** which is the same as the **Filters** area, we can move it to **Axis Fields (Categories)** which is the same as moving it to the **Rows** area, we can move it to **Legend Fields (Series)** which is the same as moving it to the **Columns** area or we can move it to **Values** which is the same as moving it to the Σ **Values** area.

It is the same functionality as the one we have in the **PivotTable Fields List** and note that any changes made here are reflected automatically in the Pivot Table and the **PivotTable Fields List**.

We can also choose to **Hide Value Field Buttons** or **Hide All Field Buttons**. If we do so we can still make changes to the **Pivot Chart** by making changes to the Pivot Table.

And last but not least, we can access **Value Fields Settings** or just **Field Settings** depending on which field's button we right click upon.

8.1 Filtering a Pivot Chart

By clicking the field buttons on **Axis** or **Legend Fields** we can access filters just like we do when we click the drop-down button next to field names in Rows or Columns on a Pivot Table. Through this we can access manual, label and value filters.

We can apply these filters just like we would in a Pivot Table. This enables us to instantly visualize filtered data in a **Pivot Chart**. Any filters applied to the **Pivot Chart** will also be applied to the Pivot Table beneath.

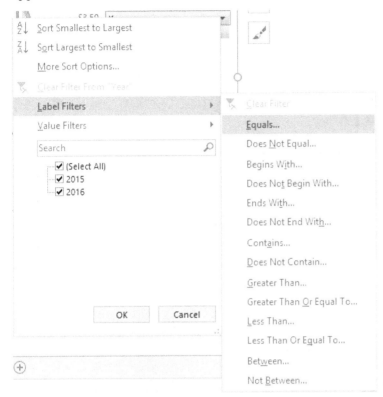

Fig 8.8: Filtering options through the **Axis** or **Legend** buttons

8.1.1 Filtering using Report Filter Buttons

Let's click on the Pivot Table above and using the **PivotTable Fields List** let's put *Shift* and *Production Line* in the **Filters** area.

This will change the **Pivot Chart** as in Fig 8.9.

Now let's apply both filters to see how the chart will update. Let's pick the *Day Shift* in *Production Line A*. To select these simply click on each **Report Filter button** and in the box that appears select the appropriate filter and click **OK**. (See Fig 8.10)

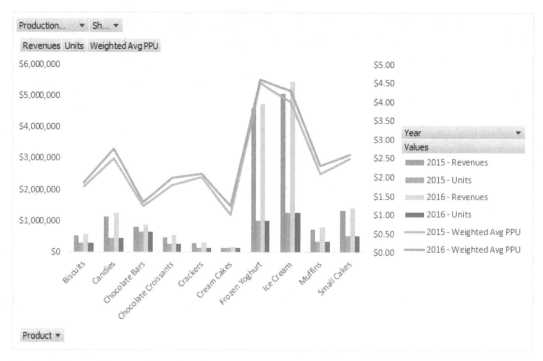

Fig 8.9: Pivot Chart with **Filter buttons** on top

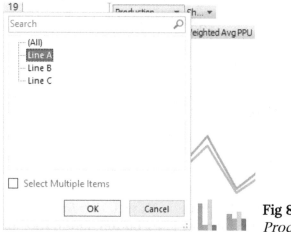

Fig 8.10: Filtering by *Production Line* using the *Production Line* **Filter button** in the **Pivot Chart**

After applying both filters the **Pivot Chart** will look like in Fig 8.11.

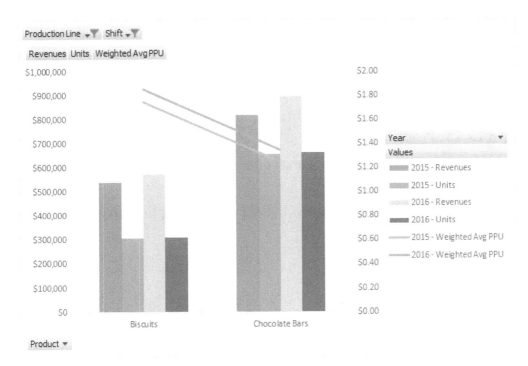

Fig 8.11: How the **Pivot Chart** looks like after both filters have been applied

8.2 PivotChart Tools

If you click on a **Pivot Chart** the **PivotChart Tools** tabs become available as in Fig 8.12.

Fig 8.12: PivotChart Tools tabs

PivotChart Tools has three tabs: The **Analyze**, **Design** and **Format** tabs.

Of these, **Design** and **Format** tabs are the same as those of normal Excel charts, whereas the **Analyze** tab is mostly the same as the **PivotTable Tools Analyze** tab but with some additional features related to **Pivot Charts** which will be covered below. The rest has been covered already.

The **Active Field**, **Filter**, **Data** and **Calculations** groups are the same as those in the **PivotTable Tools Analyze** tab.

8.2.1 PivotChart group

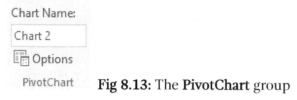

Chart Name:

Chart 2

Options

PivotChart   **Fig 8.13:** The **PivotChart** group

In this group you can give your chart a name or keep the one that is automatically generated for you.

Clicking the **Options** button will give you access to the **PivotTable Options** dialog box.

8.2.2 Actions group

Clear   Move
        Chart

Actions   **Fig 8.14:** The **Actions** group

In the **Actions** group the **Clear** feature is the same as the one for the Pivot Table. In fact, by using it you will be clearing the Pivot Table.

The **Move Chart** feature is peculiar to the **Pivot Chart**. By clicking the **Move Chart** button, you get access to the **Move Chart** dialog box which looks like in Fig 8.15.

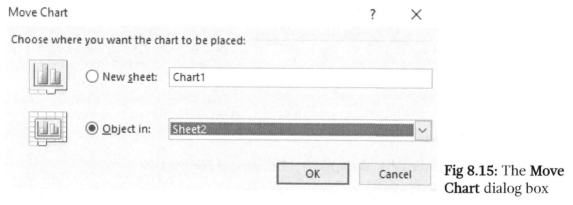

Fig 8.15: The **Move Chart** dialog box

In the **Move Chart** dialog box, you can move the chart to another sheet that already exists or you can move it to a new sheet which will be built for the chart.

If you move the chart to a new sheet, this sheet will be exclusive for the chart. You can move other charts to this sheet however this is not recommended as they will be placed on top of one another. You can give the worksheet a name of your choice or keep the recommended one which in the above figure is Chart1.

The **Move Chart** dialog box is also accessible by right clicking on the chart and then selecting **Move Chart...** .

8.2.3 Show/Hide group

Fig 8.16: The **Show/Hide** group

Field List

When a Pivot Chart is selected the **PivotTable Fields List** automatically becomes available and opens in the sheet. By clicking on the **Field List** button in the **Show/Hide** group you can activate/deactivate this feature. When this feature is active the **Field List** button is highlighted in grey as in Fig 8.16. When not active the **Field List** button will be light grey.

Field Buttons

✓	Show <u>R</u>eport Filter Field Buttons
✓	Show <u>L</u>egend Field Buttons
✓	Show A<u>x</u>is Field Buttons
✓	Show <u>V</u>alue Field Buttons
✓	Show <u>E</u>xpand/Collapse Entire Field Buttons
	Hide <u>A</u>ll

Fig 8.17: Field Buttons list

Lastly, in the **Show/Hide** group you can choose to show or hide each of the four types of **Field Buttons** that are found in a Pivot Chart. You also have the option to **Hide All**.

If we click on **Hide All** then the chart in Fig 8.11 will now look like the one in Fig 8.18.

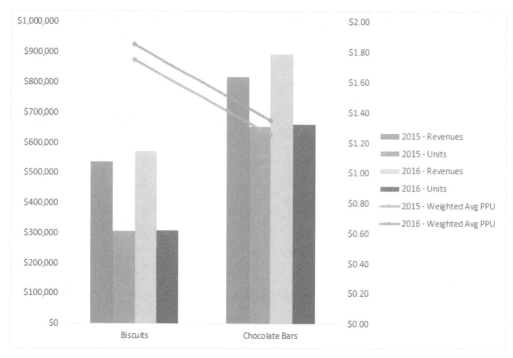

Fig 8.18: Pivot Chart without **Field Buttons**

Expand/Collapse Entire Field Buttons

If in the **Rows** area we have more than one field, when building a **Pivot Chart** Excel offers you the ability to expand or collapse the fields in the chart just like the expand and collapse buttons in a Pivot Table when in compact form. This feature is only available for the **Axis Fields** which is the equivalent of the **Rows** area.

Let's proceed with an example to understand this feature better. Let's build a simple Pivot Table with *Shift* and *Product* in **Rows**, *Year* in **Columns** and *Revenue* in Σ **Values**. Rename *Sum of Revenue* to *Total Revenue* and change the number format to $ with no decimal places. Note that we are not rebuilding a Pivot Table from scratch but merely rearranging the fields in the previous Pivot Table which already has a Pivot Chart built.

Once you have completed this you will notice that the **Pivot Chart** has been updated automatically and now looks like in Fig 8.19.

In the bottom right corner of the **Pivot Chart** we can see the **expand/collapse entire field buttons** showing automatically when we have more than one field in the **Axis Fields** (i.e. **Rows** area). We can choose to show or hide the **expand/collapse entire field buttons** by selecting the **Pivot Chart** and then clicking on **Field Buttons** in the **Show/Hide** group of the **Analyze** tab and in the list that shows make sure that there is no tick in front of **Show Expand/Collapse Entire Field Buttons**.

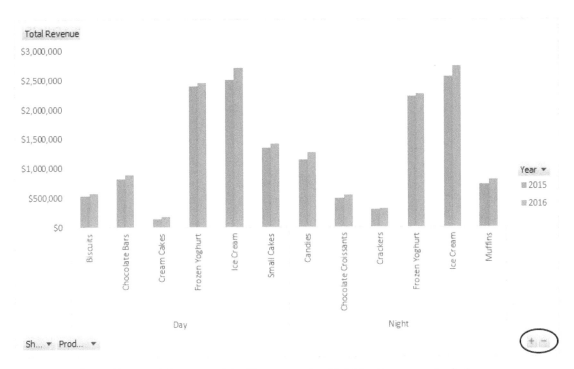

Fig 8.19: Pivot Chart with **expand/collapse entire field buttons** encircled

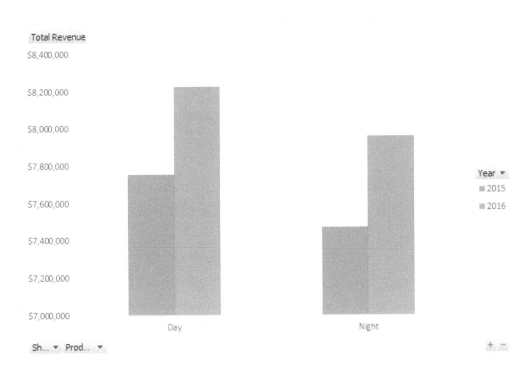

Fig 8.20: Pivot Chart showing only *Shift* in **Axis Fields** after collapse button has been pressed

Now getting back to our chart above if we click the (-) button from the **expand/collapse entire field buttons** the **Pivot Chart** will be updated as in Fig 8.20.

Notice that the same has happened to the Pivot Table. If we want to revert to the previous **Pivot Chart** click on the (+) expand button in the chart or alternatively click on the expand button in the Pivot Table.

CHAPTER 9

Miscellaneous features

We have already covered many features of Pivot Tables that are accessible from the **Analyze** and **Design** tabs. In this chapter we will cover most of what's left except for OLAP related features which will be covered in the next chapter.

9.1 Sorting a Pivot Table

Row, Column or Value fields including Grand Totals can be sorted in a Pivot Table. They can be sorted alphabetically A to Z or Z to A, smallest to largest or largest to smallest or manually in any order you may like.

9.1.1 Sorting A-Z, Z-A

This type of sorting can be accessed through the drop-down button next to **Row** or **Column Labels** when a Pivot Table is in compact form or next to the **Row** or **Column Field's** name when it is in outline or tabular form.

It can also be accessed by right clicking on any row or column item or anywhere in the value area including the grand total value area and then clicking on **Sort** and selecting one of the three options below:

- **Sort A to Z**, **Sort Z to A** or **More Sort Options** if we click on a non-numerical field

- **Sort Smallest to Largest**, **Sort Largest to Smallest** or **More Sort Options** if we click on a numerical field.

To see how this is done let's look at an example. Let's build a Pivot Table with *Product* in **Rows**, *Shift* in **Columns** and *Revenue* in ∑ **Values**. Rename *Revenue* as *Total Revenue* and change the number format to US($) with no decimal places.

The Pivot Table should look like in Fig 9.1:

Total Revenue	Column Labels		
Row Labels	Day	Night	Grand Total
Small Cakes	$2,766,238		$2,766,238
Muffins		$1,544,165	$1,544,165
Ice Cream	$5,221,139	$5,302,657	$10,523,796
Frozen Yoghurt	$4,851,777	$4,494,188	$9,345,965
Cream Cakes	$319,829		$319,829
Crackers		$626,166	$626,166
Chocolate Croissants		$1,044,430	$1,044,430
Chocolate Bars	$1,712,667		$1,712,667
Candies		$2,424,153	$2,424,153
Biscuits	$1,110,637		$1,110,637
Grand Total	$15,982,286	$15,435,759	$31,418,045

Fig 9.1: Pivot Table with *Product* in **Rows** and *Shift* in **Columns** ready to be sorted

Let's say that we want the *Product* field sorted by name in ascending order. To do this click on the drop-down button next to **Row Labels** and in the list that ensues select **Sort A to Z** as in Fig 9.2. We can also right click on any *Product* item and then select **Sort** and finally click on **Sort A to Z**. Once we do this the *Product* field will be sorted **A to Z** as in Fig 9.3.

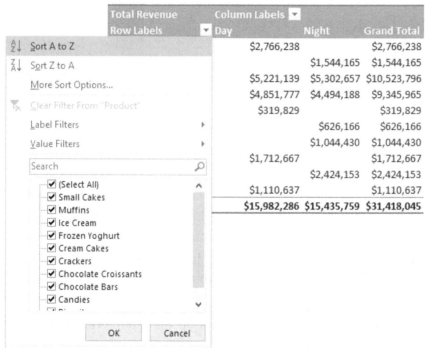

Fig 9.2: Accessing sort options for the *Product* field

If we want to sort in descending order, we simply select **Sort Z to A**.

Now let's say that I wanted the Pivot Table sorted by *Revenue* instead.

Let's click on the drop-down button next to **Row Labels** and in the list that drops down click on **More Sort Options...** . Once we do this the **Sort (Name of Field)** dialog box pops up where we have more options. In this dialog box in the drop-down list under **Ascending (A to Z) by:** select *Total Revenue* as in Fig 9.4 and click **OK**.

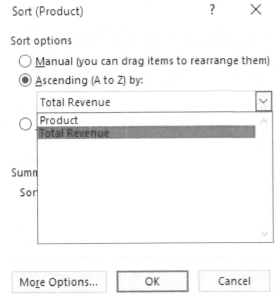

Total Revenue	Column Labels ▼		
Row Labels ▼	Day	Night	Grand Total
Biscuits	$1,110,637		$1,110,637
Candies		$2,424,153	$2,424,153
Chocolate Bars	$1,712,667		$1,712,667
Chocolate Croissants		$1,044,430	$1,044,430
Crackers		$626,166	$626,166
Cream Cakes	$319,829		$319,829
Frozen Yoghurt	$4,851,777	$4,494,188	$9,345,965
Ice Cream	$5,221,139	$5,302,657	$10,523,796
Muffins		$1,544,165	$1,544,165
Small Cakes	$2,766,238		$2,766,238
Grand Total	**$15,982,286**	**$15,435,759**	**$31,418,045**

Fig 9.3: Pivot Table with *Product* sorted A to Z

Sort (Product)   ?   ✕

Sort options
- ○ Manual (you can drag items to rearrange them)
- ◉ Ascending (A to Z) by:

  Total Revenue   ⌄

- ○   Product
       Total Revenue

  Summ
  Sor

More Options...   OK   Cancel

Fig 9.4: Sorting by *Total Revenue*

Now that we sorted by *Total Revenue* in ascending order the Pivot Table will look like in Fig 9.5:

Alternatively, instead of going through **More Sort Options** you can right click on any value cell and select **Sort** and then **Smallest to Largest** or **Largest to Smallest**. This way you can choose the *Revenue* column you want to use for sorting whereas, with **More Sort Options** you can't.

If you want to revert back to the unsorted Pivot Table you can click the Undo button (CRTL + Z) or if you prefer a different arrangement of field items, you can open the **Sort**

(Field Name) dialog box as shown above, select the **Manual** option and click **OK**. You can now drag items to rearrange them.

Total Revenue	Column Labels		
Row Labels	Day	Night	Grand Total
Cream Cakes	$319,829		$319,829
Crackers		$626,166	$626,166
Chocolate Croissants		$1,044,430	$1,044,430
Biscuits	$1,110,637		$1,110,637
Muffins		$1,544,165	$1,544,165
Chocolate Bars	$1,712,667		$1,712,667
Candies		$2,424,153	$2,424,153
Small Cakes	$2,766,238		$2,766,238
Frozen Yoghurt	$4,851,777	$4,494,188	$9,345,965
Ice Cream	$5,221,139	$5,302,657	$10,523,796
Grand Total	$15,982,286	$15,435,759	$31,418,045

Fig 9.5: *Total Revenue* sorted in ascending order

9.1.2 Manually sorting a Pivot Table

If you still want to sort a Pivot Table but not in an ascending or descending order then you have the option to sort it manually. This means that you can drag row items up and down or column items to the left or to the right.

To do this simply select the item you wish to drag and move the mouse to any of the selected cell's corners until the pointer changes to a four-headed arrow. When this happens click, hold and drag the item to the new position. Fig 9.6 shows how this is done.

Total Revenue	Column Labels		
Row Labels	Day	Night	Grand Total
Cream Cakes	$319,829		$319,829
Crackers		$626,166	$626,166
Chocolate Croissants		$1,044,430	$1,044,430
Biscuits	$1,110,637		$1,110,637
Muffins		$1,544,165	$1,544,165
Chocolate Bars	$1,712,667		$1,712,667
Candies		$2,424,153	$2,424,153
Small Cakes	$2,766,238		$2,766,238
Frozen Yoghurt	$4,851,777	$4,494,188	$9,345,965
Ice Cream	$5,221,139	$5,302,657	$10,523,796
Grand Total	$15,982,286	$15,435,759	$31,418,045

Fig 9.6: Manually sorting a row item

9.2 What can you do when you don't have value fields?

There can be occasions when all you have is a list of data with categories and no value fields in it. For e.g. in Fig 9.7 we have a list of students, the courses they are attending and their gender.

	A	B	C
1	**Name**	**Course**	**Gender**
2	Abbie J. Miller	Environmental science	Female
3	Alain Jesse Leicht	Art	Male
4	Alicia K. Hofer	History and social research	Female
5	Alisha Dawn	Mathematics	Female
6	Allison Suzanne Beit	Mathematics	Female
7	Anna Victoria Looks	Molecular biology and biochemistry	Female
8	Andrew Jr. Glick	Biology	Male
9	Andrew Tom Shenk	Art	Male
10	Anne Jan Pierre	Nursing	Female
11	Annika Betty Miller	Business	Female
12	Arielle C. Zerger	Molecular biology and biochemistry	Female
13	Aspen Juliette Schmidt	Business	Female
14	Audrey E. Hill	Accounting	Female
15	Barrett William Donnabianca	Molecular biology and biochemistry	Male
16	Benjamin Oscar Breckbill	Psychology	Male
17	Benjamin Adams James	Mathematics	Male
18	Beth Anne Wonder	Nursing	Female
19	Bianca Magali Bimba	Accounting	Female
20	Bojana Jankovic	Biology	Female
21	Brook Amaris Amaretti	Chemistry	Male
22	Caleb J. Frey Miller	Business	Male
23	Carina Bela Zehr	Biology	Female

StudentList ⊕

Fig 9.7: List of students together with their course and gender

Despite that we have no numeric data we can still use a Pivot Table to analyse the above data however, the only calculation we will be able to use is **Count**.

Let's build a Pivot Table.

- Select all data

- Go to the **Insert** tab and click on **PivotTable**

- In the **Create PivotTable** dialog box place the table in a new worksheet and click **OK**.

- Move *Course* to the **Rows** area, *Gender* to the **Columns** area and *Name* in the Σ **Values** area.

- Once the Pivot Table has been built go to the **Design** tab and select a format of your liking.

Now you should have a Pivot Table that looks like the one in Fig 9.8.

Count of Name	Column Labels		
Row Labels	Female	Male	Grand Total
Accounting	4	4	8
Art	5	3	8
Biology	5	3	8
Business	6	2	8
Chemistry	5	3	8
Computer science	4	4	8
Environmental science	6	2	8
History and social research	5	2	7
Mathematics	6	1	7
Molecular biology and biochemistry	5	3	8
Nursing	6	1	7
Psychology	2	6	8
Grand Total	59	34	93

Fig 9.8: Pivot Table built only on category data

In this Pivot Table, we have a count of students by course and gender.

If you go to **Value Field Settings** for the *Count of Name* field and try and choose another metric such as **Sum, Average, Max** etc. you will find that you either get Error or 0 values. _This is pretty much the main limitation of this Pivot Table i.e. that you can only use the Count metric._ Everything else applies so we can use Slicers, Groupings, Calculated Items but not Calculated Fields since there are no value fields, Filters, some but not all Custom Calculations and so on.

9.3 Active Field group

Fig 9.9: Active Field group

In the **Active Field** group of the **Analyze** tab we have a few features such as the displaying of the **Active Field** which is the field whose item or items are selected in a Pivot Table, access to **Field Settings** or **Value Field Settings** for the **Active Field**, **Drilling Up/Down** the data when dealing with OLAP data sources and the **Expand/Collapse Field** feature. We will be looking at each of these below.

9.3.1 Active Field

If we click anywhere on a Pivot Table, in the **Active Field** box we can see which field the selected cell belongs to. This can be a row field, a column field or a value field (e.g. *Sum of Revenue*) if we select a cell in the values area.

9.3.2 Field Settings

These are **Field Settings** and **Value Field Settings** accessible from a right click on any Pivot Table cell (except empty header cells) and depend on the field selected. These options are also accessible form the drop-down button next to a field's name in the **PivotTable Fields List**. We have already covered these settings in extensive detail.

Once a cell is selected in a Pivot Table by clicking on **Field Settings** in **Active Field** group the **Field Settings** or **Value Field Settings** dialog box will pop up depending on the field that cell belong to.

9.3.3 Drill Up & Down

This feature is available with OLAP data sources.

9.3.4 Expand/Collapse Field

The ability of this feature to **Show Detail** is already covered when we talked about **PivotTable Options** in chapter 7. There is however another detail not covered there which we will cover in this chapter.

Let's build a Pivot Table with *Production Line, Shift & Product* in **Rows**, *Year* in **Columns** and *Revenue* in $\sum$ **Values.**

In this new Pivot Table if we click on any *Product* item or on any *Year* item and then click on **Expand Field** the **Show Detail** dialog box will pop up ready to do what we have already covered in chapter 7.

However, if we select higher level fields' items such as items from *Shift* or *Production Line* and we click the **Collapse Field button** Excel will hide items in the lower fields under a collapse button. If we then click on the **Expand Field button** Excel will expand these items. Fig 9.10 shows the original Pivot Table whereas Figures 9.11 and 9.12 show the Pivot Table collapsed using the collapse field button in **Active Field** group.

Total Revenue	Column Labels		
Row Labels	2015	2016	Grand Total
⊟ Line A	$2,814,586	$3,059,037	$5,873,623
⊟ Day	$1,356,136	$1,467,168	$2,823,304
Biscuits	$538,395	$572,242	$1,110,637
Chocolate Bars	$817,741	$894,926	$1,712,667
⊟ Night	$1,458,450	$1,591,869	$3,050,319
Candies	$1,153,840	$1,270,313	$2,424,153
Crackers	$304,610	$321,556	$626,166
⊟ Line B	$2,719,726	$2,954,936	$5,674,662
⊟ Day	$1,492,041	$1,594,026	$3,086,067
Cream Cakes	$141,893	$177,936	$319,829
Small Cakes	$1,350,148	$1,416,090	$2,766,238
⊟ Night	$1,227,685	$1,360,910	$2,588,595
Chocolate Croissants	$494,613	$549,817	$1,044,430
Muffins	$733,072	$811,093	$1,544,165
⊟ Line C	$9,695,400	$10,174,361	$19,869,760
⊟ Day	$4,906,800	$5,166,116	$10,072,916
Frozen Yoghurt	$2,394,360	$2,457,417	$4,851,777
Ice Cream	$2,512,440	$2,708,699	$5,221,139
⊟ Night	$4,788,600	$5,008,245	$9,796,845
Frozen Yoghurt	$2,226,200	$2,267,989	$4,494,188
Ice Cream	$2,562,400	$2,740,257	$5,302,657
Grand Total	$15,229,711	$16,188,334	$31,418,045

Fig 9.10: Original Pivot Table

Total Revenue	Column Labels		
Row Labels	2015	2016	Grand Total
⊟ Line A	$2,814,586	$3,059,037	$5,873,623
⊞ Day	$1,356,136	$1,467,168	$2,823,304
⊞ Night	$1,458,450	$1,591,869	$3,050,319
⊟ Line B	$2,719,726	$2,954,936	$5,674,662
⊞ Day	$1,492,041	$1,594,026	$3,086,067
⊞ Night	$1,227,685	$1,360,910	$2,588,595
⊟ Line C	$9,695,400	$10,174,361	$19,869,760
⊞ Day	$4,906,800	$5,166,116	$10,072,916
⊞ Night	$4,788,600	$5,008,245	$9,796,845
Grand Total	$15,229,711	$16,188,334	$31,418,045

Fig 9.11: Same Pivot Table with *Product* collapsed

Total Revenue	Column Labels		
Row Labels	2015	2016	Grand Total
⊞ Line A	$2,814,586	$3,059,037	$5,873,623
⊞ Line B	$2,719,726	$2,954,936	$5,674,662
⊞ Line C	$9,695,400	$10,174,361	$19,869,760
Grand Total	$15,229,711	$16,188,334	$31,418,045

Fig 9.12: Same Pivot Table with both *Shift* and *Product* collapsed

9.4 Filter group

Fig 9.13: Filter group in the **Analyze** tab

From the **Filter** group we have already covered **Slicers** and **Timelines** in chapter 3. Below we will look at **Filter Connections**.

9.4.1 Filter Connections

If we have one or more **Slicers** or **Timelines** in a workbook, which may or may not be connected to one or more Pivot Tables, we are able to see which **Slicers** or **Timelines** are connected to a Pivot Table by clicking on the **Filter Connections** button once at least one cell of this Pivot Table has been selected. Apart from this we are also able to connect or disconnect a **Slicer** or **Timeline** from the selected Pivot Table.

We should already have two **Slicers** and a **Timeline** from chapter 3 in our workbook. If not rebuild these or any other you like. Then select the Pivot Table for which we have built the **Slicers** and **Timeline** and go to the **Analyze** tab and in the **Filter** group click on **Filter Connections**.

The **Filter Connections** dialog box will pop up as in Fig 9.14 displaying the names of all **Slicers** and/or **Timelines** in the workbook with a tick in front indicating whether they are connected or not to the selected Pivot Table.

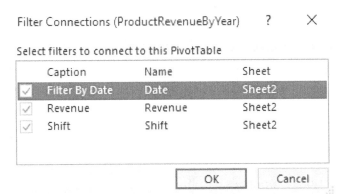

Fig 9.14: Filter Connections for the selected Pivot Table

In the **Filter Connections** dialog box you can disconnect a **Slicer** or **Timeline** from the selected Pivot Table by clearing the checkbox before its name. If you do this your Pivot Table won't be filtered by this **Slicer** or **Timeline** any more unless you connect it again by ticking the checkbox before its name.

The **Filter Connections** feature is only available if we have **Slicers** or **Timelines** in the workbook, otherwise it will be greyed out.

9.5 Data group

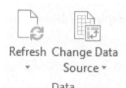

Fig 9.15: **Data** group in the **Analyze** tab

In the **Data** group we have the ability to refresh a Pivot Table and change its data source.

9.5.1 Refresh

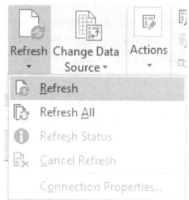

Fig 9.16: Refresh options under the **Refresh** button

A **Refresh** of the Pivot Table retrieves any data updates i.e. it gets the latest version of the data including changes that were made to the data since the last **Refresh**.

By clicking the **Refresh** button we get further refresh options. We can **Refresh** the current Pivot Table only or we can **Refresh All** Pivot Tables in the workbook. Click on the button that meets your requirement.

Further down the list we have **Connection Properties...** which is available only when building Pivot Tables from external/OLAP data sources.

9.5.2 Change Data Source

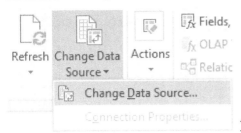

Fig 9.17: Change Data Source under **Data** group

Excel gives you the ability to change the data source of a Pivot Table. This could just be because you received a new data range or it can be for any other reason.

To change a Pivot Table's data source, click on **Change Data Source...** under **Change Data Source** in the **Data** group of the **Analyze** tab. Upon doing this Excel directs you to the current data source for the Pivot Table and the **Change PivotTable Data Source** dialog box pops up where you can select the new data range. After selecting the new data range click **OK** and the Pivot Table will be updated with the new data.

	A	B	C	D	E	F	G	H	I	J
1	Ye	Month	Date	Production Li	Manager	Shi	Product	Units produce	Price per ur	Reveni
2	2015	January	01/01/2015	Line A	Steven Robertson	Day	Chocolate Bars	54,300	$1.25	$67,875
3	2015	January	01/01/2015	Line A	Steven Robertson	Day	Biscuits	25,600	$1.75	$44,800
4	2015	January	01/01/2015	Line A	Douglass Robinson	Night	Crackers	12,356	$2.00	$24,712
5	2015	January	01/01/2015	Line A	Douglass Robinson	Night	Candies	38,000	$2.50	$95,000
6	2015	January	01/01/2015	Line B	Asim Khan	Day	Cream Cakes	11,500	$1.00	$11,500
7	2015	January	01/01/2015	Line B	Asim Khan	Day	Small Cakes	45,000	$2.50	$112,500
8	2015	January	01/01/2015					22,478	$1.80	$40,460
9	2015	January	01/01/2015					28,700	$2.10	$60,270
10	2015	January	01/01/2015					52,000	$4.00	$208,000
11	2015	January	01/01/2015					44,000	$4.50	$198,000
12	2015	January	01/01/2015					53,200	$4.00	$212,800
13	2015	January	01/01/2015					41,000	$4.50	$184,500
14	2015	February	01/02/2015					49,990	$1.25	$62,488
15	2015	February	01/02/2015					23,200	$1.75	$40,600
16	2015	February	01/02/2015					11,200	$2.00	$22,400
17	2015	February	01/02/2015					35,000	$2.50	$87,500
18	2015	February	01/02/2015	Line B	Steve Black	Day	Cream Cakes	10,000	$1.00	$10,000
19	2015	February	01/02/2015	Line B	Steve Black	Day	Small Cakes	42,000	$2.50	$105,000
20	2015	February	01/02/2015	Line B	Asim Khan	Night	Chocolate Croissants	21,765	$1.80	$39,177
21	2015	February	01/02/2015	Line B	Asim Khan	Night	Muffins	26,123	$2.10	$54,858
22	2015	February	01/02/2015	Line C	Julian Teacher	Day	Ice Cream	50,000	$4.00	$200,000
23	2015	February	01/02/2015	Line C	Julian Teacher	Day	Frozen Yoghurt	41,000	$4.50	$184,500

Sheet1 | Warehouse

Dialog box text: Change PivotTable Data Source. Choose the data that you want to analyze. Select a table or range. Table/Range: Warehouse!$A$1:$J$289. Use an external data source. Choose Connection... Connection name:. OK. Cancel.

Fig 9.18: Change PivotTable Data Source dialog box

If there are filters connected to the Pivot Table, which are also connected to other Pivot Tables the following error will pop up:

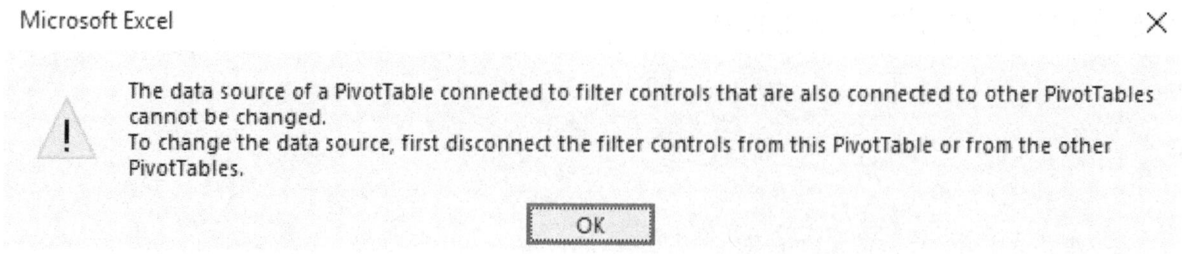

Microsoft Excel   ✕

> ⚠ The data source of a PivotTable connected to filter controls that are also connected to other PivotTables cannot be changed.
> To change the data source, first disconnect the filter controls from this PivotTable or from the other PivotTables.
>
> [OK]

Fig 9.19: Error message when trying to change data source while having filters connected to the selected Pivot Table as well as to other Pivot Tables

Filters connected to multiple Pivot Tables can only be **Slicers** or **Timelines**. You can go to the **Filter Connections** (see section 9.4) of your Pivot Table and disconnect all **Slicers** or **Timelines** that are connected to the selected Pivot Table and other Pivot Tables.

Alternatively, select each required **Slicer** or **Timeline** in your workbook and click on **Report Connections** in the options of each and disconnect your Pivot Table in the **Report Connections** dialog box.

Now try to change the data source again. It should work correctly.

Connection Properties... under **Change Data Source** are available only when using external/OLAP data sources.

9.6 Actions group

Actions

Fig 9.20: The **Actions** group

Fig 9.21: Features of **Actions** group

In the **Actions** group we can **Clear, Select** or **Move** a Pivot Table. These options become available upon clicking on the **Actions** button as in Fig 9.21.

9.6.1 Clear

The **Clear** feature offers the possibility to **Clear All** or **Clear Filters** as in Fig 9.22.

Fig 9.22: Options under the **Clear** button

Clear All

Clear All removes fields, all types of custom fields and custom items, formatting and filters from a Pivot Table. If we have multiple Pivot Tables connected to the same data source, we get the following warning when clicking on **Clear All**:

Fig 9.23: Warning when **Clear All** is applied to a Pivot Table that shares the same data source as other Pivot Tables.

If we click on **Clear PivotTable,** fields, formatting and filters are cleared from the current Pivot Table only. **Groupings, Calculated items, Calculated Fields** and **Custom Items** are cleared from all Pivot Tables connected to the data source.

Clear Filters

Whenever we have filters applied to a Pivot Table and we want all of them cleared then we go to the **Actions** group in the **Analyze** tab, click on **Actions**, **Clear** and then **Clear Filters**. When no filters are applied to a Pivot Table this option is greyed out.

9.6.2 Select

This part of the **Actions** group enables the selection of the entire Pivot Table or parts of it. As it can be seen in Fig 9.24 we have a few options to choose from.

Fig 9.24: Options available under the **Select** button

Entire PivotTable

If we select this option, we will be selecting the entire Pivot Table. By selecting the entire Pivot Table we also automatically enable the other three options which are selecting **Labels and Values** i.e. entire Pivot Table, **Values** and **Labels** (Fig 9.25).

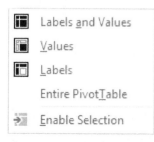

Fig 9.25: **Labels and Values**, **Values** and **Labels** enabled after selecting **Entire PivotTable**

For **Labels and Values**, **Values** or **Labels** select options to be available, either the entire Pivot Table must be selected using the **Entire PivotTable** button or parts of it selected using the selection arrow once **Enable Selection** has been activated.

Labels and Values

This is essentially the same as clicking the **Entire PivotTable** button. By clicking it we select the entire Pivot Table as in Fig 9.26.

Count of Name	Column Labels		
Row Labels	Female	Male	Grand Total
Accounting	4	4	8
Art	5	3	8
Biology	5	3	8
Business	6	2	8
Chemistry	5	3	8
Computer science	4	4	8
Environmental science	6	2	8
History and social research	5	2	7
Mathematics	6	1	7
Molecular biology and biochemistry	5	3	8
Nursing	6	1	7
Psychology	2	6	8
Grand Total	59	34	93

Fig 9.26: Labels and Values selected

Values

Clicking on **Values** selects only the **Values** part of the Pivot Table as in Fig 9.27.

Count of Name	Column Labels		
Row Labels	Female	Male	Grand Total
Accounting	4	4	8
Art	5	3	8
Biology	5	3	8
Business	6	2	8
Chemistry	5	3	8
Computer science	4	4	8
Environmental science	6	2	8
History and social research	5	2	7
Mathematics	6	1	7
Molecular biology and biochemistry	5	3	8
Nursing	6	1	7
Psychology	2	6	8
Grand Total	59	34	93

Fig 9.27: **Values** only selected

Labels

Clicking on **Labels** selects only the **Labels** part of the Pivot Table as in Fig 9.28.

Count of Name	Column Labels		
Row Labels	Female	Male	Grand Total
Accounting	4	4	8
Art	5	3	8
Biology	5	3	8
Business	6	2	8
Chemistry	5	3	8
Computer science	4	4	8
Environmental science	6	2	8
History and social research	5	2	7
Mathematics	6	1	7
Molecular biology and biochemistry	5	3	8
Nursing	6	1	7
Psychology	2	6	8
Grand Total	59	34	93

Fig 9.28: Labels only selected

Enable Selection

You can use the **Selection Arrow** to select parts of a Pivot Table. However, before using this feature you need to enable it by going to the **Analyze** tab, clicking on the **Actions** group and then clicking on **Select** and finally on **Enable Selection**. Fig 9.29 shows how the **Enable Selection** button looks when this feature is or isn't activated.

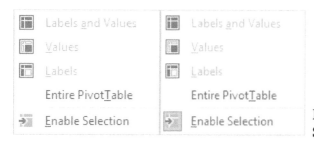

Fig 9.29: Not enabled vs enabled **Enable Selection**

Now that **Enable Selection** is enabled we can use the **Selection Arrow** to select parts of a Pivot Table. Fig 9.30 shows an attempt to select the column under the *Male* item with the **Selection Arrow** (encircled).

Once the **Selection Arrow** is visible, we simply click and it will select the entire column or row depending on what we want to select.

Count of Name	Column Labels ▾	⬇	
Row Labels ▾	Female	Male	Grand Total
Accounting	4	4	8
Art	5	3	8
Biology	5	3	8
Business	6	2	8
Chemistry	5	3	8
Computer science	4	4	8
Environmental science	6	2	8
History and social research	5	2	7
Mathematics	6	1	7
Molecular biology and biochemistry	5	3	8
Nursing	6	1	7
Psychology	2	6	8
Grand Total	59	34	93

Fig 9.30: Selection Arrow visible above the *Male* column

To select the entire Pivot Table with the **Selection Arrow** simply go to the first cell, where a description of the value field is found in this case *Count of Name*. Once the **Selection Arrow** is visible simply click and the entire Pivot Table will be selected.

You might have noticed that once a selection is done with the **Selection Arrow**, even if it is a partial selection of a Pivot Table, the **Labels and Values**, **Labels** and **Values** buttons become visible as in Fig 9.25. This is not the case if the same selection is done manually.

In the Pivot table above, if we select the column under the *Male* item using the **Selection Arrow** and then test each of **Labels and Values**, **Labels** or **Values** buttons we will notice that Excel will treat this selection as a Pivot Table on its own.

9.6.3 Move PivotTable

Move PivotTable is the last feature in the **Actions** group.

Fig 9.31: The **Move PivotTable** button

To move a Pivot Table click anywhere on it and then go to the **Analyze** tab, **Actions** group and click on **Move PivotTable**. Once you do this the **Move PivotTable** dialog box will appear as in Fig 9.32 asking you where you want the Pivot Table to be moved.

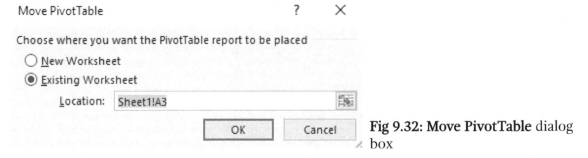

Fig 9.32: Move PivotTable dialog box

The dialog box offers you two options. The first is to place the new Pivot Table in a new worksheet and the second is to place it in a different location in the existing worksheet. If you want a different location in the existing worksheet you need to specify the location of the first cell of the Pivot Table only, which is the first cell in the top left corner of a Pivot Table.

Once you decide on where you want your Pivot Table moved and specify its new location click on the **OK** button and the Pivot Table will be moved to the new location.

9.7 Recommended Pivot Tables

Once you build your first Pivot Table, based on your data source, Excel offers you a selection of recommended Pivot Tables which you can quickly build and use.

To access this selection click on any cell in your Pivot Table and then go to the **Analyze** tab, **Tools** group and click on **Recommended PivotTables**. Once you do this the **Recommended PivotTables** dialog box will pop up as in Fig 9.33 with a list of suggested Pivot Tables.

If you have **Slicers** or **Timelines** connected to multiple Pivot Tables including the one selected a warning will be shown in the dialog box as in Fig 9.33. If you don't have any **Slicers** or **Timelines** connected then there will be no warnings.

Select the Pivot Table you like and click **OK**.

Once you click **OK** the recommended Pivot Table will replace your previous Pivot Table. If you had a **Pivot Chart** connected to the old Pivot table this will be updated with the new Pivot Table data.

The Pivot Table name will remain the same. Any number formats you had on value fields will be lost.

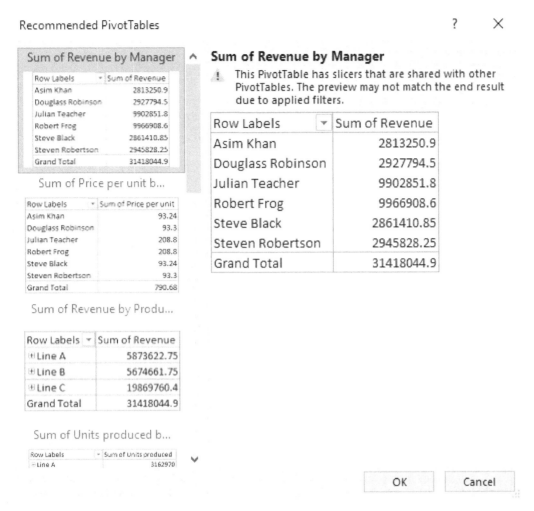

Fig 9.33: Recommended PivotTables dialog box with warning on top

Any **Slicers** or **Timelines** you had, will remain connected to the new Pivot Table however any filters applied through these will be cleared.

The advantage of **Recommended PivotTables** is that you are offered a different perspective (albeit not always useful) and you get to see how a few Pivot Tables will look like without having to build them.

9.8 Show Group

The **Show** group serves the purpose of showing or hiding the following:

- Field List

- +/- Buttons

- Field Headers

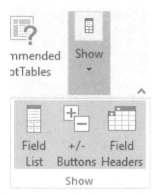

Fig 9.34: The Show group

9.8.1 Field List

Whenever you click anywhere on a Pivot Table the **PivotTable Fields List** appears in the worksheet. If you don't want the **PivotTable Fields List** shown then deselect **Field List** in the **Show** group of the **Analyze** tab.

9.8.2 +/- Buttons

When a Pivot Table is in compact form and has more that one field in rows or columns or when you group one or more Pivot Table items, the **+/- buttons** become visible in the Pivot Table through which you can collapse or expand items within fields. If you don't want these shown then deselect **+/- buttons** in the **Show** group of the **Analyze** tab.

9.8.3 Field Headers

When in compact form, **Field Headers** are **Row Labels** and **Column Labels**. In other layouts (outline and tabular) **Field Headers** are the names of the fields in the **Rows** or **Columns** areas and are shown in a Pivot Table in rows or columns. Whenever you build a Pivot Table **Field Headers** are automatically visible. If you don't want them shown in the Pivot Table then deselect **Field Headers** in the **Show** group of the **Analyze** tab.

If you remove **Field Headers** then manual filtering will need to be done from the **PivotTable Fields List's** fields section. **Label** and **Value Filters** can be set by right clicking on row or column items and selecting **Filter** or through the **PivotTable Fields List's** fields section.

9.9 PivotTable Fields List's Layout Options

In Excel 2016 there exist a few layout options for your **PivotTable Fields List**. These are accessible through the settings button found in the top right corner of the **PivotTable Fields List**.

If we click this button these layout options become available (Fig 9.35).

1. Fields Section and Areas Section Stacked

2. Fields Section and Areas Section Side-By-Side

3. Fields section only

4. Areas Section only (2 by 2)

5. Areas Section only (1 by 4)

6. Expand All (OLAP only)

7. Collapse All (OLAP only)

8. Sort A to Z

9. Sort in data source order

10. Group Related Tables (OLAP only)

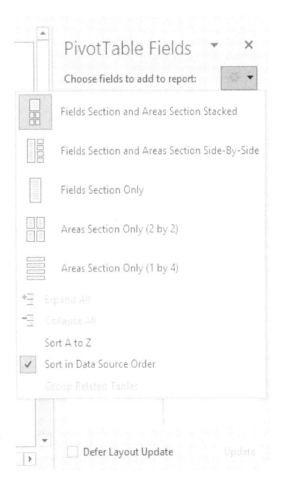

Fig 9.35: Layout options for the **PivotTable Fields List**

1. Fields Section and Areas Section Stacked

This is the standard layout of the panel and looks like in Fig 9.36.

2. Fields Section and Areas Section Side-By-Side

This layout looks like in Fig 9.37. It can be more suited to occasions when you have a long list of fields and want to see all or most of them on screen.

3. Fields Section Only

This layout displays the fields section only as in Fig 9.38.

4. Areas Section Only (2 by 2)

This layout displays the areas section only in a 2 columns 2 rows layout as in Fig 9.39.

5. Areas Section Only (1 by 4)

This layout displays the areas section only in a 1 column 4 rows layout as in Fig 9.40.

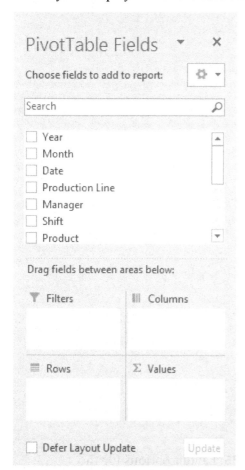

Fig 9.36: Fields Section and Areas Section Stacked

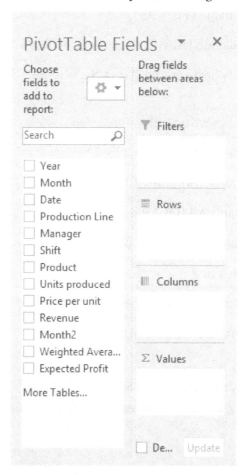

Fig 9.37: Fields Section and Areas Section Side-By-Side

PivotTable Fields

Choose fields to add to report:

Search

- [ ] Year
- [ ] Month
- [ ] Date
- [ ] Production Line
- [ ] Manager
- [ ] Shift
- [ ] Product
- [ ] Units produced
- [ ] Price per unit
- [ ] Revenue
- [ ] Month2
- [ ] Weighted Average Price per Unit
- [ ] Expected Profit

More Tables...

PivotTable Fields

Drag fields between areas below:

▼ Filters   ⫿⫿ Columns

≣ Rows   Σ Values

- [ ] Defer Layout Update   Update

Fig 9.38: Fields Section Only 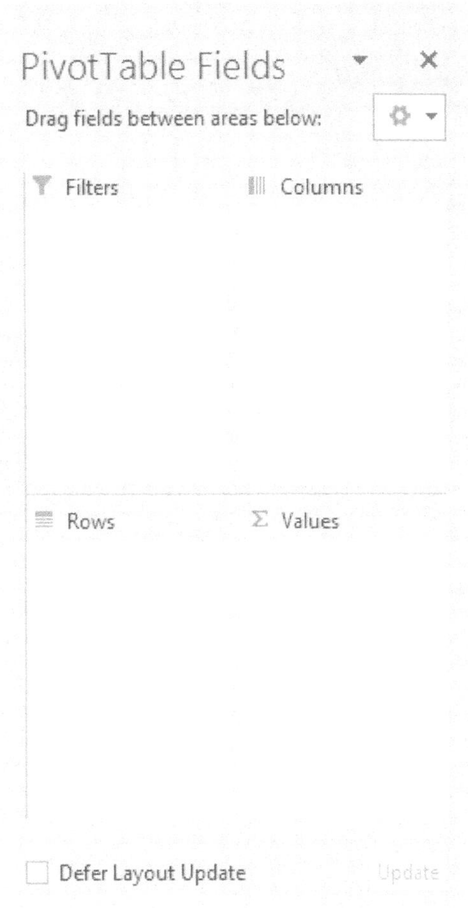   **Fig 9.39:** Areas Section Only (2 by 2)

6. Expand All (OLAP only)

When we have multiple tables in the **PivotTable Fields List** which will be used to build a Pivot Table and we can only see the table names and not the fields within each table by clicking the **Expand All** button the table names together with all fields' names within are displayed.

7. Collapse All (OLAP only)

When we have multiple tables in the **PivotTable Fields List** and we can see the table names and the fields' names within each table but we only want to see the table names, by clicking the **Collapse All** button only the table names will be displayed on the **PivotTable Fields List**.

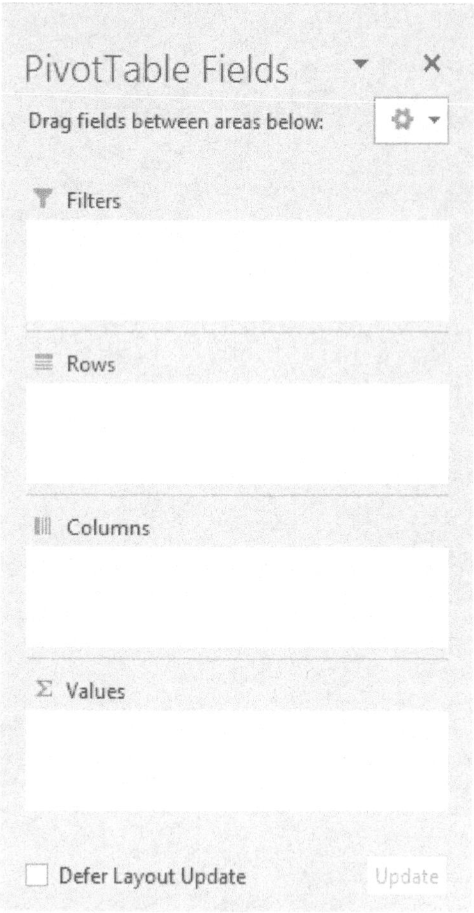

Fig 9.40: Area Section Only (1 by 4)

8. Sort A to Z

This option will sort fields in the fields section in an A to Z order (including any calculated fields) as in Fig 9.43.

9. Sort in data source order

This option will sort fields in the order they are in the data source as in Fig 9.44. Any calculated fields will go at the end of the list sorted in the order they were built.

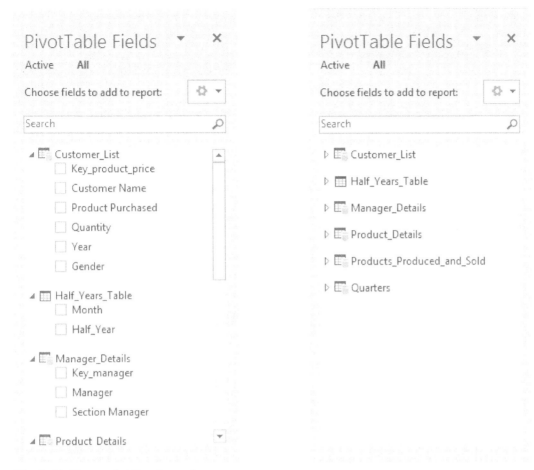

Fig 9.41: Expand All selected   **Fig 9.42: Collapse All** selected

10. Group Related Tables (OLAP only)

This option, if selected, groups tables between which there is a relationship defined using the **Create Relationship** dialog box which is accessible through the **Analyze** tab, **Calculations** group, **Relationships** and then in the **Manage Relationships** dialog box by clicking on the **New...** button.

Figures 9.45 and 9.46 show how the **PivotTable Fields List** displays tables when grouped and ungrouped.

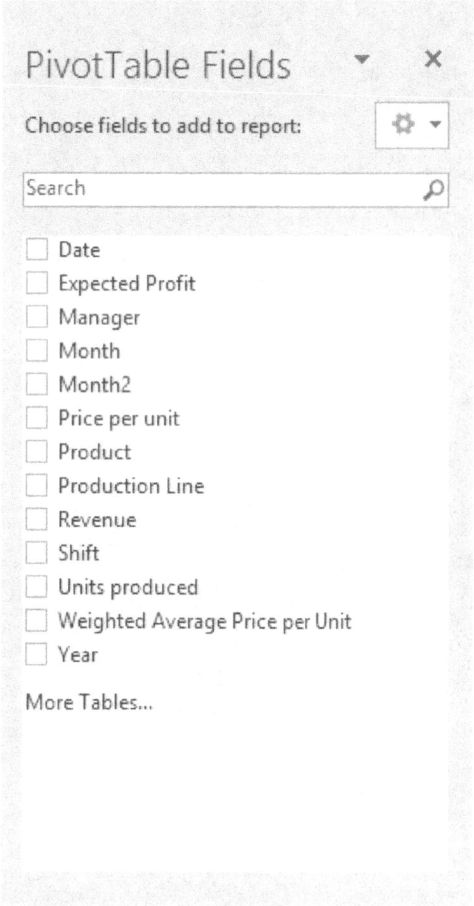

Fig 9.43: A to Z sorted

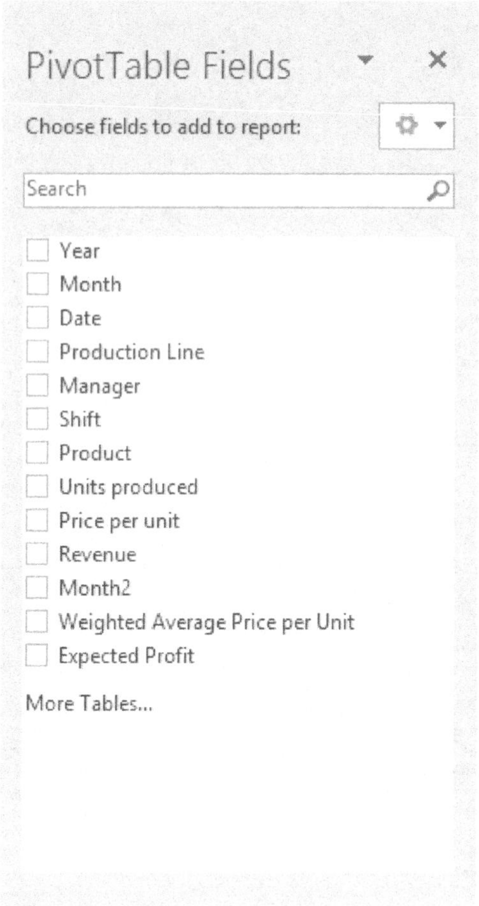

Fig 9.44: Data source sorted

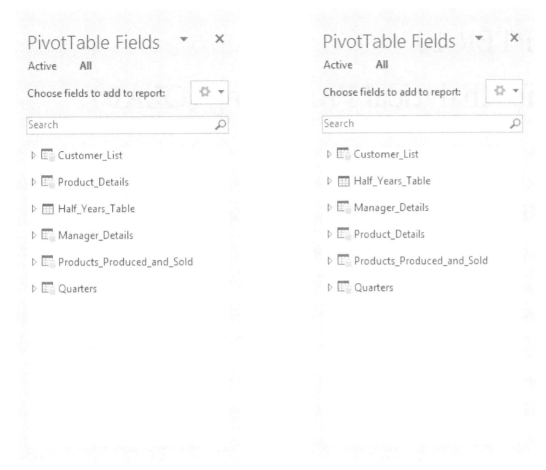

Fig 9.45: Grouped tables   **Fig 9.46**: Ungrouped tables

 Since in fact all the tables used in this example are related I had to deactivate a relationship between *Product_Details* and *Products_Produced_and_Sold* to show how the grouping works.

To understand relationships between tables check the next chapter.

CHAPTER 10

Online Analytical Processing (OLAP)

10.1 What is OLAP?

Online Analytical Processing referred to as **OLAP**, consists of software that produce views of data along multiple dimensions by allowing the user to drill down, therefore giving access to a vast array of analyses and potentially useful information.

Drilling down from summaries to detailed views can give rise to interesting findings, thus **OLAP** requires manual navigation through many reports, requiring the user to notice any details of interest.

Examples of **OLAP** use:

- Management Reporting KPIs, profit, cost, defect, risk, quality analysis etc.

- CRM, customer segmentation, customer retention, customer value analysis

OLAP tools may be seen as a way of presenting data in the form of cubes that have axes and dimensions each representing a category or subcategory of the data available.

Common measures used in **OLAP** analysis:

- Units sold/produced

- Revenue

- Cost

- Discount

- Units returned

- Value of units returned

- Customer churn rate

- Etc.

10.2 How is OLAP done?

OLAP has three main steps: Aggregate data, drill down and slice and dice the data.

10.2.1 Aggregate all data

Put your data into groups of different hierarchies. This can involve simple roll-ups or more complex aggregations of interrelated data. For e.g. a sales office can be rolled up to towns, towns can be rolled up to counties and counties can be rolled up to regions and regions to countries.

Some examples:

Product -----> Department -----> Subgroup -----> Merchant group

Day -----> Week -----> Month -----> Quarter -----> Year

Town -----> County -----> Region -----> Country

For each of these groups, including combinations that are not in the same roll-up, produce summaries.

In the case of Pivot Tables this is done automatically after choosing the combinations for your report. You also have the option to explore data using **Quick Explore** which allows you to drill down and includes the use of fields that are not in a roll-up.

10.2.2 Drill Down

When analysing data using **OLAP** start from the highest level of summary data, then drill down into greater levels of detail to find the information you are looking for.

For e.g. you can look at sales by merchant group and then for each merchant group you can look at sales by subgroup and so on.

10.2.3 Slice and Dice the data

OLAP gives you the ability to look at data from different viewpoints. For e.g. you can look at sales by product, by town and by day. At the same time you can look at sales by department, region and month.

So basically, you can use any combination of categories (or fields, using Pivot Table terminology) you have in your data sources to produce summaries and find potentially useful information.

10.3 Connecting to databases

To run Pivot Table reports on data from multiple tables sourced from a database we need to first establish a connection with that database. I have built a series of tables based on the Warehouse spreadsheet we have been using so far and I have put them into a Microsoft Access database.

This database has four tables:

- Product_Details

- Products_Produced_and_Sold

- Quarters

- Manager_Details

Figures 10.1-10.4 show a few snapshots of this data:

	Key_product_price	Product	Price per unit	Product Subgroup	Merchant Group
+	2015Biscuits	Biscuits	£1.75	Biscuits & Crackers	Sweet Snacks
+	2015Candies	Candies	£2.50	Candies	Sweet Snacks
+	2015Chocolate Bars	Chocolate Bars	£1.25	Chocolate Flavoured	Sweet Snacks
+	2015Chocolate Croissants	Chocolate Croissants	£1.80	Chocolate Flavoured	Sweet Snacks
+	2015Crackers	Crackers	£2.00	Biscuits & Crackers	Sweet Snacks
+	2015Cream Cakes	Cream Cakes	£1.00	Cakes	Sweet Snacks
+	2015Frozen Yoghurt	Frozen Yoghurt	£4.50	Frozen desserts	Frozen
+	2015Ice Cream	Ice Cream	£4.00	Frozen desserts	Frozen
+	2015Muffins	Muffins	£2.10	Cakes	Sweet Snacks
+	2015Small Cakes	Small Cakes	£2.50	Cakes	Sweet Snacks
+	2016Biscuits	Biscuits	£1.85	Biscuits & Crackers	Sweet Snacks
+	2016Candies	Candies	£2.75	Candies	Sweet Snacks
+	2016Chocolate Bars	Chocolate Bars	£1.35	Chocolate Flavoured	Sweet Snacks
+	2016Chocolate Croissants	Chocolate Croissants	£1.99	Chocolate Flavoured	Sweet Snacks
+	2016Crackers	Crackers	£2.10	Biscuits & Crackers	Sweet Snacks
+	2016Cream Cakes	Cream Cakes	£1.25	Cakes	Sweet Snacks
+	2016Frozen Yoghurt	Frozen Yoghurt	£4.60	Frozen desserts	Frozen
+	2016Ice Cream	Ice Cream	£4.30	Frozen desserts	Frozen
+	2016Muffins	Muffins	£2.30	Cakes	Sweet Snacks
+	2016Small Cakes	Small Cakes	£2.60	Cakes	Sweet Snacks

Fig 10.1: Product_Details table

Products_Produced_and_Sold								
Key_manager	Key_product_price	Year	Month	Date	Produ	Shift	Units	Revenu
AprilLine ADay	2015Chocolate Bars	2015	April	01/04/2015	Line A	Day	53,700	67,125
AprilLine ADay	2015Biscuits	2015	April	01/04/2015	Line A	Day	24,500	42,875
AprilLine ADay	2016Chocolate Bars	2016	April	01/04/2016	Line A	Day	54,502	73,578
AprilLine ADay	2016Biscuits	2016	April	01/04/2016	Line A	Day	25,115	46,463
AprilLine ANight	2015Crackers	2015	April	01/04/2015	Line A	Night	12,250	24,500
AprilLine ANight	2015Candies	2015	April	01/04/2015	Line A	Night	37,700	94,250
AprilLine ANight	2016Crackers	2016	April	01/04/2016	Line A	Night	12,329	25,891
AprilLine ANight	2016Candies	2016	April	01/04/2016	Line A	Night	38,624	106,216
AprilLine BDay	2015Cream Cakes	2015	April	01/04/2015	Line B	Day	11,450	11,450
AprilLine BDay	2015Small Cakes	2015	April	01/04/2015	Line B	Day	43,500	108,750
AprilLine BDay	2016Cream Cakes	2016	April	01/04/2016	Line B	Day	11,771	14,714
AprilLine BDay	2016Small Cakes	2016	April	01/04/2016	Line B	Day	42,919	111,589
AprilLine BNight	2015Chocolate Croissants	2015	April	01/04/2015	Line B	Night	22,000	39,600
AprilLine BNight	2015Muffins	2015	April	01/04/2015	Line B	Night	28,600	60,060
AprilLine BNight	2016Chocolate Croissants	2016	April	01/04/2016	Line B	Night	22,368	44,512
AprilLine BNight	2016Muffins	2016	April	01/04/2016	Line B	Night	28,559	65,686
AprilLine CDay	2015Ice Cream	2015	April	01/04/2015	Line C	Day	50,500	202,000
AprilLine CDay	2015Frozen Yoghurt	2015	April	01/04/2015	Line C	Day	42,700	192,150
AprilLine CDay	2016Ice Cream	2016	April	01/04/2016	Line C	Day	51,113	219,786
AprilLine CDay	2016Frozen Yoghurt	2016	April	01/04/2016	Line C	Day	41,248	189,741
AprilLine CNight	2015Ice Cream	2015	April	01/04/2015	Line C	Night	53,000	212,000
AprilLine CNight	2015Frozen Yoghurt	2015	April	01/04/2015	Line C	Night	40,500	182,250
AprilLine CNight	2016Ice Cream	2016	April	01/04/2016	Line C	Night	50,422	216,815
AprilLine CNight	2016Frozen Yoghurt	2016	April	01/04/2016	Line C	Night	41,281	189,893

Record: I◄ 1 of 288 ► ►I ►□ ▨ No Filter Search

Fig 10.2: Products_Produced_and_Sold table

Quarters	
Month	Quarter
+ April	Q2
+ August	Q3
+ December	Q4
+ February	Q1
+ January	Q1
+ July	Q3
+ June	Q2
+ March	Q1
+ May	Q2
+ November	Q4
+ October	Q4
+ September	Q3

Fig 10.3: Quarters table

Manager_Details			
Key_manager ▾	Manager ▾	Section Manager ▾	Click to Add ▾
⊞ AprilLine ADay	Douglass Robinson	Anne Lighthouse	
⊞ AprilLine ANight	Steven Robertson	Anne Lighthouse	
⊞ AprilLine BDay	Steve Black	Anne Lighthouse	
⊞ AprilLine BNight	Asim Khan	Anne Lighthouse	
⊞ AprilLine CDay	Julian Teacher	Bill Ferguson	
⊞ AprilLine CNight	Robert Frog	Bill Ferguson	
⊞ AugustLine ADay	Douglass Robinson	Anne Lighthouse	
⊞ AugustLine ANight	Steven Robertson	Anne Lighthouse	
⊞ AugustLine BDay	Steve Black	Anne Lighthouse	
⊞ AugustLine BNight	Asim Khan	Anne Lighthouse	
⊞ AugustLine CDay	Julian Teacher	Bill Ferguson	
⊞ AugustLine CNight	Robert Frog	Bill Ferguson	
⊞ DecemberLine ADay	Douglass Robinson	Anne Lighthouse	
⊞ DecemberLine ANight	Steven Robertson	Anne Lighthouse	
⊞ DecemberLine BDay	Steve Black	Anne Lighthouse	
⊞ DecemberLine BNight	Asim Khan	Anne Lighthouse	
⊞ DecemberLine CDay	Julian Teacher	Bill Ferguson	
⊞ DecemberLine CNight	Robert Frog	Bill Ferguson	
⊞ FebruaryLine ADay	Douglass Robinson	Anne Lighthouse	
⊞ FebruaryLine ANight	Steven Robertson	Anne Lighthouse	
⊞ FebruaryLine BDay	Steve Black	Anne Lighthouse	
⊞ FebruaryLine BNight	Asim Khan	Anne Lighthouse	
⊞ FebruaryLine CDay	Julian Teacher	Bill Ferguson	
⊞ FebruaryLine CNight	Robert Frog	Bill Ferguson	

Fig 10.4: Manager_Details table

In order to use these tables as a data source for building Pivot Tables we need to establish a connection to the database they are part of.

To do this open a new Excel workbook and then go to the **Data** tab, click on the **Get External Data** group and then click on **From Access** (Fig 10.5).

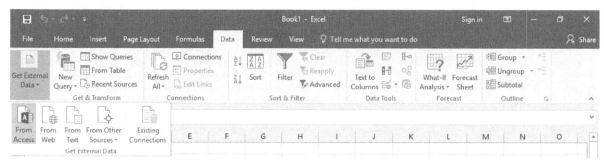

Fig 10.5: Establishing connection to a Microsoft Access database

The **Select Data Source** dialog box will pop up asking you to browse to the location of your database. Go to the folder where your database is found, select it and then click the **Open** button.

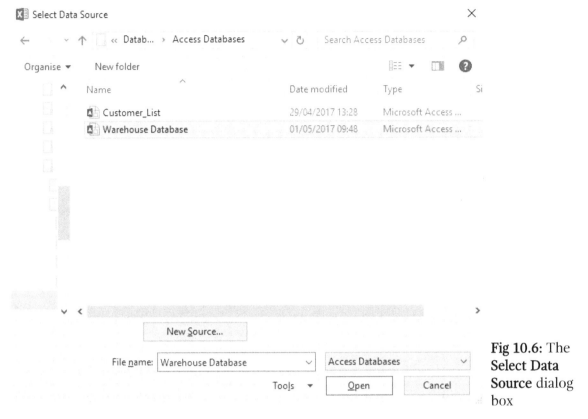

Fig 10.6: The **Select Data Source** dialog box

Once you click the **Open** button the **Select Table** dialog box will appear. In here you can select the tables you need to build your Pivot Table. In our case, we have 4 tables and we need all of them hence select all 4 and then click the **OK** button.

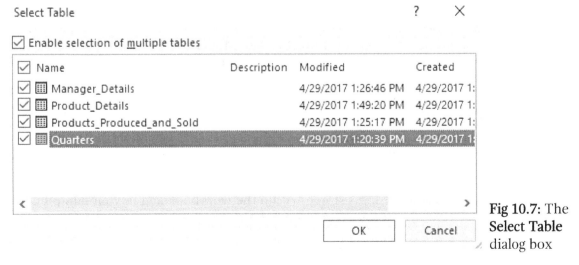

Fig 10.7: The **Select Table** dialog box

After you have done this the **Import Data** dialog box will pop up asking you what to do with the data. If we wanted to build a Pivot Table immediately we would have selected the

PivotTable Report option and clicked **OK**. All the tables would get added to the **Workbook Data Model** automatically and we would be able to use all 4 of them in building our Pivot Table.

In this case however we only want to establish a connection to the database so let's select the '**Only Create Connection**' option and click **OK** (Fig 10.8).

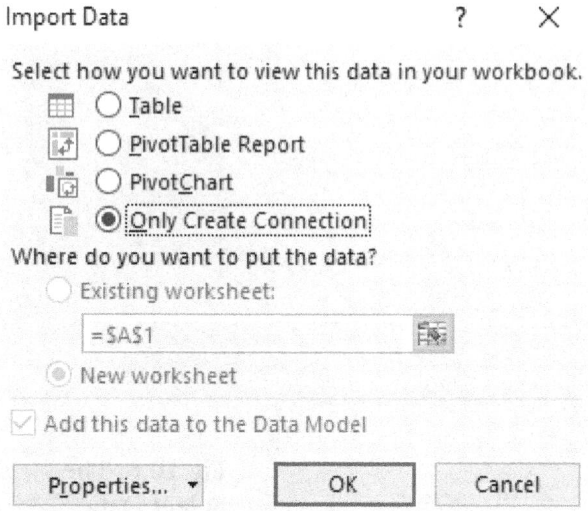

Fig 10.8: The **Import Data** dialog box

So this is it. Now we have a connection between our Excel workbook and our Microsoft Access database.

Note that whenever establishing a connection to multiple tables of a database the tables are added automatically to the **Workbook Data Model**. If we establish connection to only one table in a database then this is not the case. To add this table to the **Workbook Data Model** when establishing a connection or building a Pivot Table we need to tick the box before **Add this data to the Data Model** which in this case will not be greyed out. If importing a single table from a database and if we don't add it to the **Data Model** this table will be treated just like any single Excel table we would have used as a data source.

We can connect to most databases using the **ODBC** and **OLEDB** methods however I don't cover these in this book. If you have such requirements I suggest that you talk to someone in your IT department to help you or you can do some research online.

These connection methods can be accessed by going to the **Get External Data** group in the **Data** tab and then clicking on **From Other Sources**.

Once a connection is established it is stored within the workbook and in your computer so you can access it from other workbooks if you wanted to.

10.4 Building a Pivot Table from a database connected to your workbook

Once we have a connection to our database it is time to build a Pivot Table. It is important to know that when a connection is established with a database two things happen. First, all the tables selected from the database are automatically added to the **Workbook Data Model** and second, a connection file is created in your computer which can be used to create a connection to the database in other workbooks.

To build a Pivot Table from the connection we established in the previous section go to the **Insert** tab and in the **Tables** group click on **PivotTable**.

In the **Create PivotTable** dialog box click on **Use this workbook's Data Model** and then click **OK** to build a Pivot Table in a new worksheet. The **PivotTable Fields List** will look like in Fig 10.12.

Alternatively, (this is how it is done in Excel 2013), click on **Use an external data source** and then click on the **Choose Connection** button.

In the **Existing Connections** dialog box that pops up, in the **Connections** tab under **Connections in this Workbook** choose the *Warehouse Database* and click **Open**.

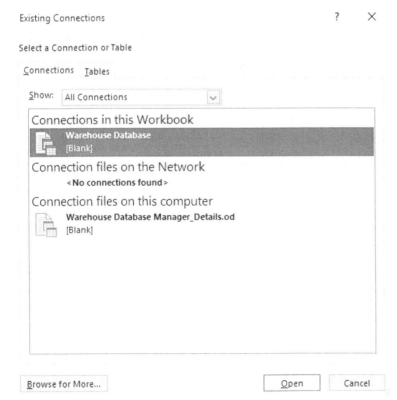

Fig 10.9: **Connections tab** in the **Existing Connections** dialog box

This will get you back to the **Create PivotTable** dialog box which now has a **Connection name**.

 Note that in the same tab you have **Connection files on this computer** and under it you have **Warehouse Database Manager_Details**. This is the same connection as the one under **Connections in this Workbook** except that Excel has saved it with a different name automatically. **Manager_Details** is the first table of the database. If you open another workbook instead of building a new connection you can use **Connection files on this computer** to access the same database.

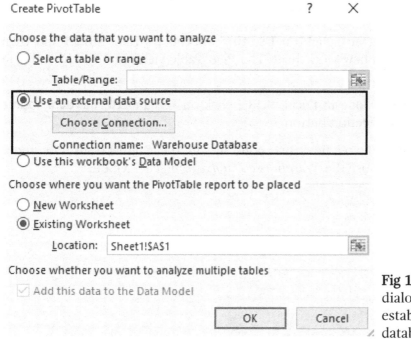

Fig 10.10: Create PivotTable dialog box with a connection established to the Access database

Click **OK** and the Pivot Table will be built with the **PivotTable Fields List** showing automatically (see Fig 10.12).

There are two more ways you could build a Pivot Table using the database from the connection we established in 10.3.

The first is instead of using the **Warehouse Database** under **Connections in this workbook** in Fig 10.9 use the **Warehouse Database Manager_Details.od** under **Connection Files on this computer**. This would be the same as opening a new workbook and building a Pivot Table using a connection file.

The second is by going to the **Tables** tab, selecting **Tables in Workbook Data Model** under **This Workbook Data Model** and clicking **Open**. See Fig 10.11.

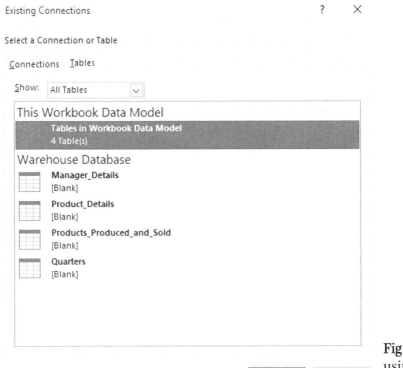

Select a Connection or Table

Connections Tables

Show: All Tables ⌄

This Workbook Data Model

Tables in Workbook Data Model
4 Table(s)

Warehouse Database

Manager_Details
[Blank]

Product_Details
[Blank]

Products_Produced_and_Sold
[Blank]

Quarters
[Blank]

Open   Cancel

Fig 10.11: Building a Pivot Table using all tables in **This Workbook Data Model**

In Fig 10.12 you can see the tables from the **Warehouse Database** and their fields in the **PivotTable Fields List**.

10.5 Using the Workbook Data Model to analyse multiple Excel tables

You can run **OLAP** analysis using multiple tables in Excel. The Excel tables can be in the same workbook or in different ones.

To do this you need to add these tables (data ranges) to the **Workbook Data Model** when they are in a different workbook, or identify them as tables when they are in the same workbook. You need to be aware though that the **Workbook Data Model** built with tables in Excel is only available in the current workbook, whereas a connection to a database can be stored on your computer and accessed from any workbook, this is why the latter is a better way to run **OLAP** analysis.

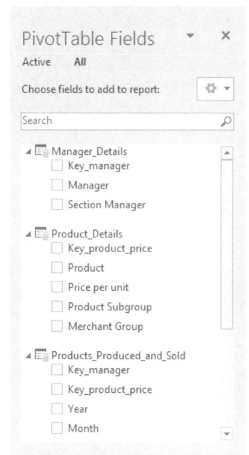

Fig 10.12: **PivotTable Fields List** in **Fields Section Only** layout showing the tables from the database

10.5.1 When data ranges (tables) are in a different workbook

To add data ranges that are in a different workbook or different workbooks to the **Data Model** you need to build a Pivot Table for each data range. If you have 4 data ranges you will need to build 4 empty Pivot Tables just to add each range to the **Data Model**.

Let's add these ranges to the **Workbook Data Model**. We will be using the same tables as in the Warehouse Database except that now they are in an Excel workbook.

Open a <u>new workbook</u>. Go to the **Insert** tab and then in the **Tables** group click on **PivotTable**. In the **Create PivotTable** dialog box select the data range you want to add to the **Workbook Data Model**. In our case the data range we will be adding is in a different workbook so we will open that workbook and select it.

After selecting the data range make sure that you tick the box in front of **Add this data to the Data Model**. The **Create PivotTable** dialog box should look like in Fig 10.13.

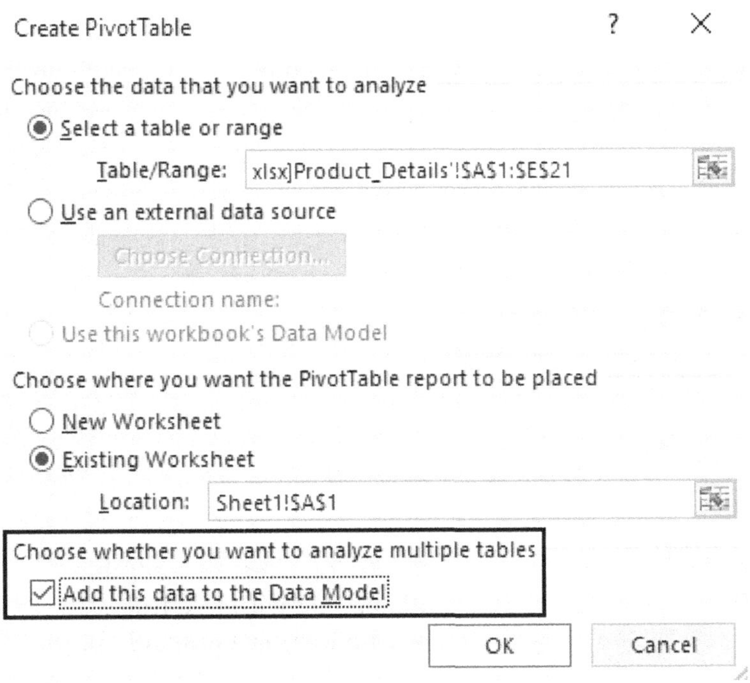

Create PivotTable   ?   ✕

Choose the data that you want to analyze

◉ Select a table or range

   Table/Range: xlsx]Product_Details'!$A$1:$E$21   [icon]

○ Use an external data source

      Choose Connection...

      Connection name:

   ○ Use this workbook's Data Model

Choose where you want the PivotTable report to be placed

○ New Worksheet

◉ Existing Worksheet

   Location: Sheet1!$A$1   [icon]

┌───┐
│ Choose whether you want to analyze multiple tables │
│ ☑ Add this data to the Data Model   │
└───┘

            OK   Cancel

Fig 10.13: Create PivotTable dialog box with **Add this data to the Data Model** option selected

Click **OK** and an empty Pivot Table will be built.

Repeat the process for the other data ranges that you want to add to the **Data Model**.

After adding all the tables to the **Data Model** build the actual Pivot Table that you will be using for your report.

In the **Create PivotTable** dialog box instead of using '**Select a table or range**' select the **Use this workbook's Data Model** option and click **OK**. See Fig 10.14.

Alternatively, select the '**Use an external data source**' option and click on the **Choose Connection...** button.

In the **Existing Connections** dialog box go to the **Tables** tab and select '**Tables in Workbook Data Model** 4 Table(s)' and then click **Open** (Fig 10.15).

This will get you back to the **Create PivotTable** dialog box which now displays a **Connection name** (Fig 10.16).

Click **OK** and now you will have your Pivot Table connected to all 4 tables. This is the equivalent of importing data from a database. The only difference is that the tables don't have their actual names but are named as Range, Range1, Range2 and so on.

The **PivotTable Fields List** will look like in Fig 10.17.

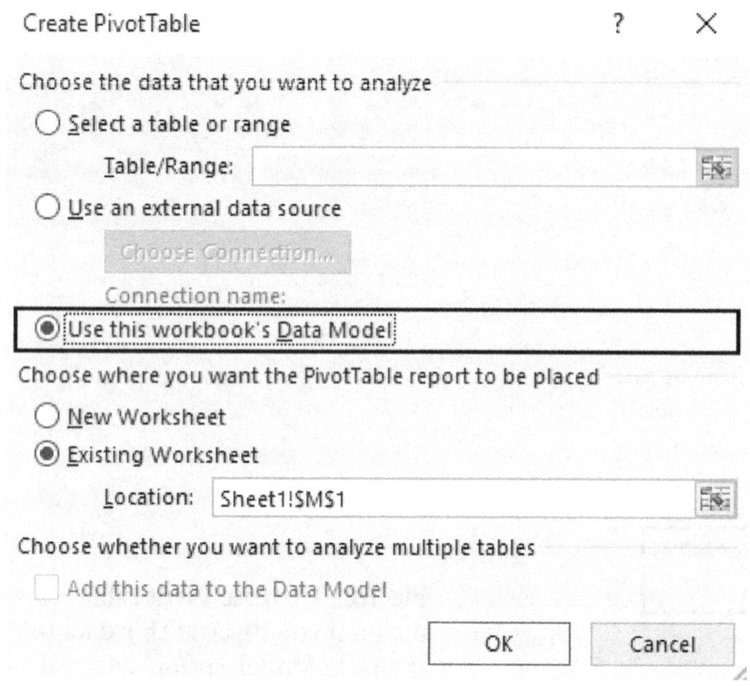

Create PivotTable   ?   ✕

Choose the data that you want to analyze

○ Select a table or range

   Table/Range: [   ] 🔢

○ Use an external data source

   [Choose Connection...]

   Connection name:

⦿ Use this workbook's Data Model

Choose where you want the PivotTable report to be placed

○ New Worksheet

⦿ Existing Worksheet

   Location: [Sheet1!$M$1   ] 🔢

Choose whether you want to analyze multiple tables

☐ Add this data to the Data Model

              [OK   ]   [Cancel]

Fig 10.14: Create PivotTable dialog box with **Use this workbook's Data Model** option selected

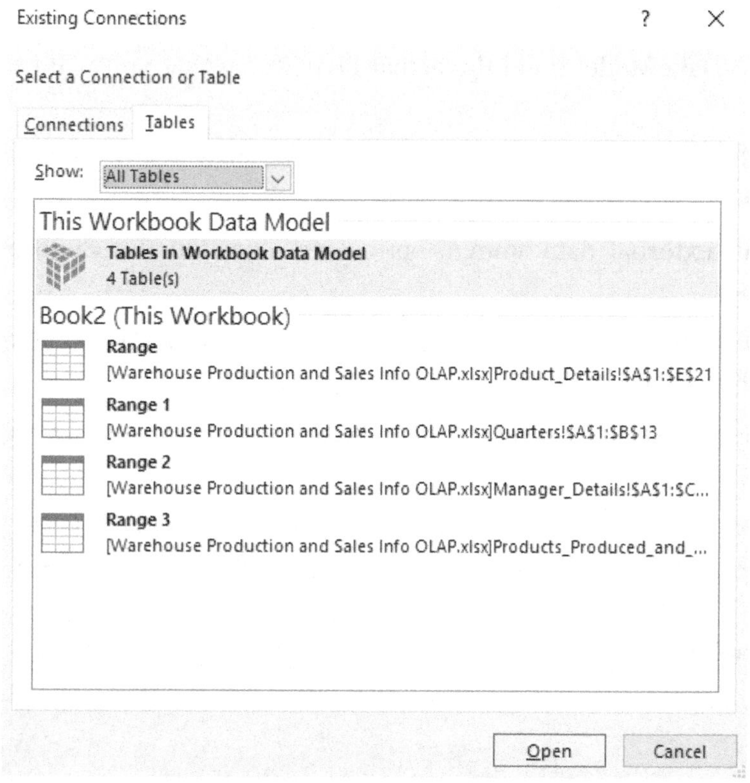

Existing Connections   ?   ✕

Select a Connection or Table

Connections | Tables

   Show: [All Tables   ▽]

┌───┐
│ This Workbook Data Model   │
│ 🧊 **Tables in Workbook Data Model**   │
│   4 Table(s)   │
│   │
│ Book2 (This Workbook)   │
│ ▦   **Range**   │
│   [Warehouse Production and Sales Info OLAP.xlsx]Product_Details!$A$1:$E$21 │
│ ▦   **Range 1**   │
│   [Warehouse Production and Sales Info OLAP.xlsx]Quarters!$A$1:$B$13 │
│ ▦   **Range 2**   │
│   [Warehouse Production and Sales Info OLAP.xlsx]Manager_Details!$A$1:$C... │
│ ▦   **Range 3**   │
│   [Warehouse Production and Sales Info OLAP.xlsx]Products_Produced_and_... │
│   │
└───┘

              [Open   ]   [Cancel]

Fig 10.15: Tables tab in the **Existing Connections** dialog box

Create PivotTable   ?   ✕

Choose the data that you want to analyze

○ Select a table or range

    Table/Range: [   ] 📊

◉ Use an external data source

    [Choose Connection...]

    Connection name: ThisWorkbookDataModel

○ Use this workbook's Data Model

Choose where you want the PivotTable report to be placed

○ New Worksheet

◉ Existing Worksheet

    Location: Sheet1!$M$1   📊

Choose whether you want to analyze multiple tables

☑ Add this data to the Data Model

[OK]   [Cancel]

Fig 10.16: Create PivotTable dialog box with **Workbook Data Model** connection established

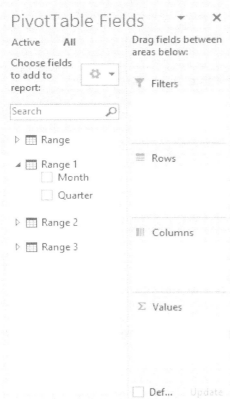

PivotTable Fields   ▾   ✕

Active   **All**   Drag fields between
                           areas below:
Choose fields
to add to   ⚙ ▾
report: ▼ Filters

[Search   🔎]

▷ ▦ Range

◢ ▦ Range 1   ≡ Rows
   ☐ Month
   ☐ Quarter

▷ ▦ Range 2

▷ ▦ Range 3   ▥ Columns

           Σ Values

☐ Def...   Update

Fig 10.17: The **PivotTable Fields List** with tables from another workbook

Now you can delete the previous empty Pivot Tables since you don't need them any more. Don't delete these before building the final Pivot Table as the data will be deleted from the **Data Model** automatically.

10.5.2 When tables (data ranges) are in the same workbook

When tables or data ranges are in the same workbook it is much easier to build a Pivot Table using multiple tables.

What you need to do, is to identify each data range as a table and give it a name unless it has been done so already.

To do this click anywhere on a data range and then in the **Insert** tab's **Tables** group click on **Table**.

The **Create Table** dialog box will appear. Make sure that the data range is selected correctly and if your table has headers tick the '**My table has headers**' box. Now click **OK**.

Create Table   ?   X

Where is the data for your table?

  =$A$1:$E$21

☑ My table has headers

          OK   Cancel   **Fig 10.18:** The **Create Table** dialog box

Once the table has been built the **Table Tools Design** tab will appear automatically. In the **Properties** group of this tab give the table a name.

Table Name:

Product_Details

Resize Table

Properties   **Fig 10.19:** Naming the table

Repeat this process for all the other data ranges you want to use.

Now that you have all the tables set up, go to the **Insert Tab** and in the **Tables** group click on **PivotTable**.

In the **Create PivotTable** dialog box select one of the tables you have named. Make sure you tick the '**Add this data to the Data Model**' option. Finally click **OK**.

Create PivotTable   ?   ✕

Choose the data that you want to analyze

◉ Select a table or range

    Table/Range: Product_Details   ▦

○ Use an external data source

        Choose Connection...

    Connection name:

    ○ Use this workbook's Data Model

Choose where you want the PivotTable report to be placed

◉ New Worksheet

○ Existing Worksheet

    Location: ▦

Choose whether you want to analyze multiple tables

☑ Add this data to the Data Model

                    OK   Cancel

Fig 10.20: Building a Pivot Table with a named table and adding it to the **Data Model**

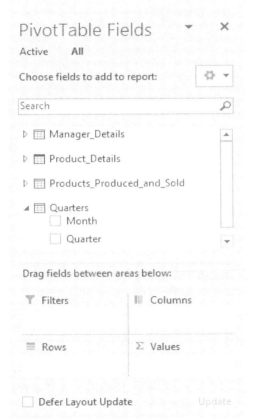

PivotTable Fields   ▾   ✕

Active   **All**

Choose fields to add to report: ⚙ ▾

Search   🔍

▷ ▦ Manager_Details

▷ ▦ Product_Details

▷ ▦ Products_Produced_and_Sold

▲ ▦ Quarters
      ☐ Month
      ☐ Quarter

Drag fields between areas below:

▼ Filters   ▌▌▌ Columns

≡ Rows   Σ Values

☐ Defer Layout Update   Update

Fig 10.21: PivotTable Fields List with all 4 tables listed

Once you click **OK** a Pivot Table will be built and the **PivotTable Fields List** will appear automatically. In here you will notice two buttons Active and All. Upon clicking on the All button you will find all the tables already listed and ready to use (See Fig 10.21).

10.6 Building a Pivot Table using multiple data sources

You can build a Pivot Table using multiple data sources. In this section we will build a Pivot Table using two databases, the Warehouse Database and Customer_List, and an Excel table as data sources.

To add another database to the workbook from **10.3** we first need to establish a connection to it. To do that follow the same steps as we did with the Warehouse Database. Go to the **Data** tab, click on the **Get External Data** group and then click on **From Access**. In the **Select Data Source** dialog box locate the *Customer_List.accdb* database file and click **Open**. This database has only one table to select.

In the **Import Data** dialog box select **Only Create Connection.**

To add the new table from the new database to the **Workbook Data Model** tick the checkbox in front of **Add this Data to the Data Model** and then click **OK**.

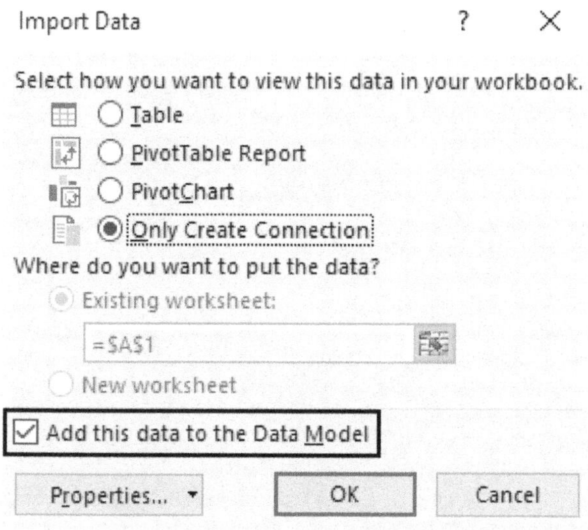

Fig 10.22: **Import Data** dialog box when connection to a single table is established

Now the connection has been established and the new table from the new database has been added to the **Workbook Data Model**.

To check that we can access all tables from both databases let's build a new Pivot Table. Let's go to the **Insert** tab and click on **PivotTable**. In the **Create PivotTable** dialog box choose

Use this workbook's Data Model and then click **OK**. The new Pivot Table will be built and we will have access to all five tables from both databases to select our fields from.

If we click the ALL button in the **PivotTable Fields List** we will notice the table from the Customer_List database alongside the tables from the Warehouse database.

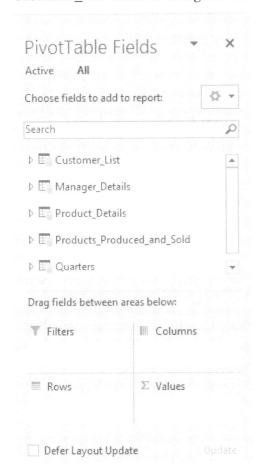

Fig 10.23: PivotTable Fields List with tables from both databases listed

10.6.1 Adding an Excel table to the Data Model

If you have categorized data (or any other data for that matter) in one or more Excel tables which you want to include in your **OLAP** analysis you can add them to the **Workbook Data Model** and use them to build Pivot Tables and conduct **OLAP** analysis together with tables from other data sources.

To add an Excel table to the **Data Model** is simple. All you need to do is define the data range you want to use as a table. This data range needs to be in the same workbook as your **Data Model**. Give the table a meaningful name unless you want to keep the automatically generated one which is **Table#** where **#** is the number of the table. Once you have done this the table will automatically be shown together with tables from other data sources (if you have any) when you click on the ALL button on the **PivotTable Fields List**.

In Fig 10.24 we have a data range which we want to use together with the two databases.

Month	Half_Year
January	H1
February	H1
March	H1
April	H1
May	H1
June	H1
July	H2
August	H2
September	H2
October	H2
November	H2
December	H2

Fig 10.24: A data range which will be defined as a table

To define the above data range as a table click on any cell in it. Go to the **Insert** tab, **Tables** group and click on **Table**.

The **Create Table** dialog box will pop up as in Fig 10.25. Check that the range has been selected correctly and if your table has headers leave the **My table has headers** checkbox ticked. Now click **OK**.

Fig 10.25: The **Create Table** dialog box

After clicking **OK** the table will be created and the **Table Tools Design** tab will appear automatically. In the **Properties** group give the table a name.

Fig 10.26: Giving the table a suitable name

If you go to the **PivotTable Fields List** of the Pivot Table we built earlier and click the ALL button you should see the new table listed together with the databases' tables.

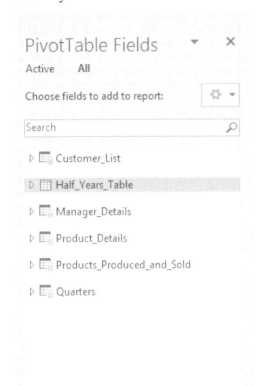

Fig 10.27: Half_Years_Table showing on the **PivotTable Fields List**

10.7 Building Pivot Tables using fields from multiple tables

Let's say that we want to build a simple Pivot Table using the tables from 10.6 where we have *Half_Year* from the ***Half_Years_Table*** table in the **Rows** area, *Year* from the ***Products_Produced_and_Sold*** table in the **Columns** area and *Revenue* from the same table in the Σ **Values** area.

After we put all these fields in their respective areas we get a notification from Excel on the **PivotTable Fields List** that **"Relationships between tables may be needed."** together with an **Auto-Detect...** and a **CREATE** button.

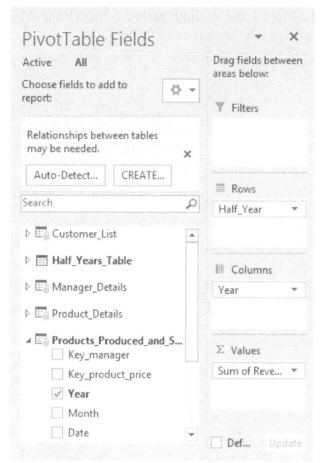

Fig 10.28: PivotTable Fields List with **"Relationships between tables may be needed."** warning

10.7.1 Building relationships between tables

Building relationships between data is essentially the same as connecting tables in the **Workbook Data Model** so that calculations are computed correctly. Without establishing these relationships Excel won't be able to know that a field in one table is the same as in another and that through these fields two or more tables can be merged into a bigger one that can be used to build a Pivot Table.

Therefore, we need to tell Excel how our tables are connected. In the Pivot Tables feature two tables can only be connected through a single common field. Excel also requires that at least one of the fields in one of the tables to be related be unique i.e. should not contain duplicate rows. And just like in databases, relationships can be defined between multiple tables.

Below is how our tables are connected:

- *Product_Details* table is connected to *Products_Produced_and_Sold* table through the *Key_product_price* field which is common to both and unique in *Product_Details* only.

- *Half_Years_Table* table is connected to *Products_Produced_and_Sold* table through the *Month* field which is common to both and unique in *Half_Years_Table* only.

- *Quarters* table is connected to *Products_Produced_and_Sold* table through the *Month* field which is common to both and unique in *Quarters* only.

- *Manager_Details* table is connected to *Products_Produced_and_Sold* table through the *Key_manager* field which is common to both and unique in *Manager_Details* only.

- *Customer_List* table is connected to *Product_Details* table through the *Key_product_price* field which is common to both and unique in *Product_Details* only.

Now that we have defined our relationships let's put them in Excel so that we can start building our first Pivot Table.

If you have many tables, I recommend that you define all relationships before building a Pivot Table. You will then keep building the Pivot Tables you want without worrying about relationships.

Click on the **CREATE** button in the **PivotTable Fields List** and in the **Create Relationship** dialog box input the details of the first relationship as in Fig 10.29 and click **OK**.

A few things to keep in mind:

- One of the tables' columns needs to contain unique values i.e. no duplicate rows.

- Both columns chosen need to contain the same type of data.

- The **Related Column (Primary)** should always be the one that contains the unique values.

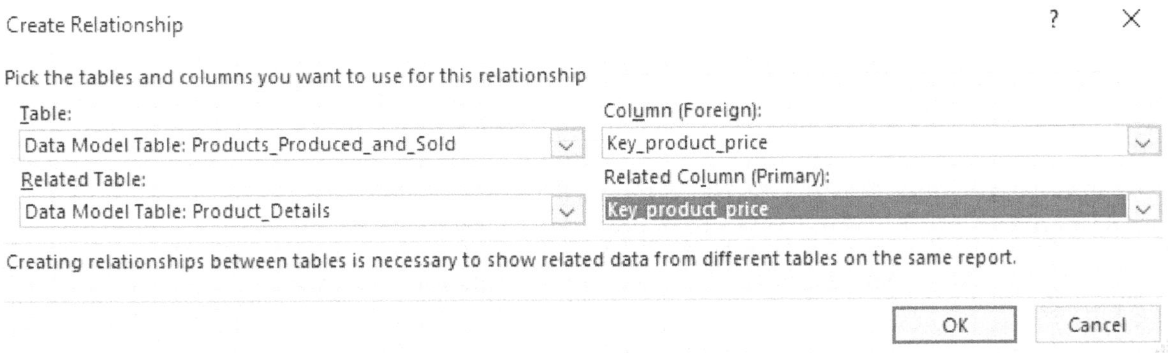

Fig 10.29: The **Create Relationship** dialog box filled with the first relationship details

To add the other four relationships, click on the **New** button in the **Manage Relationships** dialog box to access the **Create Relationship** dialog box. Repeat the process until all relationships are created.

Once you have finished adding all the relationships, the **Manage Relationships** dialog box will list all of them as in Fig 10.30. Now we are ready to build our Pivot Table.

Manage Relationships			? ✕
Status	Table ▲	Related Lookup Table	New...
Active	Customer_List (Key_product_price)	Product_Details (Key_product_price)	Auto-Detect...
Active	Products_Produced_and_Sold (Key_manager)	Manager_Details (Key_manager)	
Active	Products_Produced_and_Sold (Key_product_p...	Product_Details (Key_product_price)	Edit...
Active	Products_Produced_and_Sold (Month)	Quarters (Month)	Activate
Active	Products_Produced_and_Sold (Month)	Half_Years_Table (Month)	Deactivate
			Delete
			Close

Fig 10.30: The **Manage Relationships** dialog box with all our relationships listed

Note that in this dialog box you can **Edit, Deactivate** or **Delete** a relationship and you can also **Auto-Detect** relationships.

The **Manage Relationships** dialog box can also be accessed by going to the **Analyze** tab, **Calculations** group and clicking on **Relationships**.

Using the Auto-Detect feature

Creating relationships can be time consuming if there are many tables to connect. Here is when the **Auto-Detect** feature comes in handy.

To use the **Auto-Detect** feature let's delete all relationships we built in the previous section.

After we do this the **Auto-Detect** button on the **PivotTable Fields List** will become visible again. Click on it.

Once clicked, Excel will start building relationships and at the end of the process the **Auto-Detect Relationships** dialog box will look as in Fig 10.31.

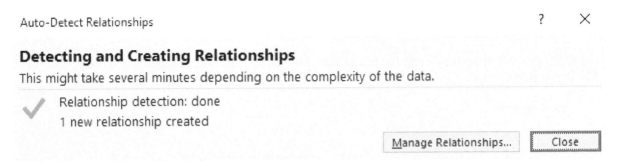

Fig 10.31: The **Auto-Detect Relationships** dialog box notifying that a relationship has been created

Now click on the **Manage Relationships** button to go to the **Manage Relationships** dialog box.

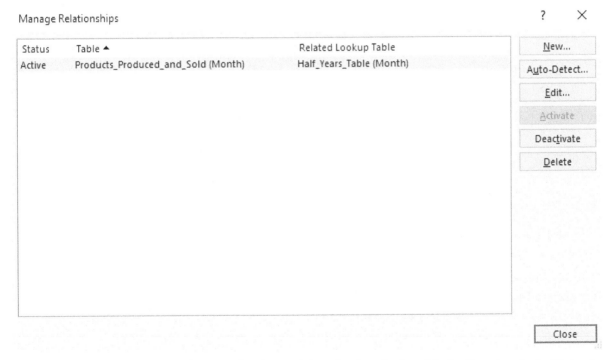

Fig 10.32: Manage Relationships dialog box with a single relationship built using **Auto-Detect**

We can see that only one relationship has been built between *Half_Years_Table* and *Products_Produced_and_Sold* tables. This is because we used fields from both tables when attempting to build our Pivot Table. If we were to use more fields from more tables more relationships would have been built.

Auto-Detect is very handy when you want to build your Pivot Table quickly and are not interested in building all the relationships between all your tables in the beginning.

Let's add *Manager* from **Manager_Details** and *Product* from **Product_Details** to the **Rows** area. The **Auto-Detect** button will become visible again. Click on it.

Two more relationships will be built and the **Manage Relationships** dialog box will look like in Fig 10.33.

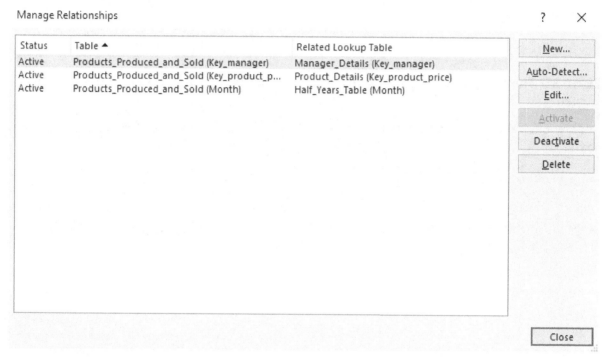

Fig 10.33: Two more relationships added

It is a good idea to quickly sense check the automatically generated relationships. The relationships built above are connected correctly.

It is important to note that once relationships have been built between tables in the **Workbook Data Model** they don't need to be rebuilt each time you build a new Pivot Table using the **Workbook Data Model** as data source.

10.7.2 Building Pivot Tables

Build the other two relationships manually so that we can start to build a few Pivot Tables with fields from different tables.

Example 1: *Half_Year* in **Rows**, *Year* in **Columns**, *Revenue* <u>twice</u> in Σ **Values** once shown as *SUM* and once as *% of Total Revenue* in the *Year*.

Year	Values					
	2015		2016		Total Revenue	Total % Tot Revenue
Half_Year	Revenue	% Tot Revenue	Revenue	% Tot Revenue		
H1	$7,445,006	48.9%	$7,914,250	48.9%	$15,359,255	48.9%
H2	$7,784,705	51.1%	$8,274,084	51.1%	$16,058,790	51.1%
Grand Total	$15,229,711	100.0%	$16,188,334	100.0%	$31,418,045	100.0%

Fig 10.34: Pivot Table with a custom calculation

Example 2: *Merchant Group, Product Subgroup and Product* in **Rows**, *Quarter* in **Columns**, *Revenue* in ∑ **Values** shown as *SUM*.

Revenue			Quarter				
Merchant Group	Product Subgroup	Product	Q1	Q2	Q3	Q4	Grand Total
⊟ Frozen							
	⊟ Frozen desserts						
		Frozen Yoghurt	$2,261,391	$2,309,388	$2,352,889	$2,422,297	$9,345,965
		Ice Cream	$2,564,039	$2,601,028	$2,645,914	$2,712,816	$10,523,796
	Frozen desserts Total		$4,825,430	$4,910,416	$4,998,803	$5,135,112	$19,869,760
Frozen Total			$4,825,430	$4,910,416	$4,998,803	$5,135,112	$19,869,760
⊟ Sweet Snacks							
	⊟ Biscuits & Crackers						
		Biscuits	$263,741	$273,194	$284,945	$288,756	$1,110,637
		Crackers	$147,709	$153,946	$160,803	$163,708	$626,166
	Biscuits & Crackers Total		$411,450	$427,140	$445,748	$452,464	$1,736,803
	⊟ Cakes						
		Cream Cakes	$73,854	$79,001	$81,047	$85,928	$319,829
		Muffins	$368,250	$380,224	$382,627	$413,064	$1,544,165
		Small Cakes	$678,074	$665,101	$696,515	$726,548	$2,766,238
	Cakes Total		$1,120,177	$1,124,326	$1,160,189	$1,225,540	$4,630,232
	⊟ Candies						
		Candies	$588,941	$607,339	$601,833	$626,041	$2,424,153
	Candies Total		$588,941	$607,339	$601,833	$626,041	$2,424,153
	⊟ Chocolate Flavoured						
		Chocolate Bars	$413,962	$420,518	$430,447	$447,740	$1,712,667
		Chocolate Croissants	$254,686	$254,870	$267,215	$267,658	$1,044,430
	Chocolate Flavoured Total		$668,648	$675,389	$697,662	$715,399	$2,757,097
Sweet Snacks Total			$2,789,216	$2,834,193	$2,905,432	$3,019,443	$11,548,285
Grand Total			$7,614,646	$7,744,610	$7,904,234	$8,154,555	$31,418,045

Fig 10.35: Pivot Table with three fields in **Rows** and one in **Columns**

Example 3: *Section Manager, Manager* in **Rows**, *Half_Year, Quarter* in **Columns**, *Units produced* in ∑ **Values** shown as *SUM*.

Units Produced	Half_Year ▼ Quarter ▼							
	⊟H1		H1 Total	⊟H2		H2 Total	Grand Total
Section Manager ▼ Manager ▼	Q1	Q2		Q3	Q4		
⊟Anne Lighthouse							
Asim Khan	321,970	314,010	635,980	331,256	332,935	664,191	1,300,171
Douglass Robinson	348,536	415,371	763,907	369,170	445,463	814,633	1,578,540
Steve Black	311,243	324,344	635,587	328,897	357,102	685,999	1,321,586
Steven Robertson	412,676	366,308	778,984	428,005	377,441	805,446	1,584,430
Anne Lighthouse Total	1,394,425	1,420,033	2,814,458	1,457,328	1,512,941	2,970,269	5,784,727
⊟Bill Ferguson							
Julian Teacher	557,574	569,389	1,126,963	577,226	583,307	1,160,533	2,287,496
Robert Frog	557,400	564,815	1,122,215	577,368	602,883	1,180,251	2,302,466
Bill Ferguson Total	1,114,974	1,134,204	2,249,178	1,154,594	1,186,190	2,340,784	4,589,962
Grand Total	2,509,399	2,554,237	5,063,636	2,611,922	2,699,131	5,311,053	10,374,689

Fig 10.36: Pivot Table with two fields in **Rows** and two fields in **Columns**. Fields sourced from different tables

10.8 Building Named Sets

A **Named Set** is essentially a grouping of rows or columns in a Pivot Table. Once you build a Pivot Table, by using sets you can decide which rows or columns you want to display. You can then use this set to build a Pivot Table again and again using the same combination of rows or columns. It basically enables you to do asymmetric reporting.

Excel has the capability to use **Multidimensional Expressions (MDX)** query language to build **Named Sets.** This however is beyond the scope if this book.

Named Sets are only available to use with the **Workbook Data Model.** The best way to understand **Named Sets** is through examples.

Using the same workbook we have used so far let's build a Pivot Table where we have *Production Line* and *Shift* in **Rows**, *Quarter, Half_Year* and *Year* in **Columns** and *Revenue* and *Units produced* in Σ **Values.** The Pivot Table will look like in Fig 10.37.

A Pivot Table with this many fields is large and we may not need all rows or columns for our report.

Let's say that in **Rows** we want to remove *Revenue* from each *Shift* and only keep it for each *Production Line* subtotal and the **Grand Total.**

Whereas for **Columns** we want to keep *Q1, Q2, H2 Total, Year Total* and **Grand Total.**

To do this we will need to build two **Named Sets.** One set for rows and one set for columns.

Production Line	Shift	Values	Year Half_Year Quarter 2015 H1 Q1	Q2	H1 Total	H2 Q3	Q4	H2 Total	2015 Total
Line A									
	Day								
		Revenue	$326,538	$335,431	$661,969	$343,300	$350,867	$694,167	$1,356,136
		Units produced	231,790	237,883	469,673	243,200	248,974	492,174	961,847
	Night								
		Revenue	$349,787	$362,956	$712,743	$369,000	$376,708	$745,708	$1,458,450
		Units produced	147,106	152,681	299,787	155,400	158,654	314,054	613,841
Line A Revenue			$676,325	$698,387	$1,374,711	$712,300	$727,575	$1,439,875	$2,814,586
Line A Units produced			378,896	390,564	769,460	398,600	407,628	806,228	1,575,688
Line B									
	Day								
		Revenue	$360,375	$363,480	$723,855	$379,784	$388,402	$768,186	$1,492,041
		Units produced	163,875	166,530	330,405	173,534	178,013	351,547	681,952
	Night								
		Revenue	$295,296	$300,841	$596,137	$309,780	$321,768	$631,548	$1,227,685
		Units produced	150,166	152,818	302,984	157,500	163,383	320,883	623,867
Line B Revenue			$655,671	$664,321	$1,319,992	$689,564	$710,170	$1,399,734	$2,719,726
Line B Units produced			314,041	319,348	633,389	331,034	341,396	672,430	1,305,819

Fig 10.37: Part of the Pivot Table built for use with **Named Sets**

10.8.1 Building the Rows Set

Click on any cell in the Pivot Table and then in the **Analyze** tab, **Calculations** group click on **Fields, Items & Sets** and then on **Create Set Based on Row Items...** .

The **New Set (ThisWorkbookDataModel)** dialog box will pop up. In this dialog box you can keep the rows you want and delete the ones you don't want. You can also add new rows with the combination of items you like or you can copy an existing row.

In our case we want to delete all rows with *Revenue* for each *Shift* but keep the *Revenue* measure for each *Production Line* and the **Grand Total**.

Let's delete these rows and let's also name this set as *Row_Set*.

Untick the checkbox before **Replace the fields currently in the row area with the new set** as we don't want the Pivot Table to be updated automatically this time.

The **New Set (ThisWorkbookDataModel)** dialog box will now look as in Fig 10.39.

Click **OK** and the *Row_Set* will be built

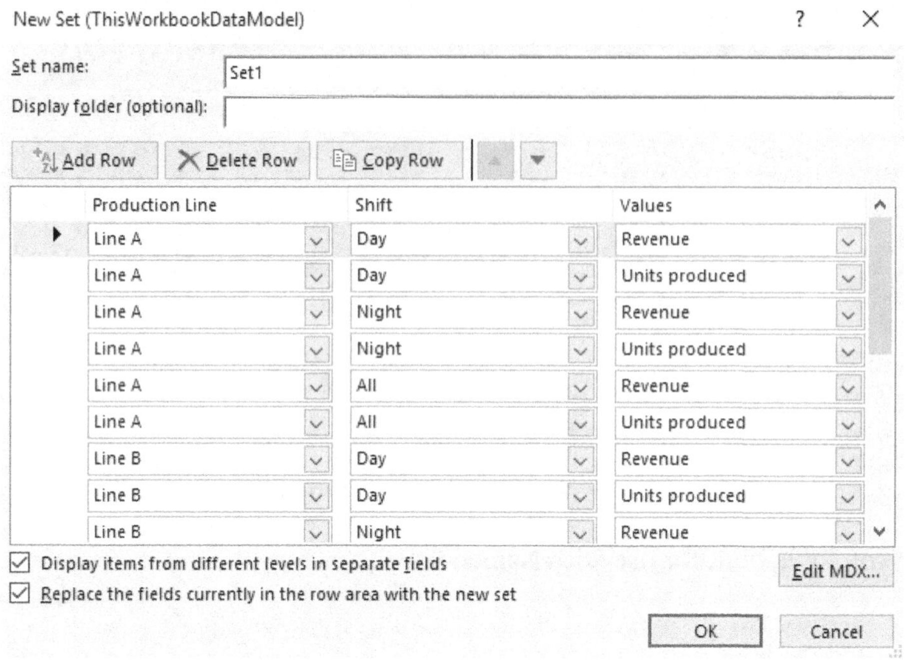

Fig 10.38: The **New Set (ThisWorkbookDataModel)** dialog box

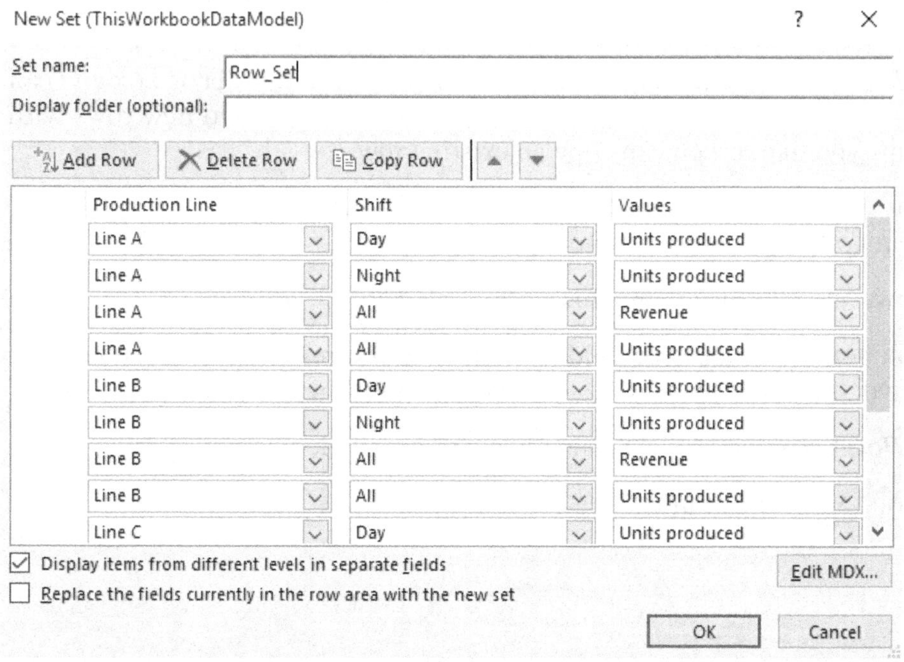

Fig 10.39: New Set **(ThisWorkbookDataModel)** filled

10.8.2 Building the Columns Set

Go again to the **Analyze** tab, **Calculations** group and click on **Fields, Items & Sets** and then on **Create Set Based on Column Items...** .

The **New Set (ThisWorkbookDataModel)** dialog box will pop up again but now with column items.

In our case we want to delete all columns that are **NOT** in the following list:

- 2015 H1 Q1; 2015 H1 Q2; 2015 H2 All; 2015 All All;

- 2016 H1 Q1; 2016 H1 Q2; 2016 H2 All; 2016 All All;

- All All All;

Let's delete the required columns and let's also name this set as *Column_Set*.

Untick the checkbox before **Replace the fields currently in the column area with the new set** as we don't want the Pivot Table to be updated automatically this time as well.

The **New Set (ThisWorkbookDataModel)** dialog box will now look as in Fig 10.40.

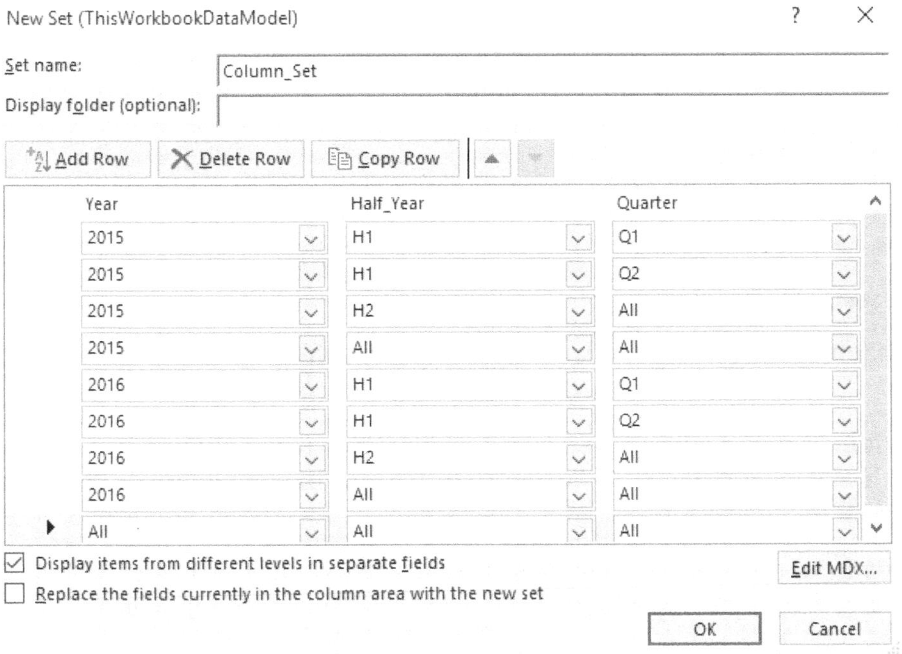

Fig 10.40: New Set (ThisWorkbookDataModel) filled with *Column_Set*

Click **OK** and the *Column_Set* will be built.

10.8.3 Managing Sets

If you click anywhere in the Pivot Table and go to the **Analyze** tab, **Fields, Items, & Sets** and then click on **Manage Sets...** the **Set Manager** will pop up as in Fig 10.41.

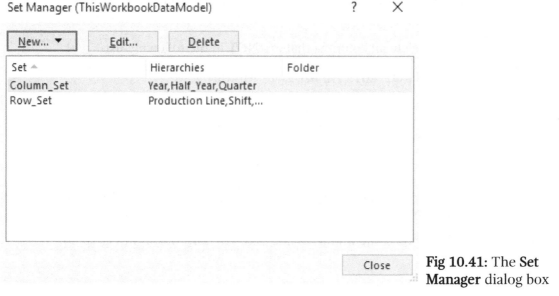

Fig 10.41: The **Set Manager** dialog box

The **Set Manager** can be used to edit existing sets, delete them, or build new ones by giving you access to the **New Set** dialog box for columns or rows when you click on the **New...** button.

10.8.4 Using Named Sets

Once you build **Named Sets** they appear automatically on the **PivotTable Fields List** as in Fig 10.44.

From the **Fields Section**, **Named Sets** can be placed in either **Rows** or **Columns** and can be used on their own in either area, in conjunction with other fields or in conjunction with other **Named Sets**.

Let's show this with an example. Let's remove all fields from the current Pivot Table and put *Row_Set* in **Rows** and *Column_Set* in **Columns**. Don't put anything in the Σ **Values** area.

Once the Pivot Table has been built go ahead and edit value fields' number formats and custom names as in the Pivot Table below. **Value Field Settings** for each field can be accessed by right clicking above any cell in the Pivot Table that contains the value field of interest.

Production Line	Shift	Values	Year 2015 H1 Q1	Q2	H2	2015	2016 H1 Q1	Q2	H2	2016	Grand Total
Line A	Day	Units produced	231,790	237,883	492,174	961,847	233,107	237,381	501,740	972,228	1,934,075
	Night	Units produced	147,106	152,681	314,054	613,841	149,209	153,734	312,111	615,054	1,228,895
Line A Revenue			$676,325	$698,387	$1,439,875	$2,814,586	$738,029	$756,611	$1,564,398	$3,059,037	$5,873,623
Line A Units produced			378,896	390,564	806,228	1,575,688	382,316	391,115	813,851	1,587,282	3,162,970
Line B	Day	Units produced	163,875	166,530	351,547	681,952	167,619	164,575	354,805	686,999	1,368,951
	Night	Units produced	150,166	152,818	320,883	623,867	151,553	154,431	322,955	628,939	1,252,806
Line B Revenue			$655,671	$664,321	$1,399,734	$2,719,726	$719,192	$714,875	$1,520,869	$2,954,936	$5,674,662
Line B Units produced			314,041	319,348	672,430	1,305,819	319,172	319,006	677,760	1,315,938	2,621,757
Line C	Day	Units produced	281,960	282,845	595,385	1,160,190	282,773	285,307	596,071	1,164,151	2,324,341
	Night	Units produced	276,900	283,090	575,321	1,135,311	273,341	282,962	574,007	1,130,310	2,265,621
Line C Revenue			$2,359,440	$2,390,863	$4,945,097	$9,695,400	$2,465,990	$2,519,554	$5,188,818	$10,174,361	$19,869,760
Line C Units produced			558,860	565,935	1,170,706	2,295,501	556,114	568,269	1,170,078	2,294,461	4,589,962
Total Revenue			$3,691,435	$3,753,570	$7,784,705	$15,229,711	$3,923,211	$3,991,039	$8,274,084	$16,188,334	$31,418,045
Total Units produced			1,251,797	1,275,847	2,649,364	5,177,008	1,257,602	1,278,390	2,661,689	5,197,681	10,374,689

Fig 10.42: Pivot Table built by using the two **Named Sets** we built earlier

Here is another Pivot Table example built using only the *Column_Set*.

Put *Section Manager* and *Manager* from **Manager_Details** in **Rows**, *Column_Set* in **Columns** and *Revenue* from **Products_Produced_and_Sold** in Σ **Values** to get the Pivot Table shown in Fig 10.43.

Revenue Section Manager	Manager	Year 2015 H1 Q1	Q2	H2	2015	2016 H1 Q1	Q2	H2	2016	Grand Total
⊟ Anne Lighthouse		$1,331,995	$1,362,708	$2,839,608	$5,534,311	$1,457,221	$1,471,486	$3,085,267	$6,013,973	$11,548,285
	Asim Khan	$339,410	$321,840	$694,111	$1,355,361	$369,678	$345,853	$742,359	$1,457,890	$2,813,251
	Douglass Robinson	$342,975	$344,096	$719,274	$1,406,344	$372,414	$367,328	$781,709	$1,521,451	$2,927,795
	Steve Black	$316,260	$342,482	$705,623	$1,364,365	$349,515	$369,022	$778,509	$1,497,046	$2,861,411
	Steven Robertson	$333,350	$354,291	$720,601	$1,408,242	$365,615	$389,282	$782,689	$1,537,587	$2,945,828
⊟ Bill Ferguson		$2,359,440	$2,390,863	$4,945,097	$9,695,400	$2,465,990	$2,519,554	$5,188,818	$10,174,361	$19,869,760
	Julian Teacher	$1,175,800	$1,195,728	$2,454,221	$4,825,749	$1,236,552	$1,270,822	$2,569,729	$5,077,103	$9,902,852
	Robert Frog	$1,183,640	$1,195,135	$2,490,877	$4,869,651	$1,229,438	$1,248,732	$2,619,089	$5,097,258	$9,966,909
Grand Total		$3,691,435	$3,753,570	$7,784,705	$15,229,711	$3,923,211	$3,991,039	$8,274,084	$16,188,334	$31,418,045

Fig 10.43: Pivot Table built with *Column_Set* and *Section Manager*, *Manager* and *Revenue* fields

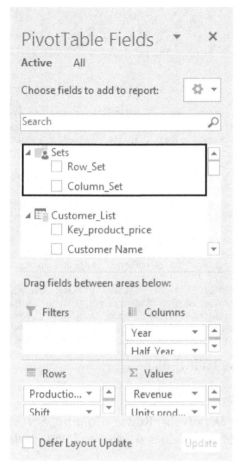

Fig 10.44: Pivot Table **Named Sets** listed in the PivotTable Fields List

10.8.5 Things to know when using Named Sets

If a **Named Set** <u>contains more than 1 value field</u> then you cannot add any value fields to the Σ **Values** area. In our case the *Row_Set* contains 2 value fields hence if you place this **Named Set** in **Rows** or **Columns** and try to add a field to the Σ **Values** area you will get an error message as in the figure below.

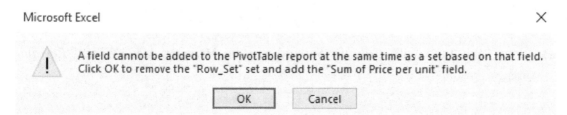

Fig 10.45: Error message when trying to add a field to the Σ **Values** area

If the same field is added to the **Columns** area for e.g. you won't be getting this error.

If a **Named Set** (or **Named Sets**) <u>contains 1 or no value fields</u> like our *Column_Set* for e.g. then you can put one or more fields in the **∑ Values** area <u>as long as</u> this set is not used in conjunction with other **Named Sets** that have more than one value field.

You cannot use the fields that you are using in a **Named Set** in another area together with that **Named Set**.

If a **Named Set** is based only on one field and one value field, then on the **Fields Section** of the **PivotTable Fields List** it will show as the last field in the table where the field (not the value field) is from. Otherwise **Named Sets** are shown at the top of the **PivotTable Fields List** as shown in Fig 10.42.

10.9 Quick Explore

At the beginning of this chapter we talked about what **OLAP** is and how it is used. So far we have learned how to build Pivot Tables using multiple tables as a data source whether they are sourced from Excel or external data sources such as a Microsoft Access database. While this is useful and important on its own, the power of **OLAP** analysis comes from drilling through the data so that we can discover interesting and useful insights and facts. This drilling through in Pivot Tables is done through **Quick Explore**.

To access **Quick Explore** right click on any cell in the **Labels** or **Values** areas of a Pivot Table (i.e. where you have value fields or items from row and column fields) and then click on **Quick Explore**. Alternatively, once you click on a cell in these areas of a Pivot Table or once the mouse pointer moves to the vicinity of a cell that is already selected the **Quick Explore** icon becomes visible on the right side of the cell.

Fig 10.46 shows how to access **Quick Explore** through a right click whereas Fig 10.47 shows how to access **Quick Explore** through its icon next to a selected cell.

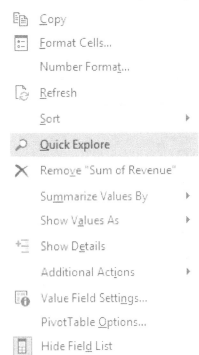

Fig 10.46: Accessing **Quick Explore** through a right click

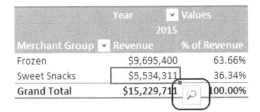

Fig 10.47: Accessing **Quick Explore** through its icon

Now let's build a Pivot Table on which we are going to drill through using **Quick Explore** so that we can understand this feature better and use it effectively.

Let's put *Merchant Group* from **Product_Details** in **Rows**, *Year* from **Products_Produced_and_Sold** in **Columns** and *Revenue* from the same table <u>twice</u> in ∑ **Values**.

Rename the first occurrence of *Revenue* from *Sum of Revenue* to *Revenue* and change the number format to $ (United States) with no decimal places.

For the second occurrence of *Revenue* go to **Value Fields Settings** by clicking on *Sum of Revenue2* in the ∑ **Values** area and then selecting **Value Field Settings**. In the **Show Values As** tab select **Show values as: % of Column Total**. Rename this field as *% of Revenue*.

Next move ∑ *Values* from **Rows** to **Columns**.

The Pivot Table will now look like in Fig 10.48.

Merchant Group	Year	Values				Total Revenue	Total % of Revenue
	2015		2016				
	Revenue	% of Revenue	Revenue	% of Revenue			
Frozen	$9,695,400	63.66%	$10,174,361	62.85%		$19,869,760	63.24%
Sweet Snacks	$5,534,311	36.34%	$6,013,973	37.15%		$11,548,285	36.76%
Grand Total	**$15,229,711**	**100.00%**	**$16,188,334**	**100.00%**		**$31,418,045**	**100.00%**

Fig 10.48: Pivot Table ready to drill through

Let's say that we wanted to drill down on *Sweet Snacks* to see *Revenue* by *Product Subgroup*. To do this click on any cell in the *Sweet Snacks* row and then once the **Quick Explore** icon becomes visible click on it.

When we do this the **Explore** dialog box will pop up as in Fig 10.49.

Fig 10.49: Explore dialog box

Under the **Explore** title the name of the item that will be drilled down is displayed. In this case this is *Sweet Snacks*.

On the left hand side we find the list of tables the Pivot Table is connected to. If we click on the small arrow before the name of any of the tables we get a list of fields for that table that are not in the Pivot Table.

We can then select the field that we want to drill down to. In this case it is *Product Subgroup*. Once we click on it the name will show on the right hand side of the dialog box under **Drill To**.

If we click on the green area around **Drill To** or press Enter then our **Drill To** choice has been made and now a new Pivot Table with *Product Subgroup* in **Rows** and *Merchant Group* in the **Filters** area filtered to *Sweet Snacks* will be built as in Fig 10.50.

Merchant Group   Sweet Snacks ⫟

| Product Subgroup | Year | | | | Total Revenue | Total % of Revenue |
| | 2015 | | 2016 | | | |
	Revenue	% of Revenue	Revenue	% of Revenue		
Biscuits & Crackers	$843,005	15.23%	$893,798	14.86%	$1,736,803	15.04%
Cakes	$2,225,113	40.21%	$2,405,119	39.99%	$4,630,232	40.09%
Candies	$1,153,840	20.85%	$1,270,313	21.12%	$2,424,153	20.99%
Chocolate Flavoured	$1,312,354	23.71%	$1,444,743	24.02%	$2,757,097	23.87%
Grand Total	$5,534,311	100.00%	$6,013,973	100.00%	$11,548,285	100.00%

Fig 10.50: Drilled To Pivot Table

This is our first **Drill To** operation. We can keep going and pick another item under *Product Subgroup* for *Sweet Snacks*. Click anywhere on the *Cakes* item row and then on the **Quick Explore** icon. In the **Explore** dialog box click on *Product* from **Product_Details** table and then click on **Drill To** on the left hand side of the dialog box or press Enter. A new Pivot Table as in Fig 10.51 will be built.

Merchant Group   Sweet Snacks ⫟
Product Subgroup   Cakes   ⫟

| Product | Year | | | | Total Revenue | Total % of Revenue |
| | 2015 | | 2016 | | | |
	Revenue	% of Revenue	Revenue	% of Revenue		
Cream Cakes	$141,893	6.38%	$177,936	7.40%	$319,829	6.91%
Muffins	$733,072	32.95%	$811,093	33.72%	$1,544,165	33.35%
Small Cakes	$1,350,148	60.68%	$1,416,090	58.88%	$2,766,238	59.74%
Grand Total	$2,225,113	100.00%	$2,405,119	100.00%	$4,630,232	100.00%

Fig 10.51: Drilled To Product

Let's do another **Drill To** operation. Click anywhere on the *Small Cakes* item row and then on the **Quick Explore** icon. In the **Explore** dialog box click on *Quarter* from **Quarters** table and then click on **Drill To** on the left hand side of the dialog box or press Enter. A new Pivot Table as in Fig 10.52 will be built.

Merchant Group	Sweet Snacks	▼
Product Subgroup	Cakes	▼
Product	Small Cakes	▼

Quarter ▼	Year ▼ Values					
	2015		2016		Total Revenue	Total % of Revenue
	Revenue	% of Revenue	Revenue	% of Revenue		
Q1	$327,500	24.26%	$350,574	24.76%	$678,074	24.51%
Q2	$328,250	24.31%	$336,851	23.79%	$665,101	24.04%
Q3	$343,750	25.46%	$352,765	24.91%	$696,515	25.18%
Q4	$350,648	25.97%	$375,900	26.54%	$726,548	26.26%
Grand Total	$1,350,148	100.00%	$1,416,090	100.00%	$2,766,238	100.00%

Fig 10.52: Pivot table further drilled to *Quarter*

To go back after a **Drill To** simply press the **Undo** button ↶▾ or **CRTL + Z**. The **Undo** command goes back up to 100 actions. Another way is to use the **PivotTable Fields List** and keep the fields you want to in the areas that you want to.

10.9.1 A few final points on Quick Explore

First you must have noticed that whenever you click on a Pivot Table cell and then on **Quick Explore** it is always the *Row Item* that is **Drilled To**. To **Drill To** a *Column Item* you need to click on a *Column Item* cell. In Fig 10.52 these cells are the ones containing the values **2015** and **2016**.

Second if a *Row Item* or *Column Item* has a parent field, then the parent field is also placed in the **Filter** area. In Fig 10.54 we have a Pivot Table which is the same as the one in Fig 10.48 except that we have added *Shift* from **Products_Produced_and_Sold** in the **Rows** area above *Merchant Group*.

Shift ▼	Merchant Group ▼	Year ▼ Values					
		2015		2016		Total Revenue	Total % of Revenue
		Revenue	% of Revenue	Revenue	% of Revenue		
⊟Day		$7,754,976	50.92%	$8,227,310	50.82%	$15,982,286	50.87%
	Frozen	$4,906,800	32.22%	$5,166,116	31.91%	$10,072,916	32.06%
	Sweet Snacks	$2,848,176	18.70%	$3,061,194	18.91%	$5,909,370	18.81%
⊟Night		$7,474,735	49.08%	$7,961,024	49.18%	$15,435,759	49.13%
	Frozen	$4,788,600	31.44%	$5,008,245	30.94%	$9,796,845	31.18%
	Sweet Snacks	$2,686,135	17.64%	$2,952,779	18.24%	$5,638,914	17.95%
Grand Total		$15,229,711	100.00%	$16,188,334	100.00%	$31,418,045	100.00%

Fig 10.54: Pivot Table with two fields in **Rows**

If we select a cell with a *Merchant Group* item and then click on the **Quick Explore** icon and then **Drill To** *Product Subgroup* from the **Product_Details** table we will get the following Pivot Table.

Shift   Day   ▼
Merchant Group   Sweet Snacks ▼

Product Subgroup ▼	Year ▼ Values				Total Revenue	Total % of Revenue
	2015		2016			
	Revenue	% of Revenue	Revenue	% of Revenue		
Biscuits & Crackers	$538,395	18.90%	$572,242	18.69%	$1,110,637	18.79%
Cakes	$1,492,041	52.39%	$1,594,026	52.07%	$3,086,067	52.22%
Chocolate Flavoured	$817,741	28.71%	$894,926	29.23%	$1,712,667	28.98%
Grand Total	$2,848,176	100.00%	$3,061,194	100.00%	$5,909,370	100.00%

Fig 10.55: Pivot Table with both parent field and field moved to the **Filters** area

As you can see not only the *Merchant Group* has been moved to the **Filters** area but also *Shift*. Both have been filtered as per selection in the previous Pivot Table.

10.10 Including Filtered Items in Totals

When filtering an OLAP Pivot Table we have the option to either let the subtotal and total calculations be done on the filtered items only or on all items whether filtered or not.

Fig 10.56 shows a Pivot Table where we have *Shift* from **Products_Produced_and_Sold** and *Product* from **Product_Details** in **Rows**, *Year* from **Products_Produced_and_Sold** in **Columns** and *Revenue* from **Products_Produced_and_Sold** twice in ∑ **Values**.

For the second occurrence of *Revenue* go to **Value Fields Settings** by clicking on the field name in the ∑ **Values** area and then selecting **Value Field Settings** and then in the **Show Values As** tab select **Show values as: % of Column Total**. Rename this field as *% of Revenue*.

For the first occurrence of *Revenue* go to **Value Field Settings** and rename the value field from *Sum of Revenue* to *Revenue* and change the number format to $ (United States) with no decimal places.

Next move ∑ *Values* from **Rows** to **Columns**. The Pivot Table will now look like in Fig 10.56.

Let's manually filter out *Frozen Yoghurt* and *Ice Cream* from the *Product* field in the Pivot Table from Fig 10.56. Once we do this the Pivot Table will look as in Fig 10.57.

Notice that now that we have removed *Frozen Yoghurt* and *Ice Cream* from the Pivot Table we have also reduced the **Subtotals** and **Totals**.

If we want **Subtotals** and **Totals** to include *Frozen Yoghurt* and *Ice Cream* even though they are not shown in the Pivot Table we can go to the **Design** tab, click on **Subtotals** in the **Layout** group and then click on the **Include Filtered Items in Totals** button as in Fig 10.58.

Shift	Product	2015 Revenue	2015 % of Revenue	2016 Revenue	2016 % of Revenue	Total Revenue	Total % of Revenue
Day		$7,754,976	50.92%	$8,227,310	50.82%	$15,982,286	50.87%
	Biscuits	$538,395	3.54%	$572,242	3.53%	$1,110,637	3.54%
	Chocolate Bars	$817,741	5.37%	$894,926	5.53%	$1,712,667	5.45%
	Cream Cakes	$141,893	0.93%	$177,936	1.10%	$319,829	1.02%
	Frozen Yoghurt	$2,394,360	15.72%	$2,457,417	15.18%	$4,851,777	15.44%
	Ice Cream	$2,512,440	16.50%	$2,708,699	16.73%	$5,221,139	16.62%
	Small Cakes	$1,350,148	8.87%	$1,416,090	8.75%	$2,766,238	8.80%
Night		$7,474,735	49.08%	$7,961,024	49.18%	$15,435,759	49.13%
	Candies	$1,153,840	7.58%	$1,270,313	7.85%	$2,424,153	7.72%
	Chocolate Croissants	$494,613	3.25%	$549,817	3.40%	$1,044,430	3.32%
	Crackers	$304,610	2.00%	$321,556	1.99%	$626,166	1.99%
	Frozen Yoghurt	$2,226,200	14.62%	$2,267,989	14.01%	$4,494,188	14.30%
	Ice Cream	$2,562,400	16.83%	$2,740,257	16.93%	$5,302,657	16.88%
	Muffins	$733,072	4.81%	$811,093	5.01%	$1,544,165	4.91%
Grand Total		$15,229,711	100.00%	$16,188,334	100.00%	$31,418,045	100.00%

Fig 10.56: OLAP Pivot Table

Shift	Product	2015 Revenue	2015 % of Revenue	2016 Revenue	2016 % of Revenue	Total Revenue	Total % of Revenue
Day		$2,848,176	51.46%	$3,061,194	50.90%	$5,909,370	51.17%
	Biscuits	$538,395	9.73%	$572,242	9.52%	$1,110,637	9.62%
	Chocolate Bars	$817,741	14.78%	$894,926	14.88%	$1,712,667	14.83%
	Cream Cakes	$141,893	2.56%	$177,936	2.96%	$319,829	2.77%
	Small Cakes	$1,350,148	24.40%	$1,416,090	23.55%	$2,766,238	23.95%
Night		$2,686,135	48.54%	$2,952,779	49.10%	$5,638,914	48.83%
	Candies	$1,153,840	20.85%	$1,270,313	21.12%	$2,424,153	20.99%
	Chocolate Croissants	$494,613	8.94%	$549,817	9.14%	$1,044,430	9.04%
	Crackers	$304,610	5.50%	$321,556	5.35%	$626,166	5.42%
	Muffins	$733,072	13.25%	$811,093	13.49%	$1,544,165	13.37%
Grand Total		$5,534,311	100.00%	$6,013,973	100.00%	$11,548,285	100.00%

Fig 10.57: OLAP Pivot Table with *Frozen Yoghurt* and *Ice Cream* filtered

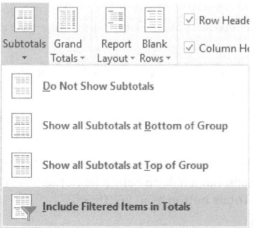

Fig 10.58: Clicking the **Include Filtered Items in Totals** button

Once we do this the **Subtotals** and **Totals** will include the filtered items and by default a star will be displayed next to the item where the totals include filtered items. The Pivot Table will look like in Fig 10.59.

Shift	Product	Year ▼ Values 2015 Revenue	% of Revenue	2016 Revenue	% of Revenue	Total Revenue *	Total % of Revenue *
⊟ Day *		$7,754,976	50.92%	$8,227,310	50.82%	$15,982,286	50.87%
	Biscuits	$538,395	3.54%	$572,242	3.53%	$1,110,637	3.54%
	Chocolate Bars	$817,741	5.37%	$894,926	5.53%	$1,712,667	5.45%
	Cream Cakes	$141,893	0.93%	$177,936	1.10%	$319,829	1.02%
	Small Cakes	$1,350,148	8.87%	$1,416,090	8.75%	$2,766,238	8.80%
⊟ Night *		$7,474,735	49.08%	$7,961,024	49.18%	$15,435,759	49.13%
	Candies	$1,153,840	7.58%	$1,270,313	7.85%	$2,424,153	7.72%
	Chocolate Croissants	$494,613	3.25%	$549,817	3.40%	$1,044,430	3.32%
	Crackers	$304,610	2.00%	$321,556	1.99%	$626,166	1.99%
	Muffins	$733,072	4.81%	$811,093	5.01%	$1,544,165	4.91%
Grand Total *		$15,229,711	100.00%	$16,188,334	100.00%	$31,418,045	100.00%

Fig 10.59: OLAP Pivot Table with filtered items included in totals

If you compare the **Subtotals** and **Totals** in the above table to the ones in Fig 10.56 you will find that they are identical.

10.11 Convert to Formulas

An **OLAP** Pivot Table can be converted into formulas. To do this click anywhere on the Pivot Table and then go to the **Analyze** tab, **Calculations** group, click on **OLAP Tools** and then click on **Convert to Formulas**.

Note that if you are using the **Show Values As** feature (from the **Show Values As** tab in **Field Settings**) you will get an error message as in Fig 10.60.

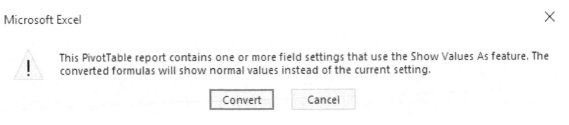

Microsoft Excel   ✕

⚠ This PivotTable report contains one or more field settings that use the Show Values As feature. The
    converted formulas will show normal values instead of the current setting.

                           [Convert]   [Cancel]

Fig 10.60: Error message when having values using the **Show Values As** feature

If you still want to convert to formulas click the **Convert** button.

Once an **OLAP** Pivot Table is converted to formulas it loses all it's formatting. Fig 10.61 shows the Pivot Table from Fig 10.59 converted to formulas.

Shift	Product	Year 2015	Values	2016		Total Revenue	Total % of Revenue
		Sum of Revenu	Sum of Revenu	Sum of Revenu	Sum of Revenue		
Day		7754976.25	7754976.25	8227309.65	8227309.65	15982285.9	15982285.9
	Biscuits	=CUBEVALUE("ThisWorkbookDataModel",$C10,D$8)				1110636.5	1110636.5
	Chocolate Bars	CUBEVALUE(connection, [member_expression1], [member_expression2], [member_expression3], ...)					1712667.05
	Cream Cakes	141893	141893	177936.25	177936.25	319829.25	319829.25
	Small Cakes	1350147.5	1350147.5	1416090	1416090	2766237.5	2766237.5
Night		7474734.7	7474734.7	7961024.3	7961024.3	15435759	15435759
	Candies	1153840	1153840	1270313	1270313	2424153	2424153
	Chocolate Croissants	494613	494613	549817.1	549817.1	1044430.1	1044430.1
	Crackers	304610	304610	321556.2	321556.2	626166.2	626166.2
	Muffins	733072.2	733072.2	811092.7	811092.7	1544164.9	1544164.9
Grand Total		15229710.95	15229710.95	16188333.95	16188333.95	31418044.9	31418044.9

Fig 10.61: OLAP Pivot Table in Fig 10.59 converted to formulas

OLAP Pivot Table formulas can be very useful because you can get any value from the above table without having to build the entire Pivot Table.

For e.g. the following formula will get *Revenue* for *Biscuits* on the *Day Shift* of the *Year 2015*.

=CUBEVALUE("ThisWorkbookDataModel",CUBEMEMBER("ThisWorkbookDataModel", {"[Products produced and sold].[Shift].&[Day]","[Product Details]. [Product].&[Biscuits]"}),CUBEMEMBER("ThisWorkbookDataModel",{"[Products produced and sold].[Year].&[2015]","[Measures].[Sum of Revenue]"}))

For this formula to work the **Workbook Data Model** must have at least *Product_Details* and *Products_Produced_and_Sold* tables added and <u>related</u>.

10.12 Refresh Control with Connection Properties

You can set how frequently to refresh the connection of an **OLAP** Pivot Table to a data source in the **Connection Properties** dialog box.

To access **Connection Properties** click anywhere on the Pivot Table and then go to the **Analyze** tab, **Data** group, click on **Refresh** and then click on **Connection Properties...** .

Once you do this the **Workbook Connection for {Pivot Table Name}** dialog box will pop up. In this dialog box select the connection you want to refresh and then click on the **Properties...** button.

On clicking the **Properties...** button the **Connection Properties** dialog box for the selected connection will pop up (Fig 10.63).

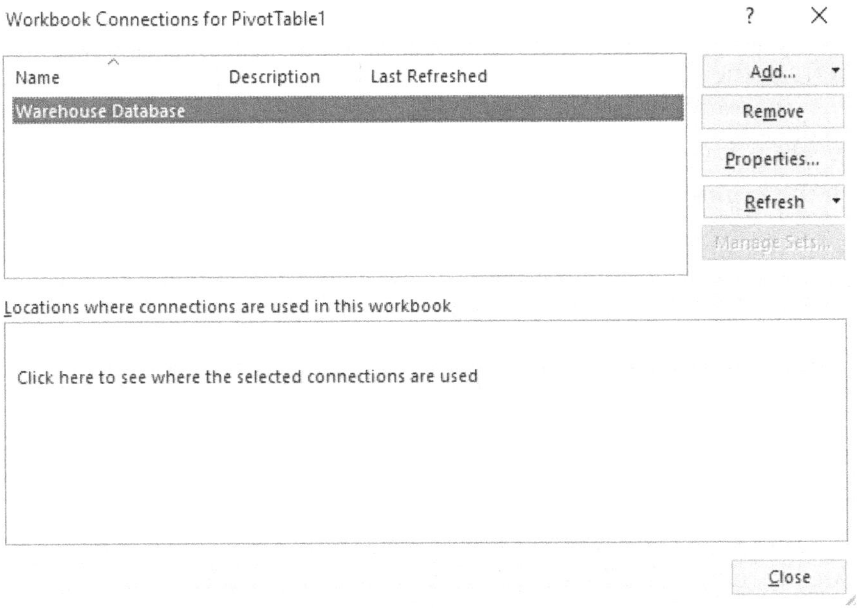

Workbook Connections for PivotTable1   ?   ✕

Name	Description	Last Refreshed	
Warehouse Database			

Add... ▾
Remove
Properties...
Refresh ▾
Manage Sets...

Locations where connections are used in this workbook

Click here to see where the selected connections are used

Close

Fig 10.62: Workbook Connections dialog box

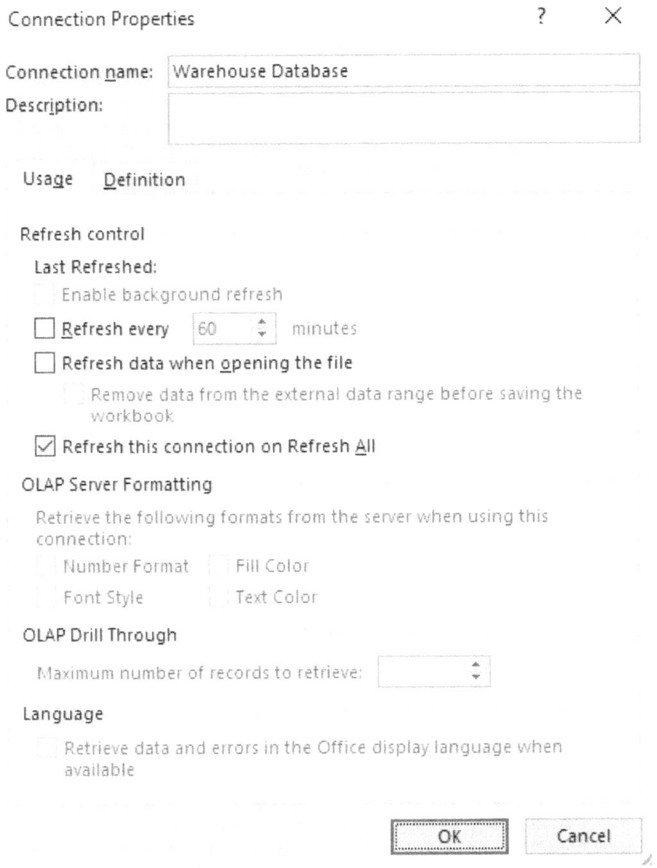

Connection Properties   ?   ✕

Connection name: Warehouse Database
Description:

Usage   Definition

Refresh control

Last Refreshed:

☐ Enable background refresh

☐ Refresh every   60 ⬍ minutes

☐ Refresh data when opening the file

☐ Remove data from the external data range before saving the workbook

☑ Refresh this connection on Refresh All

OLAP Server Formatting

Retrieve the following formats from the server when using this connection:

☐ Number Format   ☐ Fill Color
☐ Font Style   ☐ Text Color

OLAP Drill Through

Maximum number of records to retrieve: [   ] ⬍

Language

☐ Retrieve data and errors in the Office display language when available

OK   Cancel

Fig 10.63: Connection Properties dialog box

In the **Usage** tab of this dialog box under **Refresh control** you can choose:

- How frequently to refresh the connection. Refresh every X minutes.

- Whether to "Refresh data when opening the file"

- Whether to "Refresh this connection on **Refresh All**"

If you are not sure what is the best set up for you I suggest you to keep Excel's default options.

10.13 Pivot Table Options exclusive to OLAP

When we build a Pivot Table using the **Data Model** there are a few options made available in the **PivotTable Options** dialog box under the **Totals & Filters** tab and the **Display** tab.

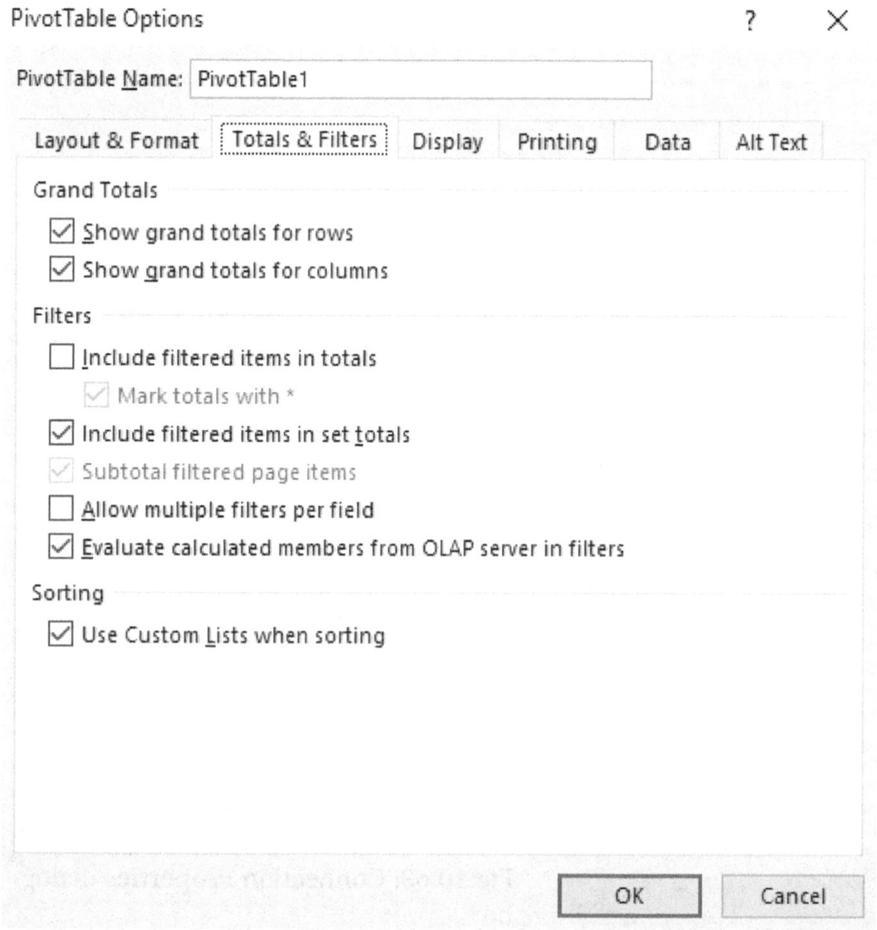

PivotTable Options   ?   ×

PivotTable Name: PivotTable1

| Layout & Format | Totals & Filters | Display | Printing | Data | Alt Text |

Grand Totals
  ☑ Show grand totals for rows
  ☑ Show grand totals for columns

Filters
  ☐ Include filtered items in totals
    ☑ Mark totals with *
  ☑ Include filtered items in set totals
  ☑ Subtotal filtered page items
  ☐ Allow multiple filters per field
  ☑ Evaluate calculated members from OLAP server in filters

Sorting
  ☑ Use Custom Lists when sorting

OK   Cancel

Fig 10.64: Totals & Filters tab in Pivot Table options

10.13.1 Totals & Filters tab

In the **Totals & Filters** tab the additional options are made available under the Filters section. They are:

☐ **Include Filtered Items in totals**

    ☒ Mark totals with *

This option is the same as the **Include Filtered Items in Totals** option accessible from the **Design** tab, **Layout** section, **Subtotals** button.

If selected it includes filtered items in subtotal and grand total calculations. When this is the case you can choose whether to mark totals with a * in the option just under. Marking totals with a * is selected by default.

☒ **Include filtered items in set totals**

This option is selected by default.

If you build a **Named Set** from a Pivot Table with filtered items, when you use this **Named Set** in another Pivot Table the filtered items will remain filtered. If this option is selected the subtotals and totals will include the filtered items.

☒ **Evaluate calculated members from OLAP server in filters**

This option relates to using **MDX (MultiDimensional Expressions)** which is not covered in this course. Ignore it unless using **MDX calculated members**.

10.13.2 Display tab

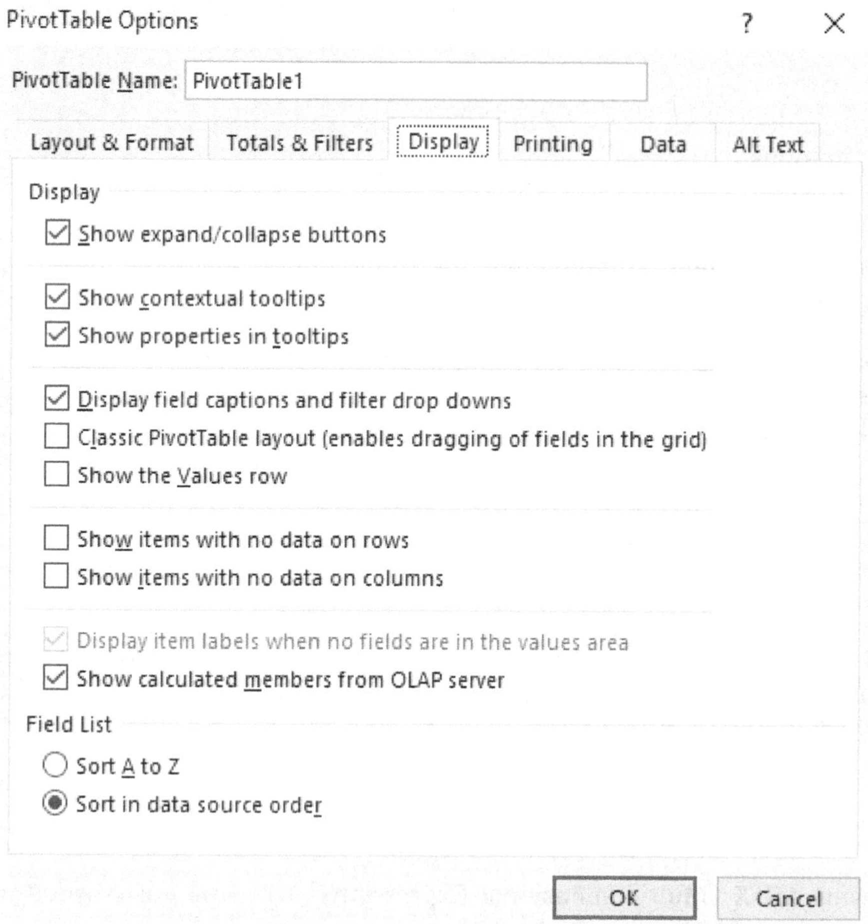

Fig 10.65: Display tab in **PivotTable Options**

☐ **Show items with no data on rows**

If a particular item within a field has no equivalent data (i.e. no data in the same row) in another field it won't be displayed in rows when placed together with this field unless this option is selected.

To understand this clearly let us look at an example. I have deleted *Revenue* data for *February* in both years in the ***Products_Produced_and_Sold*** table. Deleting means that I have deleted data in the *Revenue* column only but the other columns have the data intact. Fig 10.66 shows a simple Pivot Table with *Month* in **Rows**, *Year* in **Columns** and *Revenue* in ∑ **Values** all from the ***Products_Produced_and_Sold*** table. As you can see *February* is not in the Pivot Table.

Sum of Revenue	Year		
Month	2015	2016	Grand Total
January	$1,260,417	$1,326,231	$2,586,649
March	$1,248,195	$1,347,664	$2,595,859
April	$1,237,010	$1,304,882	$2,541,892
May	$1,268,263	$1,345,825	$2,614,088
June	$1,248,297	$1,340,332	$2,588,629
July	$1,301,202	$1,369,796	$2,670,998
August	$1,277,925	$1,346,617	$2,624,541
September	$1,256,384	$1,352,311	$2,608,695
October	$1,293,890	$1,381,815	$2,675,704
November	$1,313,026	$1,401,244	$2,714,270
December	$1,342,279	$1,422,301	$2,764,581
Grand Total	$14,046,888	$14,939,019	$28,985,907

Fig 10.66: Pivot Table with *February* not showing since it has no data

Now let's go to the **Display** tab in the **PivotTable Options** dialog box and tick the checkbox in front of **Show items with no data on rows** and click **OK**. The Pivot Table will now look like in Fig 10.67.

Sum of Revenue	Year		
Month	2015	2016	Grand Total
January	$1,260,417	$1,326,231	$2,586,649
February			
March	$1,248,195	$1,347,664	$2,595,859
April	$1,237,010	$1,304,882	$2,541,892
May	$1,268,263	$1,345,825	$2,614,088
June	$1,248,297	$1,340,332	$2,588,629
July	$1,301,202	$1,369,796	$2,670,998
August	$1,277,925	$1,346,617	$2,624,541
September	$1,256,384	$1,352,311	$2,608,695
October	$1,293,890	$1,381,815	$2,675,704
November	$1,313,026	$1,401,244	$2,714,270
December	$1,342,279	$1,422,301	$2,764,581
Grand Total	$14,046,888	$14,939,019	$28,985,907

Fig 10.67: *February* showing in rows despite having no data

☐ **Show items with no data on columns**

If a particular item within a field has no equivalent data (i.e. no data in the same row) in another field it won't be displayed on columns when placed together with this field unless this option is selected.

Continuing from the example above if we put *Month* in **Columns** and *Year* in **Rows** we will get the Pivot Table in Fig 10.68 with *February* not showing in the table.

Revenue	Month ⬇										
Year ▼	January	March	April	May	June	July	August	September	October	November	December
2015	$1,260,417	$1,248,195	$1,237,010	$1,268,263	$1,248,297	$1,301,202	$1,277,925	$1,256,384	$1,293,890	$1,313,026	$1,342,279
2016	$1,326,231	$1,347,664	$1,304,882	$1,345,825	$1,340,332	$1,369,796	$1,346,617	$1,352,311	$1,381,815	$1,401,244	$1,422,301
Grand Total	$2,586,649	$2,595,859	$2,541,892	$2,614,088	$2,588,629	$2,670,998	$2,624,541	$2,608,695	$2,675,704	$2,714,270	$2,764,581

Fig 10.68: *February* not showing in columns due to **Show items with no data on columns** not selected

Now let's go to the **Display** tab in the **PivotTable Options** dialog box and let's tick the checkbox in front of **Show items with no data on columns**. Now the Pivot Table will look like in Fig 10.69.

Revenue	Month ⬇											
Year ▼	January	February	March	April	May	June	July	August	September	October	November	December
2015	$1,260,417		$1,248,195	$1,237,010	$1,268,263	$1,248,297	$1,301,202	$1,277,925	$1,256,384	$1,293,890	$1,313,026	$1,342,279
2016	$1,326,231		$1,347,664	$1,304,882	$1,345,825	$1,340,332	$1,369,796	$1,346,617	$1,352,311	$1,381,815	$1,401,244	$1,422,301
Grand Total	$2,586,649		$2,595,859	$2,541,892	$2,614,088	$2,588,629	$2,670,998	$2,624,541	$2,608,695	$2,675,704	$2,714,270	$2,764,581

Fig 10.69: Now the Pivot Table displays *February* with no data

⊠ **Show calculated members from OLAP server**

This option relates to using **MDX (MultiDimensional Expressions)** which is not covered in this book. Ignore it unless using **MDX calculated members**.

10.14 Final words on OLAP

Here are a few more things you should know when using **OLAP**:

- A workbook can have only one Data Model
- Tables in a Data Model have no limit in terms of rows
- Any Excel table can be added to the Data Model
- A long list of data sources can be added to the Data Model
- If using the Data Model you can't group items
- If using the Data Model you can't create Calculated Fields or Calculated Items

APPENDIX

Custom Sorting

While custom sorting is not a Pivot Table feature it is an important Excel feature which can help in building better organized Pivot Tables.

Let's suppose that you have a list of items which can be anything for e.g. products, names etc. that you always want sorted in a particular way which is neither alphabetical nor numerical then what would you do? You could for e.g. add a number or letter in front of each item's name and that would help sorting, though it wouldn't be as neat and clean as using only the item's name.

The good news is that there is a way of automatically sorting these items in any order you like through **Custom Sorting**.

For example, let's say that whenever I am using our product list, from the Warehouse dataset, in a Pivot Table, I would like it sorted in a particular order, which is based on expected revenue from each product sorted in descending order.

The way I want products specifically sorted in a Pivot Table is as below:

- Ice Cream
- Frozen Yoghurt
- Small Cakes
- Candies
- Chocolate Bars
- Muffins
- Biscuits
- Chocolate Croissants
- Crackers
- Cream Cakes

Whenever *Product* field's items appear in a Pivot Table they should always be sorted as above. To do this as already mentioned we need to use **Custom Sorting**.

Custom Sorting requires a **Custom Sort List**. To build a **Custom Sort List** let's go to the **File** tab and click on **Options**. The **Excel Options** dialog box will pop up. Select **Advanced** and then scroll down until you find the **Edit Custom Lists...** button (see Fig A.1).

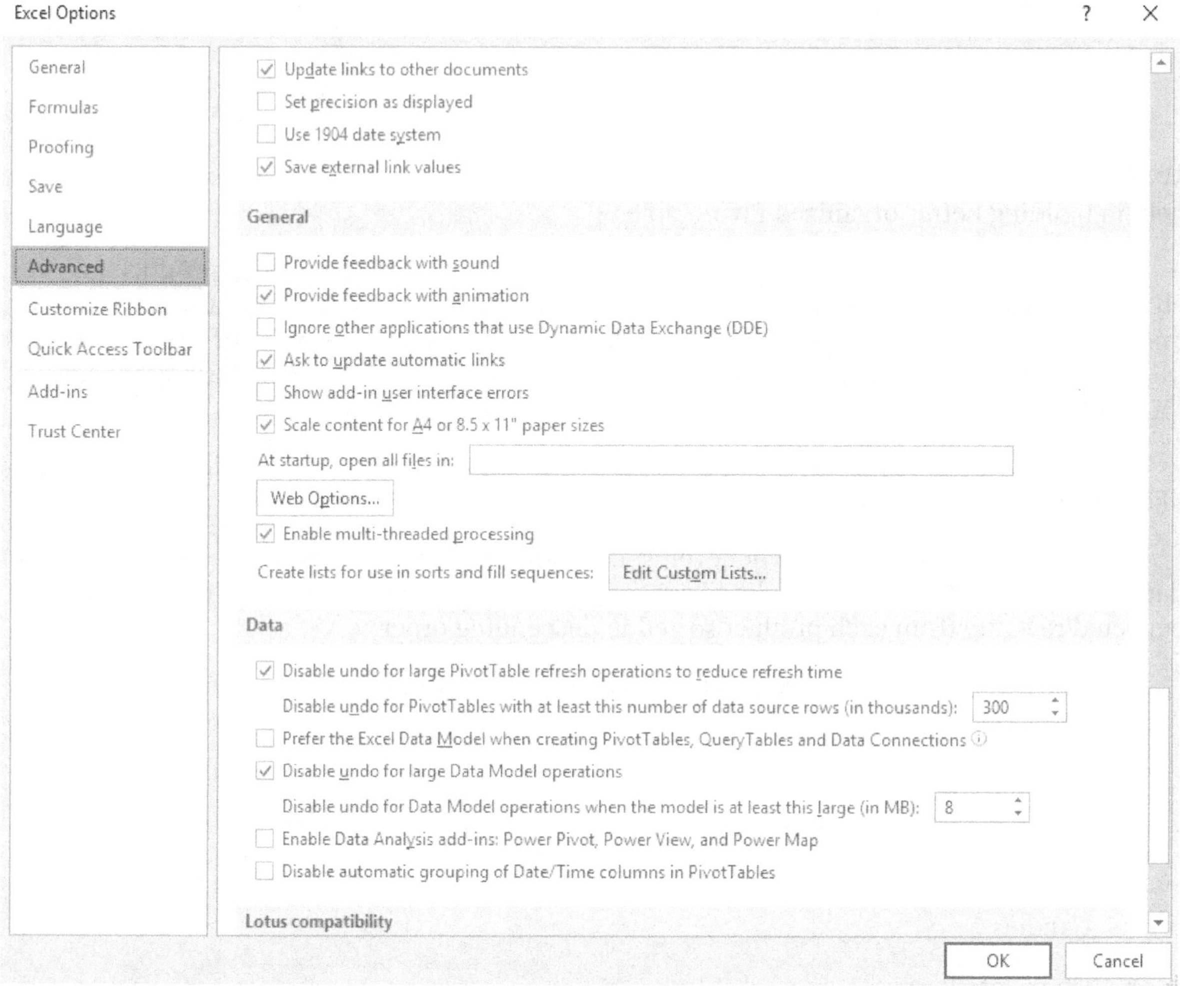

Fig A.1: Edit Custom Lists... button in **Advanced Excel Options**

Click on the **Edit Custom Lists...** button and the **Custom Lists** dialog box will pop up as in Fig A.2.

In the box under **List entries:** enter the list of products in the order specified above and then click **Add**. Once you do this your new list will appear in the **Custom lists** box as in Fig A.3.

Click **OK** and then again **OK**. Now we can use our new custom sort list.

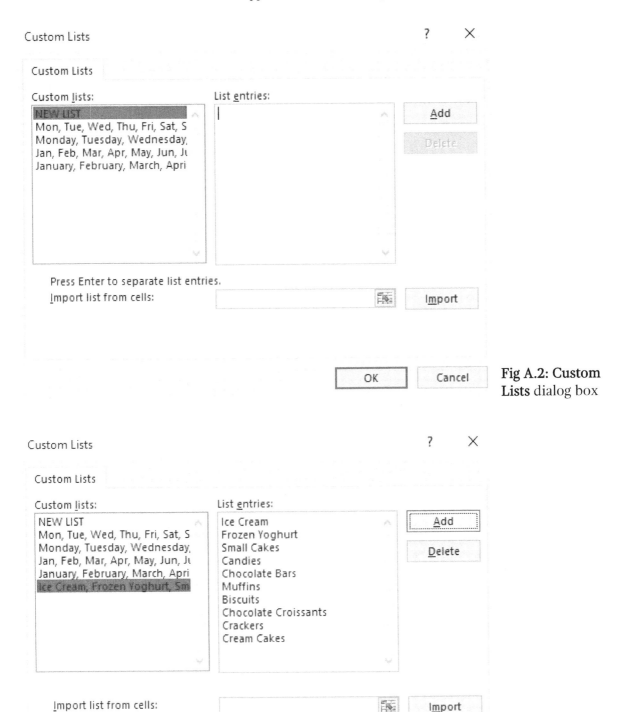

Fig A.2: Custom Lists dialog box

Fig A.3: Custom Lists dialog box after adding a new list

To sort a Pivot Table with the new custom sort list simply right click on any *Product* item and select **Sort** and then select **Sort A to Z**. If you want items sorted in reverse order then select **Sort Z to A**. To stop custom sorting *Product* go to the **Totals & Filters** tab in the **PivotTable Options** dialog box and untick the checkbox before **Use Custom Lists when sorting** and click **OK**.

Previously a Pivot Table with the *Product* field in it unsorted would look like in Fig A.4.

Total Revenue	Year		
Product	2015	2016	Grand Total
Biscuits	$538,395	$572,242	$1,110,637
Candies	$1,153,840	$1,270,313	$2,424,153
Chocolate Bars	$817,741	$894,926	$1,712,667
Chocolate Croissants	$494,613	$549,817	$1,044,430
Crackers	$304,610	$321,556	$626,166
Cream Cakes	$141,893	$177,936	$319,829
Frozen Yoghurt	$4,620,560	$4,725,405	$9,345,965
Ice Cream	$5,074,840	$5,448,956	$10,523,796
Muffins	$733,072	$811,093	$1,544,165
Small Cakes	$1,350,148	$1,416,090	$2,766,238
Grand Total	$15,229,711	$16,188,334	$31,418,045

Fig A.4: Pivot Table with the *Product* field not sorted

A new Pivot Table built with the *Product* field in it custom sorted, would look like in Fig A.5.

Total Revenue	Year		
Product	2015	2016	Grand Total
Ice Cream	$5,074,840	$5,448,956	$10,523,796
Frozen Yoghurt	$4,620,560	$4,725,405	$9,345,965
Small Cakes	$1,350,148	$1,416,090	$2,766,238
Candies	$1,153,840	$1,270,313	$2,424,153
Chocolate Bars	$817,741	$894,926	$1,712,667
Muffins	$733,072	$811,093	$1,544,165
Biscuits	$538,395	$572,242	$1,110,637
Chocolate Croissants	$494,613	$549,817	$1,044,430
Crackers	$304,610	$321,556	$626,166
Cream Cakes	$141,893	$177,936	$319,829
Grand Total	$15,229,711	$16,188,334	$31,418,045

Fig A.5: Pivot Table with the *Product* field custom sorted

INDEX

Made in the USA
Columbia, SC
31 January 2019